A Relevant War Against Poverty

A Study of Community Action Programs and Observable Social Change

A Relevant War Against Poverty

A Study of Community Action Programs and Observable Social Change

by Kenneth B. Clark and Jeannette Hopkins

1817

HARPER & ROW, PUBLISHERS
New York and Evanston

An Urban Affairs book, cosponsored by the Metropolitan Applied Research Center, Inc., and Harper & Row, Publishers, Incorporated, under the general editorship of Kenneth B. Clark.

A study conducted under the auspices of the Stern Family Fund by the director and selected staff of the Social Dynamics Research Institute of the City College of the City University of New York, and published by the Metropolitan Applied Research Center, Inc., New York, New York.

 For information address Harper & Row, Publishers, Incorporated, 49 East 33rd Street, New York, N.Y. 10016. Published simultaneously in Canada by Fitzhenry & Whiteside Limited, Toronto.

LIBRARY OF CONGRESS CATALOG CARD NUMBER: 72-88633

Preface

In rethinking the findings of *A Relevant War Against Poverty,* one is forced to realize that the pessimistic conclusions which many regarded as unduly harsh at the time were, if anything, understated. White backlash has grown, separatism has increased, the living conditions of the ghetto poor remain conditions of pathology.

On the basis of the data gathered in the first two years of the War on Poverty, *A Relevant War on Poverty* offered a prophecy of the future of that program and related programs. Events since that analysis have confirmed rather than refuted our predictions. Further analysis of factors and forces not observable at the time of study, but suggested by what we had projected, has tended to support the original findings.

Beneath the rhetoric of the Johnson Administration's brief and romantic interlude with the poor was a deep-rooted distrust of the poor themselves, manifested when the poor—and particularly the Negro poor—choose to believe the rhetoric of participatory democracy and choose to act on that belief. The poor as aggressors or as rude initiators of action, unresponsive to benevolent control, ungrateful and distrusting, and even violent, are less appealing to indulgent political leadership than the humble and apathetic poor.

Despite the high hopes of the youthful Kennedy Administration, and its holdovers under Johnson, the campaign for massive feasible participation by the poor in the anti-poverty program must now be seen as a charade, an exhilarating intellectual game whose players never understood the nature of power and the reluctance of those who have it to share it. It seems apparent that canny political leadership—national and city—never intended fundamental social reorganization. The political participation of the poor in their own affairs was not to be a serious sharing of power after all.

Congressional reaction against the challenge of community action programs, the Johnson Administration's executive preoccupation with Vietnam and its loss of interest in the War on Poverty, its refusal to acknowledge the imperatives of the Kerner Commission Report, the inadequacy of that Administration's reaction to the series of northern urban riots, and the more recent growing resistance of Congress to foundation involvement in voter education and registration—all are indicative of the superficiality of the official engagement with the poor.

One suspects that just as the civil rights movement was most successful when Southern-oriented, so President Johnson himself understood, identified with, and was capable of responding to the Southern Negro's demands for justice as he never was capable of responding to the Northern Negro's needs and demands. Further, President Johnson had more to lose politically in the North than in the South. Northern big-city mayors, who had long run their cities without addressing themselves to the fundamental inequities faced by the inhabitants of their decaying ghettos, understandably felt threatened by the effort to engage the poor in leadership and in strategy for social change, and demanded that the federal government dilute or control its community action programs.

As long as programs for the poor were philanthropic, ameliorative, welfare-oriented, based either on the hearty ward-boss political model, or on the more chaste, less corrupt, but also less compassionate social-agency model, political, social, or economic leadership felt no stirring of dread that the equation of power would shift.

But when some of the poor, particularly the Negro poor and their advocates, took the War on Poverty seriously in a few cities like Syracuse and New York, organizing voters, demanding community control of schools (a prelude to demands for community control of police and civic services), demanding that welfare recipients be treated as human beings, demanding an effective role in urban planning generally, the political forces in the cities deployed for counterattack. The War on Poverty was a national strategy that never planned for or gained support in most of the large cities where it operated. In a bipartisan effort to acknowledge common cause, a number of city mayors, both Democratic and Republican, joined with national leadership to prune and to blunt the community action program, to render it impotent.

Having encouraged and even whetted the appetite of the Negro poor—and now, more recently, the Mexican American and Puerto Rican poor—leadership now pulled back in fright at the consequences of its act—limited and even pathetic though the consequences were. One must surmise that the program had not been thought through originally by those who promulgated it, or that the energetic crusading proponents who urged it on the President did anticipate the cause-and-effect relationship, but lacked the power to do more than generate, through promises, a discontent whose demands they were not in a position to fulfill.

Some justify their role on the grounds that to motivate the poor will unleash a hunger for real participation that will not, in the long run, be susceptible of appeasement. Some justify it also on the grounds that a limited number of the poor have been helped to move out of poverty. Certainly, upward mobility of a number on the fringe of poverty has been hastened, though possibly more anti-poverty funds went to middle-class white and Negro professionals than to the poor themselves. One must point, however, to a measure of irresponsibility and cynicism that characterizes such a rationale. Those to whom promises are broken and those whose hunger and hope are reinforced can be dangerous. The anti-poverty program has given a new dimension to the "hustle," as some Negroes come to regard relatively high-salaried jobs in the program as their due—a form of reparation for past and present white sins—and seek to exploit white guilt. It is scarcely surprising that some corruption has been discovered in some anti-poverty and related programs. It may be seen by many whites as evidence that Negroes cannot be trusted with money or power. In the face of evidence of systematic Negro exclusion from the highest echelons of crime, such conclusions are naïve. The judge who urged Negroes to avoid white crimes on the grounds of inexperience and likelihood of capture did not understand that achievement in certain kinds of crime—embezzlement, rigging of contracts, and the like—is regarded by some Negroes as a badge of upward mobility. At the very least, it provides a tiny adjustment in the unequal distribution of illegal, ill-gotten gains.

More to be criticized are those who make such petty corruption easy, who pay salaries far out of line with comparable positions elsewhere, making later transition to other jobs difficult, who fail to institute guidelines and normal protections. The laxity in certain anti-poverty programs, as in school decentralization, and in double-standard programs in colleges, while posing as permissiveness and generosity, serves as a form of entrapment. The inadequate guidelines in the Ocean Hill–Brownsville school decentralization experiment in New York City, for example, may have been unconsciously, if not consciously, designed to cause confusion, chaos, and counter-response. If restless natives are shown to be irresponsible, one then may feel justified in taking away the "privilege" of power, since the anti-poverty program generally regarded the participation of the poor in their own destiny as a privilege, not a right, and, as such, susceptible to modification or withdrawal by the controlling power.

The rhetoric of involvement of the poor, combined with studied control of the poor, has led to ineffectiveness, to a substitution of rhetoric for basic social change. This ineffectiveness, in turn, has been used by public officials to justify any postponements, inaction, and decision to pull back on their commitment to change.

The involvement of the poor in the Model Cities program, in New York City, for example, has served as an effective device to excuse inaction, to postpone building of housing, to delay any serious change. In the Ocean Hill–Brownsville school decentralization dispute, disruption—caused in large part by ambiguity in guidelines and resistance from the educational establishment, especially the United Federation of Teachers—served as an excuse for indefinite postponement of any changes in the educational system itself.

The demands of Negro students, which have led to hasty concession to separatist demands, continue to obscure the basic problem of the continued limitations and excessive cost of these essentially compensatory programs, and the weakness of a public educational system that produces students who are incapable of competing on an equal basis with other students.

It would be unjust to attribute only failure and insincerity to the Johnson Administration War on Poverty, for it seems fair to conclude the program was in certain respects successful, not the least in its stated purposes, and in its stimulus to the growth of the Negro middle-class and in arousing black community leadership to the pitiful conditions of ghetto schools, ghetto housing, and the conditions of life generally. The failures, which are more easily measurable than the successes, seem rather to be due more to an inability to realize the full implications of the program's stated goals and the probable political consequences. The Administration could not pay the price.

Basically, it seems clear that the poor are not taken seriously. They have not been provided with the type of training and freedom to engage constructively in the political process. There seems rather to have been a tacit—conscious or unconscious, deliberate or inadvertent—encouraging of random emotional and nonrelevant behavior on the part of the poor. This has provided cathartic expression but has not seemed to be backed up by any satisfactory program for confronting and solving the fundamental problems of poverty.

Race seems to have played an important role in the poverty

program backlash. Observing the flight of middle-class whites from the city, the hostile reaction of the majority to school bussing programs, and rising welfare rolls, the urgent demands for law and order in the aftermath of ghetto rebellions, national and city leadership generally responded spontaneously or with strategy designed to contain the newly restless poor. Race reinforced the sense of alienation between the Johnson Administration and the urban poor, and the possibility of reprisal by each against the other in an unequal struggle in which the nearly powerless poor had few weapons but the increasingly militant fury of the young.

The demand for black separatism is a direct consequence not so much of the participation of the poor, who had been encouraged "to do their own thing," but of the failure of government and other leadership to invest that participation with genuine power and to respond to elementary demands for justice in education, housing, police protection, employment, and union membership, civic services generally. Separatism—long desired and cultivated by whites out of a false perception of self-interest and identity—is now desired and fought for by a growing number of young black militants out of similarly false perceptions. This self-destructive, despairing demand has been reinforced in certain respects by the Nixon Administration, which may, if it continues in the present trend, add a new and potentially even more dangerous dimension to the relationship of government to the poor and powerless. The Nixon emphasis on "black capitalism," the HEW rationalization of black self-segregation on campuses on the ground that race is an appropriate definition of relevance in education, the failure to enlist strong Negro leadership in executive posts in the Administration, all are ominous signs of a new romanticism of race that finds sentimental reasons for endorsing segregation. Just as the Johnson Administration's rhetoric was posed in terms of daring innovative liberalism, so the Nixon rhetoric speaks of bold support for the independence of blacks. Blacks seldom take rhetoric for the deed for long, however, and disillusioned militants may soon discover that Northern black capitalism resembles in both isolation and inequality the divided societies of the old South, and that black separatism in schools and in universities leads to unequal training for successful competition in the larger society, just as it did for a century after Emancipation.

The Nixon Administration began without the burden or the asset of black confidence. The Negro vote against Nixon was an overwhelming rejection. Most prominent Negroes approached for advice about posts in the Administration proved skeptical about its sincerity and commitment. Ironically enough, however, a few black militants thought an accommodation possible and, therefore, made it possible for the Administration to maintain a certain stance of boldness without, so far, the necessity for rigorous implementation. Whether other plans—for rehabilitation of ghetto areas destroyed in the riots, for income maintenance, for reform of welfare programs, and the like—prove productive of observable social change is still to be seen. There do seem to be indications, however, that the Nixon Administration is unlikely to disturb the status quo in Northern cities, avoiding political confrontation whenever possible, attempting instead to deal with socioeconomic conditions in the belief that nothing can be done to transform education, for example, or to share political power, without change in income levels of the poor.

This approach presents other dangers, for it may substitute a new and more sophisticated form of economic and social dependence for the old, providing subsidies of tax aid, welfare, minimum income, but failing to bring the poor effectively and productively into the economy. It may also deepen the racial divisions in American society not only by increasing resentment among whites but also by reinforcing the walls of the ghetto rather than by breaching them.

Even in a program of income maintenance, one can devise a system that robs the individual of a sense of control, a sense of dignity and worth, resulting in a system that is indistinguishable in its psychological effects from welfare itself.

Further, the present generation of children in ghetto schools

—and others after them—could be lost while society waits for economic subsidy to take effect. The Nixon Administration may find itself persuaded that economic and social class and not race are the relevant factors in the conditions of the ghetto. In this the Johnson and the Nixon Administrations have a similar perspective. The War on Poverty, by definition, was intended as such. But race proved intrusive whatever the plans to exclude it. The War came to be viewed as applying primarily to blacks. Nor will minimum income maintenance alone improve ghetto schools if they remain segregated and if teachers and administrators regard Negro and Puerto Rican and Mexican American children as inferior. It will not lead to positive self-identity if men cannot get jobs and cannot join unions, if housing is not open to minority groups everywhere in city or suburb.

One consequence of the anti-poverty program, however, has been the emergence with greater clarity of the class factor within the Negro community itself. The black militants and students have aligned themselves, verbally and in some cases directly, with the working class. The class issue they have raised places the older Negro middle-class in a position of rejection both by the Negro poor, many of whom resent their mobility and partial acceptance by the majority society, and by the young militants, who view such "making it" with contempt as evidence of group betrayal.

It seems clear that the Nixon Administration will be even more wary of political participation of the poor than the Johnson Administration, not the least because the poor are likely to vote for the opposition party. In two of the twelve cities studied for this report, Negroes have since risen to the highest political post—the mayoralty. Negroes have been elected to positions in a number of communities in the South and a number of legislatures. Whether rising political involvement will lead to effective power and whether that will lead to positive social change is still to be seen. In part, particularly in Northern cities, Negro political success is a function of white default—

the abandonment of the central city to minority poor. To the extent this continues, Negro leadership will increasingly preside over decaying, impoverished, and segregated cities; the power earned will prove of dubious value, susceptible in addition to state or federal veto in the form of withholding of funds. The recent curtailing of public school terms in several major cities is a forbidding omen in this regard.

But, there is still hope of arresting the decay if the majority society acknowledges the negative influence of racial determinations on the health of the whole society and comes to perceive that the self-interest of the whole society depends on establishing conditions of free mobility, free choice of housing, quality education, employment, equal health and sanitation, and equal police protection for all without regard to irrelevant criteria of race. Only if this is so will economic and class mobility operate in accordance with individual capacity as they must do if the society is to progress. Unless this is done, neither the economic nor the political system will work; disruptions among the powerless will continue. It is in the clear self-interest of the affluent and of the majority that conditions ensuing orderly change exist in American cities. Without such provision, no stability is possible, despite any repressive methods of containment, for artificial stability—as well as chaos—is conducive to a society's decay and death.

A genuine war on poverty is possible. This nation has the intellectual and material resources to plan and win this war. It must now find the commitment, since urban stability and national survival are both at stake.

—KENNETH B. CLARK
JEANNETTE HOPKINS

May 9, 1969

Acknowledgments

This study was made possible not only by the generosity of the Stern Family Fund, but also by the personal and professional commitment of a number of people on the professional staff as well as those who became involved through their interest in the problem. The staff of the study are Gloria Edwards and Carolyn Atkinson, who, in their role as research associates, were involved in the planning and were assigned primary responsibility for interviewing the directors and top staff of community action programs in the twelve cities studied in depth. Willie Jones and Bernard Dyer served as field investigators, with the primary responsibility of conducting tape-recorded interviews with people in the community and indigenous staff of programs studied. Frances Farber, research secretary, in addition to her secretarial duties, was responsible for the analysis of the data obtained through the questionnaires and correspondence.

Barbara Kaplan contributed invaluable help in the final stages of preparation of the manuscript for publication. Jeannette Hopkins assumed the difficult responsibility of preparing the original material and documents into publishable form. Her contributions went beyond that of editorial responsibility and, in fact, were such as to require her recognition as chief collaborator in the published report. The fact that this document is published is a testament to her insistence.

David Hunter, who conceived of the project, demonstrated a high degree of patience. He understood the complexities of the problem and showed a willingness to trust the judgment of the project's director throughout all stages—including his judgment as to timing of its publication. His role in regard to this study went beyond the usual role of personal responsibility for the grant to the delicate role of one who was involved without attempting in any way to influence findings or interpretation.

I am pleased to have this opportunity of expressing personal thanks to Jeannette Hopkins, Barbara Kaplan, and David Hunter, who persisted in seeing that I carried this study through to its conclusion in spite of competing demands.

We delayed publication because we did not want findings used to influence the political decisions that affected OEO appropriations. We felt, however, that the findings are relevant to a serious attempt at strengthening and increasing the effectiveness of anti-poverty programs. They are not intended to be used for a categorical discrediting or a truncating of the programs. The report is now offered in the spirit of helping to ensure a serious and relevant war against poverty.

—KENNETH B. CLARK
General Editor

Contents

Preface v

Acknowledgments xv

I. Foreword: Introduction, Methods, and Source of Data 1

II. Stated Purposes, Definitions, and Goals 17

1. Rationale of Programs Seen in Terms of Tradition 19
A. *The Puritan–Horatio Alger Tradition* 19
B. *The Good Samaritan–Lady Bountiful Tradition* 19
C. *The Prophet Amos–New Deal Tradition* 20

2. Stated Purposes and Definitions 21
A. *Ambiguity of Definitions* 21
B. *A Priori Model of Community Action* 23
C. *Types of Goals of Community Action* 26
(1) SERVICES 27
(2) OPPORTUNITIES 29
(3) PARTICIPATION OF THE POOR 31
(4) LEADERSHIP OF THE POOR 34
D. *Resistance to Definition* 41

3. Implications of Stated Goals 42
A. *Ambiguity of Stated Goals* 42
B. *Community Action Programs as Mediators* 43
C. *Community Action Programs as Forces for Social Cohesion and Harmony* 49

D. *The Role of Community Action Programs as Molders of Individual Behavior* 50
E. *The Role of Community Action Programs as Agents for Self-Help* 53

III. Community Action Programs and Attempts at Implementation 57

1. Classification of Community Action Programs 59

2. Changing Professional Attitudes Toward Social Welfare 71

3. Community Organization and Action 78
A. *The Community Action Training Center and the Syracuse Community Development Association* 82

4. The Participation of the Poor 88
A. *Unfamiliarity with Organization and Suspicion of Organization* 88
B. *The Search for the Indigenous* 91
C. *The Role and Effectiveness of the Indigenous* 93
D. *"Maximum Feasible Participation of the Poor"* 106
(1) ELECTIONS OF THE POOR 110
(2) ASSESSMENT OF INDIGENOUS LEADERSHIP 120

5. Empathic Professionals as Surrogates 128

IV. The Control of the Poor and Attempts to Protect the Interests of the Poor 131

1. The Control of the Poor: Political Power 133
A. *Coalition of Political Leadership and CAP Organization in Behalf of Positive Change* 134
(1) NEW HAVEN: COMMUNITY PROGRESS, INC. 134
(2) PATERSON: TASK FORCE FOR COMMUNITY ACTION 150
(3) NEWARK: UNITED COMMUNITY CORPORATION 152
B. *CAP Threats to Local and Federal Political Control* 152
(1) SYRACUSE: COMMUNITY ACTION TRAINING CENTER 152
(2) THE POLITICAL IMPLICATIONS OF PARTICIPATION OF THE POOR 156

2. The Control of the Poor: Social Agency Power 160
A. *Cleveland: Action for Youth* 161

3. The Role of Civil Rights Groups 167

4. The Role of the Churches 172

5. Programs to Protect the Interests of the Poor 175
A. Ad hoc *Groups Dealing with Specific Limited Issues* 177
B. *Counter-Programs to Protect the Poor* 178
(1) THE WOODLAWN ORGANIZATION OF CHICAGO 178
(2) THE PROTESTANT MINISTRY TO POVERTY (CLEVELAND) 181
C. *Local Coalitions between Professionals and the Poor* 185
(1) THE CITIZENS' COMMITTEE FOR AN ADEQUATE CLEVELAND COMMUNITY ACTION PROGRAM 185
(2) STUDENTS FOR A DEMOCRATIC SOCIETY PROPOSAL FOR CHICAGO 188
D. *Councils and Conventions of the Poor* 190
(1) THE PEOPLE'S WAR COUNCIL AGAINST POVERTY IN SYRACUSE AND THE PEOPLE'S CONVENTION FOR THE TOTAL PARTICIPATION OF THE POOR 190
(2) POOR PEOPLE'S CONVENTION OF THE CITIZENS' CRUSADE AGAINST POVERTY 194
E. *National Organizations of Citizens to Protect the Poor* 198

V. Criteria of Effectiveness of Community Action Programs 205

1. Ranking of Cities Studied 207

2. Characteristics of Relatively Effective Programs: Positives Dominant 212
A. *New Haven* 213
B. *Syracuse* 213
C. *Newark and Paterson, New Jersey* 215
D. *Minneapolis* 217

3. Characteristics of Presently Unclear Programs: Balance of Positive and Negative Forces 218
A. *New York City* 218
B. *Washington, D.C.* 222

C. *San Francisco* 224
D. *Los Angeles* 225

4. Characteristics of Relatively Ineffective Programs: Negatives Dominant 226
A. *Cleveland* 227
B. *Chicago* 227
C. *Boston* 228

5. A Relative Achievement 229

VI. A Relevant War Against Poverty: Summary and Conclusions 231

1. Objectives of the Study 233
A. *Inventory* 233
B. *Definitions and Goals of Programs* 233
C. *Criteria of Effectiveness* 236

2. Implications of Evaluation 238
A. *Conflict and Controversy* 239
B. *Diversion of Energies* 244
C. *Involvement of the Poor* 245
D. *Actual Change in the Conditions of the Poor* 248

3. A Coalition of Professionals and the Poor 254

Afterword: A Theory of Power 257

Appendix: Outline of a Community Action Program 261

Index 265

Tables and Charts

Chart 1: Tabulated Sample of 51 Community Action Programs by Region and State 62

Table 1: Classification of 51 Community Action Programs in Terms of Services 64

Table 2: Inventory of Community Action Program Descriptions of 51 Programs in Terms of Services and Frequency of Mention 66

Table 3: Ranking of Community Action Programs in 12 Cities in Terms of Effectiveness 210

Table 3A: Ranking by Individuals 210

I
Foreword: Introduction, Methods, and Source of Data

With the growth of our country has come opportunity for our people; opportunity to educate our children, to use our energies in productive work, to increase our leisure; opportunity for almost every American to hope that through work and talent he could create a better life for himself and his family. The path forward has not been an easy one. But we have never lost sight of our goal: An America in which every citizen shares all the opportunities of his society, in which every man has a chance to advance his welfare to the limit of his capacities.

We have come a long way toward this goal. We still have a long way to go. The distance which remains is the measure of the great unfinished work of our society. To finish that work I have called for a national war on poverty. Our objective: total victory.

. . . Through a new community action program we intend to strike at poverty at its source—in the streets of our cities and on the farms of our countryside among the very young and the impoverished old. This program asks men and women throughout the country to prepare long-range plans for the attack on poverty in their own local communities. These are not plans prepared in Washington and imposed upon hundreds of different situations. They are based on the fact that local citizens best understand their own problems and know best how to deal with those problems.

President's Message on Poverty
to the Congress of the United
States, March 16, 1964

Introduction

President Johnson's declaration of war against poverty was not abrupt, but had deep roots in recent American history. Franklin D. Roosevelt's New Deal—Emergency Relief, Works Project Administration (WPA), National Youth Administration (NYA), Civilian Conservation Corps (CCC camps)—were the earlier versions of the war or skirmishes against the prevailing poverty of the Depression years.

In spite of the last two decades of rising prosperity and general affluence, the persistence of pockets of poverty and the related pathologies of increasing crime and delinquency and other manifestations of economic and racial discrimination have demanded the development of new approaches to the solution of these long-standing social problems. The recent civil rights crisis, reflecting among other things the increasing disparity in the average economic status of whites and Negroes in America, has focused attention on the need to improve the standard of living of the masses of Negroes in our cities if legal and legislative "victories" are to prove substantive—if the pathologies and pressures which dominated the lives of these people are to be removed and if they are to be provided with the education, the jobs, the housing, and the power and the pride to take advantage of the opportunities to become constructive and contributing members of the larger society.

An approach to these larger goals emerged from President Kennedy's attack on the symptomatic problems of juvenile delinquency. Probably one of the most significant contributions of his short administration was the establishment of his President's Committee on Juvenile Delinquency (PCJD), which in large part became the foundation for the national anti-poverty program. The importance President Kennedy gave to these programs was demonstrated by his appointment of his brother, Robert Kennedy, then the Attorney General of the United States, as chairman of this interdepartmental committee. That the Kennedys were serious in this approach to the problem of the control of juvenile delinquency was reflected in the tremendous amount of time and energy which Robert Kennedy devoted to this responsibility, the rapid organization and staffing of this national effort, and the amount of funds made available for the planning of systematic delinquency control programs in various American cities.

Mobilization for Youth, on the Lower East Side of New York City, was the first of these massive community-based delinquency control programs to be funded directly by the PCJD in 1962. The theory and planning for Mobilization had preceded the establishment of the PCJD by about two or three years, and its approach to the problem of prevention and control of juvenile delinquency set the style for similar programs in other cities sponsored by the PCJD. The essence of this approach was that juvenile delinquency had to be understood in terms of larger and pervasive community problems, and could be controlled only through programs designed to ameliorate these relevant problems and pathologies.

At the same time at which the President's Committee on Juvenile Delinquency provided funds for the operation of the Mobilization for Youth program, it granted funds to Harlem Youth Opportunities Unlimited (HARYOU) to conduct a study and to plan a program for the control of delinquency in the Central Harlem area. The HARYOU approach was similar to that of Mobilization and emphasized the fact that one could not deal seriously with the problem of delinquency among Harlem's youth without assuming the task of identifying and remedying those pervasive problems in the community which stunted and dehumanized Harlem's youth.

The HARYOU document, *Youth in the Ghetto,* was therefore an analysis and diagnosis of a community—its strengths and its weaknesses, its power and its stagnation, its momentum and its inertia—and was the basis for a programmatic prescription for increasing the personal and social effectiveness of Harlem's youth. The HARYOU document went beyond the concern with the immediate community, seeking to understand the problems of the community and its youth in terms of the intensification of the civil rights struggle and the fundamental questions of social and political power and justice. Probably the most significant contribution of that document was the fact that it built into the core of its programmatic recommendations the insistence that social action on the part of the people of the community themselves was the imperative factor in obtaining desired social change. Just as the Mobilization approach expanded the perspective of juvenile delinquency control within the framework of the community, the HARYOU approach added the factor of social action and social change as necessary for any serious concern with the problems of disadvantaged youth. This emphasis on social action and social change precipitated the dilemma which has pervaded the anti-poverty program; namely, that it simultaneously demanded the mobilization of the people of a depressed community for social action and social change, and sought to finance such programs through federal and local funds. This remains a fundamental problem with which the following study of the nature, organization, operation, and effectiveness of the community action components of the anti-poverty program must concern itself.

When the Review Panel of the PCJD reviewed the HARYOU document and interviewed its top staff in April of 1964, it appeared as though this fundamental dilemma could be successfully resolved. Members of the panel raised serious and penetrating questions concerning the feasibility and realism of expecting existing political institutions and governmental agencies to finance a serious program of community social action which would necessarily involve political confrontation and the possibility of abrasive conflict between those forces seeking fundamental changes and those forces required to resist such changes. It was not possible to avoid these questions—they had to be answered directly and forthrightly. It was pointed out by those responsible for the HARYOU approach that a careful study of the nature and forces and the explosive potential of an oppressed ghetto community left no reasonable alternative to the exploration of all possibilities of obtaining desired social change through rational, systematic social planning and social action. Without this approach, there remained only the possibilities of destructive social explosions, intensification of nationalistic racism, exploitation of the real and imagined grievances of the people of the ghetto by demagogues, and the continued erosion and stagnation of the human resources—particularly the youth—of the ghetto. The shadow of Malcolm X and the possibility of destructive riots were candidly used in supporting the point that responsible government had no alternative except to adopt the HARYOU plan for intelligent and rational programs geared toward social action and social change. The HARYOU proposal was adopted unanimously by the Review Panel, which demonstrated its full acceptance of the rationale and the program by appropriating the unprecedented sum of $1,000,000 to aid in the transition from the planning to the operational stage of HARYOU.

The impact of the HARYOU approach can be most clearly seen in terms of its influence on that part of the Economic Opportunity Act which deals with community action programs. The relevant part of this act is Title II A, Section 202(a). Taking its lead from President Lyndon Johnson's message to Congress on March 16, 1964, the law programmatically defines a community action program as one:

(1) which mobilizes and utilizes resources, public or private, of any urban or rural, or combined urban and rural geographical area

(referred to in this part as a "community"), including but not limited to a state, metropolitan area, county, city, town, multicity unit, or multicounty unit in an attack on poverty;

(2) which provides services, assistance, and other activities of sufficient scope and size to give promise of progress toward elimination of poverty or a cause or causes of poverty through developing employment opportunities, improving human performance, motivation and productivity, or bettering the conditions under which people live, learn and work;

(3) which is developed, conducted and administered with the maximum feasible participation of residents of the areas and members of the group served; and

(4) which is conducted, administered or coordinated by a public or private non-profit agency (other than a political party), or a combination thereof.

Although the Economic Opportunity Act does not define community action programs explicitly and specifically, it was the first of any federal legislation concerned with matters of public welfare to require community action and to provide the basis for governmental support for this type of activity. Among the most significant of the many precedent-breaking aspects of this legislation is the fact that it marks a major break with the traditional social service, welfare, dole approach to the amelioration of the conditions of the poor.

This abandonment of the relative safety of the traditional group work, case work, and social service method brings with it the many types of risks associated with a new appraisal of long-standing social problems. Among them are the risks inherent in testing and exploring the feasibility, practicality, and validity of community action and social change emphases in "bettering the conditions under which people live, learn and work." Despite the fact that there was ample evidence that the traditional social welfare approach had not been effective in solving or even retarding the problems and the pathologies faced by the people in America's urban slums and ghettos, the new community action approach had not been tried on any large scale, and there was no way of determining its effectiveness before the fact. Though some of these programs, such as Mobilization for Youth and HARYOU, had built research and evaluation components into their over-all organizational structure and design, at the time of the present study results from these sources were not available. Furthermore, it is necessary and desirable to set up an independent approach to the study of the nature and the results of community action programs in various localities.

The basic rationale of the Mobilization and HARYOU community action programs is that underprivileged peoples must somehow be taught to define and solve for themselves their most oppressive problems; they must seek out their own leadership and determine and use those methods necessary to bring about the desired changes in their community and their lives. Given the novelty of this approach—the many obvious and subtle risks and problems inherent in any attempt on the part of disadvantaged peoples to bring about actual changes in their predicament—and recognizing the fact that such changes cannot be brought about without sometimes abrasive contacts, misunderstandings, and the possibility of conflict with existing political, social service, and other institutional interests and traditional approaches, *it is essential to study these programs objectively in order to determine as precisely as possible those factors which increase and those which decrease their chances of effectiveness.*

While many of the existing community action programs obtain or expect to obtain their major, if not all of their funds from public and governmental sources, it is quite likely that private foundations will be asked to provide grants in support of some aspects of these programs. It is conceivable that significant parts of an over-all community action program, such as those involving lobbying, or direct political protests and pressure, cannot be legitimately or practically supported or long sustained by public funds. In that event, it would be necessary for private foundations to have some basis upon which to determine which programs and what aspects of them are worthy of their own support.

In the summer of 1964, David Hunter, executive director of the Stern Family Fund, approached the director of the Social Dynamics Research Institute with the idea for a study which would seek to explore community action projects systematically, so that the Fund would have a better basis for evaluating proposals which were being and would be submitted to it. In subsequent discussions with the board of directors of the Stern Family Fund, it was agreed that such a study would be valuable in the light of the novelty, diversity and the general ambiguity of the variety of programs and projects being developed under the general heading of "community action" or "social action" programs. It was further agreed that it would be necessary to devote the first year of this study to a preliminary examination of these projects with the following objectives:

A. To develop an inventory of the various community action programs now in operation or in the planning stage.

B. To determine how each of these programs defines what is meant by a community action program.

C. To attempt to establish on the basis of systematic inquiry some objective criteria by which these programs could be evaluated.

It is necessary to seek answers to various questions:

—Under whose auspices do these programs operate—the PCJD or the Office of Economic Opportunity, local community or city, non-governmental private foundations or individual support, civil rights groups, religious groups, labor unions, or a combination of groups?

—How does each program define what is meant by community action?

—What are the basic rationale and assumptions?

—What are the limits, the scope, the emphasis for each program?

—Is the major emphasis placed upon housing, education, employment, delinquency, narcotics, family life, or varying combinations of these?

—What are the methods relied upon: organization for political action, organization for demonstrations and other forms of social and community protest, community organizations of adults and youth groups, training programs, or other forms of self-help or remediation?

—To what extent do traditional social welfare and social service approaches intrude into the definitions of community action?

—What is the role of professional community organizers, social workers, and social agencies in these various community action programs?

—To what extent are other types of personnel, such as labor organizers or indigenous leaders or workers, used in the organization of groups for community action?

—To what extent are the methods, limits, and scope of community action programs influenced by political considerations and officials, social agencies, civil rights groups, the characteristics of indigenous leaders, or combinations of these?

—What are the chances of, the nature, the determinants, and the extent of conflict among the various interest groups involved in community action programs?

—To what extent are possibilities of conflict increased or decreased by the way in which such programs are designed and organized, and the techniques and methods which are used in developing and implementing them?

—To what extent are verbal definitions translated into actual programs? To what extent can they be? If there are discrepancies between verbal and programmatic definitions of community action, what is the basis for such discrepancies?

In regard to the objective of establishing criteria for evaluating community action programs, it is necessary to seek answers to the following questions:

—What plans and techniques for evaluation exist as a part of the operation of these programs themselves?

—By what standards can one determine the extent to which the goals and objectives of these programs are actually being fulfilled?

—How can one differentiate between effective community action programs and those programs which are primarily verbal or traditional community organization programs?

—What are the differences in personnel, methodology, and results which can aid in differentiating between effective community action programs and traditional programs?

—What types of programs should be encouraged and supported financially by private foundations, and why?

—What types of programs should be left to other sources of support, such as civil rights groups, governmental agencies, labor unions, or churches, and why?

—What types of programs should be discouraged, and why?

Methods and Source of Data

The background information and basic data for this study were obtained as follows:

A. *Correspondence* was begun with appropriate governmental agencies and various projects.

A master list of all projects under its auspices was obtained from the President's Committee on Juvenile Delinquency. Subsequent correspondence sought and obtained the written proposals and other documents from individual PCJD projects. The documents from twelve urban communities were analyzed in terms of an outline prepared for this study.

After the start of this study, its scope was drastically enlarged by the passage and implementation of the Economic Opportunity Act of 1964. Because of the goals and purposes of this study and because almost all of the programs which were previously under the auspices of the PCJD were transferred to the Office of Economic Opportunity, it was necessary to obtain from the OEO a list of all the community action programs funded by that office as of March, 1965. Correspondence was initiated with the directors of these OEO projects in order to obtain their proposals and documents for analysis.

Correspondence was initiated with civil rights leaders and organizations, with relevant personnel in universities and other community groups and private institutions in order to determine their degree of involvement in community action programs and obtain from them all relevant documents, proposals, and reports.

B. *Questionnaires* were sent to 131 projects and to a list of 80 civil rights organizations and groups in selected cities.

C. *Direct observation* of a sample of Community Action Programs was made in order to determine the relationship between written definitions of community action programs and the actual programs conducted by the projects. The cities visited, observed directly, and studied in varying degrees of detail and depth were:

1. New York City
2. Boston
3. New Haven
4. Syracuse
5. Washington, D.C.
6. Newark
7. Paterson
8. Minneapolis
9. Chicago
10. Cleveland
11. Los Angeles
12. San Francisco

D. *Interviews* were conducted with a sample of project directors, other top staff, former and present staff members, former and present members of boards of directors, and others in order to determine what they considered to be the major emphases, strengths, weaknesses, problems, conflicts, and values of these programs.

E. *Field investigations and participant observers* were used in several cities in order to interview directly the "residents of the areas and members of the group served" and to determine whether their programs do in fact involve and are seen by these individuals themselves as benefiting them.

F. *Content analysis of newspaper reports and editorials* dealing with these programs, their problems and successes, in order to understand the role of the press in presenting and interpreting controversies and conflicts associated with community action programs. It was possible to compare the press treatment of a major community action program controversy in New York City with the press treatment of a similar controversy in Syracuse, New York.

The sheer bulk and variety of data collected for this study required the use of some conceptual framework or theory to serve as a basis for organizing, analyzing, and presenting the findings in coherent and systematic form. The imperatives of an essential coherence in any written or oral communication can lead to distortion, oversimplification, or other forms of inaccuracies or incompleteness when one is seeking to understand and describe complex and inconsistent phenomena—phenomena which are not themselves always coherent. Given this fact, one must depend upon the available research design and methodological safeguards together with the consistency of a relevant, integrative, and verifiable theory, which combined might help to keep the distortions and inaccuracies to a minimum. The theory which served as a basis for the design of this study, the construction of its instruments, and the analysis of its data, was essentially that used in the HARYOU planning study and presented in *Youth in the Ghetto:* namely that the basic factor involved in the extent or the degree of success or failure of community action programs, and in any observable and significant changes in the predicament of the poor, was the degree of effective social power which was available and could be mobilized by the poor themselves or by their dependable allies or surrogates. Given this rationale and theoretical perspective, this study was strongly influenced by the social science literature dealing with the questions of social power and social change; its questions and approach were determined by the desire to understand the nature, problems, conflicts, and effectiveness of these programs in terms of the dynamics of power and power conflicts; and the analysis and presentation of the findings were attempts to provide a systematic picture of this complex social phenomenon within this integrative theoretical framework.

It is possible to observe common trends and developments

among these projects and to determine which are positive or negative despite the limitations described and the additional overriding fact that at the time of this study all these programs were so new (not one of them had had more than a year of actual operation) that it would seem premature, if not presumptuous, to make definitive conclusions concerning their success or failure.

This study and its findings can contribute to the development and refinement of theories of social power and social change. The most specific goal of the study, however, remains the desire to assess as objectively as possible the nature, effectiveness, and consequences of community action programs and to contribute this knowledge to the possibility of increasing the effectiveness of these programs and thereby of increasing the chances of observable positive change in the lives of human beings.

The study is limited in a number of ways, and therefore its findings cannot be considered definitive.

First, the public officials such as mayors, councilmen, and others in the political establishment who were related directly or indirectly to the anti-poverty program in a particular city were not directly interviewed. All information concerning their attitudes or opinions was obtained either through the conversations with the professionals or other staff members associated with the anti-poverty programs or through newspaper accounts. It would have been desirable, if time or personnel permitted it, to have interviewed these political officials directly, particularly where there was evidence of a conflict between these officials and the professionals.

Second, as the study proceeded it became clear that there were important anti-poverty programs being operated in other cities such as Pittsburgh, Trenton, Detroit, St. Louis, and Houston. It is possible that an intensive study of these cities would have clarified or modified the impressions and conclusions derived from the study of the cities which were visited.

Third, it was not possible to make a survey of the attitudes and opinions of the poor themselves in all the communities studied. A small and not necessarily representative sample of individuals in target areas was interviewed, and their responses recorded on tape, in Syracuse, Washington, and New York. The crucial test of the effectiveness of an anti-poverty and community action program certainly is the response of the individuals who are allegedly the beneficiaries of such programs. The sampling of such responses suggests that at present any findings in this regard are necessarily inconclusive. Further studies could contribute to a more definitive appraisal of these programs by more systematic surveys of the opinions and reactions of the poor in selected cities.

II
Stated Purposes, Definitions, and Goals

1. Rationale of Programs Seen in Terms of Tradition

The rationale and stated purposes of the community action programs cannot be seen in isolation from the history of social welfare and social action in the United States. The defined goals of these programs reflect the diverse traditions of this history, and their frequent ambiguity of intent and inherent contradictions may in part be traced to the contradictions implicit in the traditional American attitudes toward the poor. These traditional attitudes can be briefly summarized as follows:

A. *The Puritan–Horatio Alger Tradition.* The assumption of this tradition is that thrift, firm will, and good moral character tend to insure prosperity and personal success, and that a condition of poverty is related to the lack of personal moral fiber. The further assumption is that it is the better part of wisdom to withhold public help and aid lest indulgence reinforce weakness, and limit the motivation of those others who have, by virtue of fortitude and persistence, succeeded in achieving success themselves.

B. *The Good Samaritan–Lady Bountiful Tradition.* The assumption of this tradition is that poverty is the consequence of tragic human weakness and lamentable circumstance, very possibly no fault of the victim, and that compassion is the proper attitude of the fortunate towards the less fortunate. The correlate is that it is the duty of the compassionate to give succor to the helpless that their condition be made the more endurable.

C. *The Prophet Amos–New Deal Tradition.* The assumption of this tradition is that unjust conditions of society have victimized the poor and that the prosperous are often exploitative in their relationship to the poor. The duty of the poor is to break the shackles that bind them and assert their independence and their rights as free men, and the duty of the wealthy is to compensate the victims, to lead the fight against injustice, and to transform the nature of society itself.

All three traditions have been reinforced by American religious and social and economic and political institutions; the third has been reinforced even more strongly by political institutions like the New Deal. All three traditions are explicit and implicit in the current community action programs. The fact that the community action programs are overtly political in their origins (the President's Committee on Juvenile Delinquency and the War Against Poverty) has tended to bring to these programs components of the third tradition. Many of the most serious problems in these community action programs—*e.g.,* the organization of the poor to act in their own behalf—owe their impetus to this tradition of political justice and participatory democracy inherent in the trade union, the Populist and the civil rights movements. But the responses—*e.g.,* the withdrawal of federal support when resistance to political activities of the poor becomes too threatening to other interests—are related to the fact that the first and second traditions are also part of the rationale for these programs and, even when not expressed, tend to color the implemented programs themselves. The federal government has been stimulated in its own concern not only by political realities but by the pressure of philanthropic foundations, American business leadership, religious institutions, and others, who tend strongly to reflect both the first tradition of the-Lord-helps-those-who-help-themselves and the second tradition of benevolence with its frequent overtone of paternalism and *noblesse oblige.* One finds these community action programs at the same time influenced by the social welfare tradition and yet often hostile to the social work approach. This, in turn, occasions ambivalence from the social welfare community itself, which in cities like Cleveland, tends to dominate the community action program, and in other cities tends to engage in subtle and not-so-subtle opposition to the programs.

It is possible that a newer and fourth tradition is in the making, a tradition of cold, hardheaded pragmatism that makes no moral judgments about the causes of poverty and assumes no moral responsibility for eliminating poverty, but that does assume that the interests of the nation depend on abolishing dependency and misery. There are signs in the American political and business community that such a tradition may be emerging, emphasizing rational uses of natural resources and the harnessing of whatever power is necessary to conserve and cultivate such human resources.

Which, if any, of these traditions will prove to be most effective in facilitating the process of desirable social change has still to be determined.

2. Stated Purposes and Definitions

A. *Ambiguity of Definitions*

The clarity of the earlier President's Committee on Juvenile Delinquency proposals in the definitions of and emphasis on community action was sometimes but not always found in the proposals submitted to the Office of Economic Opportunity.

There has been a variety of definitions of what is meant by the "community action program" component of anti-poverty projects. This has to be understood first in terms of the fact that "community action programs" were not specifically defined by the Economic Opportunity Act of 1964. Section 201 of that act stated that the purpose of Title II "is to provide stimulation and incentive for urban and rural communities to mobilize their resources, public and private, to combat poverty through community action programs." Section 202, then, defines community action programs' attack on poverty in terms of (1) the mobilization and utilization of public and private resources; (2) the provision of services and assistance for "improving human performance, motivation and productivity"; (3) "the maximum feasible participation" of the intended beneficiaries of these programs; and (4) the administration and coordination of these programs by a public or private non-profit agency ("community action organization") which is "broadly representative of the community."

The latitude permitted by and the ambiguity of the statutory definition of community action programs is further indicated by Section 202(b), wherein it is stated that "The director is authorized to prescribe such additional criteria for community action programs as he shall deem appropriate."

In addition to the variety of definitions, the occasional evidence of a unique or a highly personal definition or interpretation of the rationale of a community action program probably reflects the exercise of this statutory latitude on the part of directors, their boards, and advisors. On the other hand, some constraint on the range of permissible variability in the verbal definition of community action programs is found in the law, particularly that part of the act which requires "maximum feasible participation" of the poor in the development, operation, and administration of these programs. This specific statutory requirement, however, is itself and on its face also ambiguous. While it required every anti-poverty project which functioned under the law to define its community action programs in terms of some type or degree of "involvement" or "participation" of the intended beneficiaries, it does not specify the extent or nature or level of involvement, the specific goals and consequences of participation and the standards by which one judges the value or effectiveness of the participation of the poor.

Appendix A indicates that the OEO was originally, at least, inclined to emphasize the social services-opportunities aspects of community action programs as contrasted with community action-organization of the poor.

B. *A Priori Model of Community Action*

Given the ambiguity of the statutory definition and the related variety of definitions of community action programs, it is necessary to construct an ideal definition and an *a priori* model of a functioning community action program to be used as stable standards by which existing and actual definitions can be examined, compared, and eventually evaluated. The definition devised by the director as reasonable and pragmatic for purposes of this study is:

A community action program must involve the development and use of techniques whereby the victims of poverty, social injustice, or some form of exploitation and discrimination are organized to identify their problems, determine the sources and causes, mobilize their energies, resources, and collective power in seeking and obtaining remedies and the desired changes.

The above ideal definition of community action programs takes into account the fact that in reality such programs involve a process, and that individual definitions and programs can be evaluated only within a time perspective. The role of time as a factor in the evaluation of these definitions is further highlighted by the fact that most if not all of these definitions were obtained from proposals written before the actual initiation of these programs or during the first year of their operation. The problem of this study—comparing verbal definitions with actual community action programs and the related problems of understanding the role of conflict and controversy and the ultimate test of effectiveness in terms of the attainment of the desired social change—cannot be resolved and no definite evaluation can be made without taking into account the factor of time.

For these reasons, therefore, it was necessary to formulate stages in the development of community action programs. These suggested time gradients reflect both hypothetical expectations and certain empirical observations and, therefore, may be used as a basis for the evaluation or comparison of different programs in spite of differences in time of actual operation.

(1) Each community action program must arise out of the awareness and some degree of articulation of a social problem adversely affecting the lives of the particular individuals to be involved.

(2) There must be some expression of concern and desire to seek remedies ranging from sporadic verbal protests through abortive individual or collective attempts at seeking redress through demonstrations, non-violent or violent protests or destructive eruptions.

(3) There must be attempts at the organization of the concerned individuals in order to define and identify their problems, seek an understanding of their causes, and determine the agents and agencies of government which are responsible and from which remedies must be sought.

(4) Efforts must be made to assess and mobilize the individual and group power available for appropriate action—seeking leadership, determining plan and method of action, and assigning responsibilities. This stage could also include the exploration and quest for dependable allies and the anticipation and determination of the nature, power and source of opposition.

(5) Probably the most critical stage in the community action process is the actual initiation of the agreed-upon appropriate action. The success of this stage is a function of the effectiveness of the previous stages and will determine the effectiveness of subsequent stages.

(6) The community action organization must have the strength and organizational power to sustain its action program in the face of initial and intensified conflict with specific governmental authorities and agencies, the general political structure, and other forms of vested interest. This stage will test not only the apparent power of the community action organizational machinery, but also its depth, its seriousness, the quality and resilience of its leadership, and the morale and determination of its members. This stage will also be a

test of the ability of the group to work cooperatively with its allies and other social institutions and to negotiate flexibly with political officials and governmental agencies without any loss in clarity of its goals or sacrifices of its integrity and independence.

(7) The ultimate test of the effectiveness of a community action organization and program is to be found in the evidence that the desired social change or agreed-upon goal was obtained through the efforts and activity of the community action machinery.

In summary, the above stages in an effective and serious community action program may be seen in terms of (1) an initial stage of evidence of *concern* and *protest* about some remediable problem adversely affecting the lives of human beings; (2) a second stage of *organization* and *mobilization* of the power of the victims for appropriate *social action;* (3) an intermediary stage of *confrontation*—the *initiation* and *sustaining* of the necessary action in spite of *controversy* and *conflict;* and (4) a final stage of obtaining and sustaining the desired *social change.*

An outstanding finding of this survey of the verbal and proposed programmatic definitions of community action programs is that few of the existing definitions describe community action in terms of the total pattern of this formulation. Nevertheless, almost all the definitions assumed that the problems of the poor stem from their lack of services, opportunities, or power, and defined community action as some combination of programs designed either to provide the necessary services and opportunities, or demonstrate the ability to mobilize the power required to obtain the desired change. Nearly all the proposals examined defined community action primarily in terms of social services with some inclusion of one or another ingredient of the community action constellation described above. In addition to one or more of the various types of educational and social services, the most frequently mentioned community action factor found in the written or oral definitions, obtained through interviews with directors and other top staff people, and through an analysis of the proposals and program definitions of fifty-four community action projects throughout the country was that of community organization. The tendency to mention community organization programs as ends in themselves—in isolation from the other ingredients of the community action constellation—and as satisfying the statutory requirements for community action programs again suggests the ambiguity of the definition found in the Economic Opportunity Act, and the novelty of the approach to the problems of the poor. It is difficult, in the light of these facts, to determine at this time the differences, if any, between community organization as an aspect of community action—as a means to the end of social change—and the traditional form of community organization as an end in itself.

Some proposals and project directors tend to define community action programs in terms of some of the components of the above definition, and imply, if not explicitly state, some of the stages. A few tend to define community action programs in terms of the above definition and model including the acceptance of the ultimate tests of effectiveness; *i.e.*, social action, confrontation and conflict, and social change.

C. *Types of Goals of Community Action*

It is important to assess these stated goals of community action programs, as determined by their explicit proposals to the government and by their explicit and implicit statements in questionnaires and interviews and program materials, not only to determine their relationship to the *a priori* model but also to clarify the standards by which to measure effectiveness in terms of their own intent.

The stated goals and definitions of purpose tend to fall into several major categories, reflective of the previously described traditional attitudes toward social welfare:

(1) The goal of provision of help through services from the community of affluence to the community of need.

(2) The goal of opening up of opportunities by the community of affluence for the community of need so that the poor can enter the more fortunate community.

(3) The goal of provision of help through the participation of the poor to help themselves, participation in the extension and provision of services through individual effort or through organization, such organization to be provided for and guided by the community of affluence, with the assumption that the poor will then secure the services and opportunities they need, improving their condition and hopefully rising out of that condition.

(4) The goal of providing the opportunity for the poor to take the leadership themselves through independent action, primarily political, to secure power as a countervailing force in the larger community to deal with the basic cause of poverty itself toward the end of the elimination of poverty.

(1) *Services: Help through services from the community of affluence to the community of need.* The tradition of services is the traditional foundation of social welfare, both public and private, with the public agencies tending toward alleviation of gross need (abject poverty-relief checks; psychosis-hospitalization; delinquency-recreation), and the private agencies oriented toward individual casework (impending divorce-family counselling), though both engage in both activities and, in many ways, parallel each other's functions. This is essentially a paternalistic approach to need that assumes the persistence and inevitability of need, and has its roots in the second tradition stated under Section 2, I, B of the Good Samaritan–Lady Bountiful tradition of Welfare.

Analysis of the data in this study shows a strong service orientation of stated goals despite the designation of "community action," as seen in the following excerpts from CAP documents:

One of the major objectives of the program is to develop *techniques for providing services to families who need services but do not take the initiative in seeking them.* This can be achieved, in part by communication and interpretation between the center and other agencies in the community. This can be accomplished by the liaison worker to the center from such agencies as the Boston Redevelopment Authority, the Boston Housing Authority, the Public Schools, and the City's Welfare Department. A community coordination unit will reach out actively into the community *to make contact with those who need its services* and to interpret its programs to other community agencies and to people in a position to refer those in need. (Boston, ABCD, emphasis added)

Four experiments: a) Coordinated Services to Large, Low-Income Families—CPI has undertaken the responsibility for *coordination of social services* for forty large, low-income families who have been placed in subsidized private rental housing from a housing project. The purpose is *to provide equal accessibility to social services* for all families in the demonstration group and in the control group; b) Community Welfare Project—Economically dependent families will be provided with a *full range of social and casework services, broader than those usually offered by a public welfare agency;* c) Concerted Services in Public Housing—An experiment with new approaches in *improving the social services in public housing communities* so that residents might attain a more self-sufficient life and participate more productively in our society; d) Community Health Program-Task is to *coordinate health services* in the Wooster Square and Dixwell demonstration areas. Top priority was given to efforts to consolidate the *nursing services* so as to provide a single community nursing program as recommended by the American Public Health Association. (New Haven, CPI, emphasis added)

Community Services—The general design of the neighborhood services program aims to involve residents of the program areas in planning, *making sure that services are available when and where people need them, seeing that services are visible and meaningful,* and affecting the service pattern of the community so that adequate and appropriate services are available for people who need them. (Syracuse, CFO, emphasis added)

The YOB is *not primarily an agency involved in direct implementation of programs.* Rather it is a cooperative governmental body designed to provide leadership, coordination, and innovative approaches to the unprecedented problems of urbanization—by utilizing facilities and resources of existing agencies wherever possible. The signatory agencies which comprise the YOB provide a *complete spectrum of governmental services* for youth, and, in fact, for the entire community. (Los Angeles, YOB, emphasis added)

(2) *Opportunities: Availability of opportunities from the community of affluence for the community of need.* The newer tradition of social welfare has been to amend the service emphasis by an emphasis on opportunities to be made available so that the poor can make their own way. It does not assume inevitability of need.

Employment Opportunities are blocked by the supply of jobs, lack of training, *lack of equal employment opportunities* for all, and *some youth lack motivation to learn and perception of employment opportunities*. . . . If *opportunity is a major factor in youth success,* as we believe it to be, then acquisition of basic knowledge and skills is an essential prerequisite. Therefore, promotion of youth success leads us to the objective of a high school education of excellent quality for every youth who is mentally and physically capable of achieving it.

Underlying the acquisition of knowledge and skills must be a set of attitudes which form the basis for motivation to learn. If staying in school to get an education has brought occupational achievement for others, then education is likely to be valued highly. But if education has not opened doors and if adults from outside the neighborhood, such as school personnel, affirm this, attitudes favorable to education probably will not be developed. Since the latter has often been the case in the past, *opening opportunities in employment must be accompanied by efforts to change attitudes* that relate to educational and occupational achievement. (New Haven, CPI, emphasis added)

This approach has been given impetus in various programs (*e.g.,* Minneapolis Community Health and Welfare Council) with reference to Cloward and Ohlin's theoretical base of opportunity barriers (see *Delinquency and Opportunity: A Theory of Delinquent Gangs,* New York: The Free Press,

1960). Mobilization for Youth posed the Cloward-Ohlin theory as the basis of its original proposal:

In summary, it is our belief that much delinquent behavior is engendered because opportunities for conformity are limited. Delinquency therefore represents not a lack of motivation to conform but quite the opposite: the desire to meet social expectations itself becomes the source of delinquent behavior if the possibility of doing so is limited or nonexistent.

The importance of these assumptions in framing the large-scale program which is proposed here cannot be overemphasized. The essence of our approach to prevention, rehabilitation, and social control in the field of juvenile delinquency may be stated as follows: in order to reduce the incidence of delinquent behavior or to rehabilitate persons who are already enmeshed in delinquent patterns, we must provide the social and psychological resources that make conformity possible. (MFY)

The federal government and some of its foundation allies, impatient with the traditional social service approach, are far more attracted by Cloward and Ohlin's "opportunity theory" to open doors to the poor to enable them to help themselves. Their own emphasis has, therefore, increasingly been on education and on jobs. It may well be that this will be the federal government's direction in the next few years for this positive reason, but also in no small part because of the threat embodied in the countervailing power theories. The conflict and anxiety experienced by local political and civic leadership after the OEO experimentation with the participation of the poor in the achievement of power has made the opportunity theory seem the lesser of two evils.

The Youth Development Program (YDP) sees delinquency as one form of behavior resulting from a disparity between aspirations and opportunity. . . . It is presumed that delinquency reduction and prevention should occur on a probabilistic basis. Favorable side effects (e.g., reduction of dependency and drop-outs) should occur. The underlying conditions on which the YDP has focused are lack of awareness, pathology, lack of concern and a lack of capability (for solving the problems of the deprived) on the part of the dominant society. . . .

In the main, programs should be directed toward those aspects of the predominate society which *provide* (*or limit*) *opportunities*, rather than toward specific problems of individual youth. (Minneapolis, YDP, emphasis added)

Two major substantive goals underlie UPO's Community Action Program: 1. Expanding opportunities and improving the skills of the poor; 2. Active and effective participation of the poor in the development and conduct of *a program aimed at the expansion of their opportunities and the improvement of their skills.* (Washington, D.C., UPO, emphasis added)

1) The program must be *opportunity-oriented as opposed to the service orientation of the traditional social welfare agency*. Jobs and education must have program priority; 2) *Self-help* must be the guiding principle of the program; 3) The operational unit of the program must be the *neighborhood;* 4) . . . the program should be, as far as possible, a truly *democratic* program. Poor people should be directly involved in the operations and administration of the program and have a readily accessible forum for criticizing the program and suggesting new courses of action. (Trenton, UPI, emphasis added)

(3) *Participation of the Poor: Provision of help from the community of affluence to encourage participation of the poor to help them help themselves.* The tendency to revert to the verbalization of the traditional social services approach was checked by the need to recognize and assert that the poor must be somehow involved in these programs, a need accentuated by OEO's insistence on "maximum feasible participation" of the poor as a condition for allocation of funds to a community action program. As Donald Wendell, assistant director of the United Community Corporation of Newark, put it: "The poor just can't be recipients of services. They must be involved in program planning, involved in policy positions relative to that service, and, where possible, be employed in the giving of

services." In Chicago, Deton Brooks of CCUO defines the committee's purposes as involving the poor in satisfaction of their needs (education, housing, etc.): "This means services not *for* the poor, but *with* the poor," a common theme in the last decade of the more enlightened social service agencies.

This goal, like (2), is a combination of the first and second traditions in American social welfare (see p. 19). It assumes that conditions of poverty are not inevitable, but that the poor bear some responsibility for alleviating their own condition at the same time as the affluent bear responsibility for helping through services. Such self-help can be (a) individual, as in the case of teenagers seeking job training, or (b) group-oriented, as in the case of block organizations working for neighborhood rehabilitation.

[Definition of what is meant by community organization] Helping *mobilize local resources* to meet the problem involving citizens in planning and decision-making, helping neighborhoods and groups to *organize for action and/or self-help;* helping community leaders to determine needs, priorities, and programs. [Assumptions underlying definition of community organization] . . . that people are concerned about problems when they know about them and can take appropriate action to meet the need with *cooperative effort.* (San Antonio, Economic Opportunities Development Corporation, emphasis added)

Community organization or development is a process by which resources within a community are mobilized to improve the social, political, and economic status of the community, and *inhabitants are educated to the need to bring in outside help and to the means to obtain outside help. . . . The resources necessary for self-improvement lie, for the most part, within the community itself. Upper income citizens will be concerned for those less fortunate if they are informed.* Improved communication among social agencies will increase the effectiveness of their services. (Craven Operation Progress, New Bern, North Carolina, emphasis added)

[Goal] To assist disadvantaged people in the achievement of *social and economic independence.* During the first year the highest priority was given to youth employment and education. The Neighborhood Adult Participation Project calls for the establishment of a community action program through which the poor themselves would participate in finding a solution to the problems of poverty and through which the poor would 'mount an attack on the forces perpetuating the evils of poverty.' (Los Angeles, EYOA, emphasis added)

[A Community Development Program is] the process of involving local residents in the effort *to do something about their problems* which arise out of the conditions of poverty. (San Francisco, emphasis added)

The victims of poverty need to 'take greater responsibility for their own destiny.' Neighborhood Stations are suggested as the vehicle through which these goals could be achieved: 'The GATEWAY effort is based upon *the concept of helping people of the neighborhood, youth and adults, to take greater responsibility for their own destiny:* in overcoming their problems, in utilizing available opportunities, in creating opportunities.' (St. Louis, emphasis added)

In order for an attack on poverty to have integrity and be viable, it must have a substantial provision for a *mechanism through which the poor can speak for themselves* in the identification of individual and community problems, can take action to influence programs being planned in their behalf, and can assume a variety of relevant *roles* in implementing these programs. (Los Angeles, emphasis added)

People should develop their own instrument *to solve their own problems.* 'Neighborhood people should begin to have a voice on the issues that interest them and should not be expected to participate only in terms of issues designated by others.' The document of this project defines the community action machinery and purpose as follows: 'The Neighborhood Development Team will be developed to help target area residents to become aware of, and to participate in neighborhood social action.' (Minneapolis, YDP, emphasis added)

The solution of neighborhood problems requires active, organized neighborhoods. Active neighborhoods require active articulate leadership. Hence, *it is important that the neighborhood coordinator not do for the people, but work with people.* (New Haven, CPI, emphasis added)

The social service emphases of community action program definitions have been required to give way, at least in such formulations, to the community organization and the mobilization-of-the-power-of-the-poor definitions of community action. These latter definitions and their programmatic formulations are predicated upon the basic assumption that the predicament of the poor is a consequence of their lack of power to change their conditions, not primarily a matter of desire or motivation. They assume further that where opportunities are blocked and services are unavailable to the poor, then the poor, themselves, must be organized to deal with these and other common personal and community problems.

(4) *Leadership of the Poor: Provision of opportunity for leadership of the poor through the assumption of power as a countervailing force.* This goal, which owes its primary impetus to the American tradition of political action, has been stimulated by the insistence of the federal government upon the participation of the poor and upon its tendency to define participation as the inclusion of the poor not only as recipients and workers, but as policy-making collaborators on anti-poverty boards.

The available data strongly suggests that the community action approach to the solution of the problems of the poor had its origin in the Mobilization for Youth and HARYOU projects in New York City. Mobilization's emphasis on the effective organization of the poor and the origin of the statutory requirement for "maximum feasible participation" of the poor is seen in this statement of goals from the Mobilization proposal:

Organizing the Unaffiliated—Participation by adults in decision-making matters that affect their interests increases their sense of identification with the community and the larger social order. The primary objective is to stimulate the participation of lower-class persons in attempts to resolve community problems. (New York, MFY)

An even more explicit statement of the meaning of community action, with emphasis on the goal of autonomy, is found later in the Mobilization document: "The uniqueness of our approach to community action is in the encouragement of autonomy among lower-class participants."

The HARYOU proposal was organized around the general theoretical perspective of the power-powerless dimension for understanding and remedying the conditions of the poor. Its definitions and emphasis on community action programs were therefore essential to the integrity and unity of its proposal and suggested programs. *Youth in the Ghetto,* the HARYOU proposal, defined community action as:

> Social action, in its operation sense, means and demands the stimulation of concern among individuals who share a common predicament, who are the victims of long-standing community problems and injustices, who can be induced not only to identify these problems but to seek to determine the methods by which they can be resolved, and who are able to develop and sustain the initiative for the type of collective action which, in fact, does resolve or ameliorate these problems. (New York, HARYOU)

The uniqueness of the HARYOU insistence on the nuclear importance of community action programs is demonstrated by its explicit rejection of a social services emphasis. In stating that "the core of the HARYOU programs and the basis upon which any claim for innovation must be judged is the persistent emphasis upon social action rather than dependence upon mere social services," HARYOU clearly articulated the nature of the incipient and current revolution in helping the poor. An examination of the total HARYOU document, particularly the proposed programs, revealed that the rejection of services was not complete, but one of emphasis. The community action emphasis was primary; social services were seen as a means to an end rather than an end and were an integral part of a total constellation of programs with community action at its core. The community action component was seen as an important factor in maintaining the substance and relevance of all suggested programs and services. It was HARYOU's contention that individuals identified with the programs—professionals, lay, indigenous, and recipients—had "to maintain the initiative in seeing that the components and the total cluster of programs maintain their relevance and their integrity."

These more action-oriented and self-help definitions or emphases of community action are based upon one or more of the following assumptions:

(a) that the predicament of the poor is due *not* to a lack of service and "opportunity" but primarily to their condition of *powerlessness;*

(b) that poverty will never be abolished until the poor themselves gain power to reverse their condition;

(c) that the victims of long-standing injustices must be organized to identify their problems, determine methods to alleviate the perceived problem, develop and sustain the type of organization for collective action which can survive when confronted with internal or external conflicts;

(d) that their goals must be stated in terms of observable community change or change in the predicament of the poor; and

(e) that their collective community action must address itself to the achievement of these goals.

The HARYOU report stated the problem in these terms. In Paterson, and Newark, New Jersey, the identical definition of social action was used in the descriptive documents. (Not insignificant in this regard is the relationship between the leadership in Paterson and Newark and in HARYOU. The then director of the Paterson Task Force for Community Action was formerly Program Director of HARYOU during its planning stage, and the then director of the Newark program was formerly Administrative Director of HARYOU.)

The concern with the powerlessness of the poor and the

intention of reversing this condition by basic social change dominates other statements of goals.

The Community Action Training Center of Syracuse focuses on the condition of powerlessness of the poor. It maintains that organization of the poor is the best immediate hope for altering their condition: 'Experience has indicated that through organization, the poor can create social systems which begin to provide an arena for action, which motivate the poor to resolution of the tough problems which poverty imposes on their lives, which can make them leaders in a successful community effort to do the socially useful work which needs to be done. . . . The fact that their lives are controlled by persons and forces outside themselves and that there are no socially provided structures through which they can exercise control over their lives [results in the fact that] persons in areas of poverty tend to become apathetic, without confidence in or hope for themselves, without long on-going courses of action central to their lives.'

[Goals of Community Action program] . . . to develop the competence of action area residents to deal with the problems of their neighborhood and community; to provide a mechanism enabling action area residents to deal with the problems of their neighborhoods and to make decisions regarding their solution; to increase the social cohesion of action area neighborhoods through effective organization; *to overcome the feelings of alienation and powerlessness among action area residents by increasing their ability to handle their problems themselves;* and to provide a mechanism which will enable action area residents who have special talents and abilities to assume key roles in promoting the social cohesion of their neighborhoods. (Syracuse, CATC, emphasis added)

[Neighborhood development is] a continuing process in which the residents of a neighborhood or given area act, individually or collectively, purposefully to bring about desired and agreed upon results. (Houston)

[Community action is an attempt] to help residents form new social action groups to act regarding concerns whenever there is no realistic vehicle for such social action. (Minneapolis)

Strategy for Action—1. Primary emphasis should be upon prevention, especially through education, employment, and leisure-time programs, with restorative services being utilized mainly to enable youth to take advantage of these basic programs; 2. Action should be carried out through the community's basic social institutions, and *institutional changes should be brought about where necessary;* 3. As far as possible, programs should have a neighborhood base, and the strengths of inner-city neighborhoods should be utilized. (New Haven, CPI, emphasis added)

UPO realizes that any program which involves services to people will have *limited chance for success if it is imposed from above without any real involvement by those to whom the service is directed.* Crucial, therefore, is the conscious effort to enlist citizen participation from the beginning, and to continue such involvement as the program is implemented and modified according to the defined needs of the poor themselves. It is a major policy commitment of UPO to help translate the needs of the poor into an effective demand for the resources necessary to overcome their status of economic dependency and poverty. . . . Apart from needing money, what the poor people in the United States lack is a *sense of power.* In their view they cannot change their economic fortunes; they are politically impotent; and they cannot affect for the better the future of their children. *The aim of the neighborhood development program is to change this perspective of powerlessness that now obtains among the poor.* (Washington, D.C., UPO)

[Community social action is] organizing of protestors or advocates to influence goals and actions rather than community organization, which implies balancing out of competing vested interests. . . . Community organization only comes alive if it is prodded by effective social action. Community organization is the melting pot; *social action is the fuel.* (Los Angeles, Director, YOB, emphasis added)

The subtle and complex relationship between the organization and mobilization of the power of the poor and the pride and effectiveness of the poor was most starkly expressed in the HARYOU document's rejection of the social services approach to community action as encouraging dependency and further immobilization of the poor. The fact remains, however, that even the HARYOU and Mobilization for Youth programs—the earliest models of the power and organization approach—have had to recognize that the poor have to be organized at least initially through the efforts of others and not primarily through their own efforts. The efforts of others, outside skills and forces, tend, however, to retain some control or guidance over the form of organization, its pace, goals, and direction of action. This is another facet of the pathos of the poor: independence can only be achieved by initial dependence upon others.

This fact is related to the question of the extent to which *community organization* tends to be equated with *community action.* The risks involved in an effective community action program could be avoided through the device whereby professionals or other mediators for the poor settle for the comparatively limited goals of community organization. The inconvenience and abrasiveness to the middle class inherent in a serious community action program could be avoided through the efforts and direction of such programs toward community organization by middle-class agents who work with the poor.

Some of the directors of anti-poverty programs see the goals and techniques of community organization and community action programs as identical; others believe that community organization is a means toward effective community action; others are reluctant to verbalize a distinction or assume that a meaningful distinction must be observed in programs and their consequences rather than in words; still others put their primary emphasis on community action and almost totally subordinate community organization toward this end.

The director of the Hunters Point Youth Opportunity Center in San Francisco was an example of one who sees no real distinction between community organization and community action: "We see social action as part of community organization. This is one way of achieving the goals of community organization." This would seem to suggest that community organization was the dominant goal, but with some verbal attention being paid to community action through the stated intent in the document to mobilize community resources "in an effective attack on social and economic problems."

Hy Frankel, of the United Planning Organization of Washington, D.C., stated clearly the position that "community organization is one of the instrumentalities of social action." But Frankel's concern with the problem of power broke through to dominate his ideas about community organization and social services. He asserted: "Just as social services in a sense is linked to a whole system of activities aimed at obtaining power, community organization could be considered another device, another instrument for *knowing how to get power and how to use it*" (emphasis added). His specific definition of community action emphasized this concept of power: "Social action refers to the organization of constituent members in a locale, aimed at obtaining and using power in their own interest. Social action is directed at obtaining, and exercising of power, in order to participate effectively in the community. . . . Long-range goals . . . the need to give to the people living in these areas a sense of power. Not only a sense of power, but in fact a control over resources."

The verbal responses of top officials of the Cleveland (CAY) and the Boston (ABCD) programs offer clear examples of a dynamic approach to community action as dominating a more static community organization program:

[Community action is] activities engaged in by groups designed to bring about institutional, social and political change which would accrue to the benefit of residents in the community. . . . It is only through *unified social action* of this type that pressure can be brought to bear on the community power structure. . . . Community organization is the first step and a major tool toward achieving social action. (Cleveland, CAY, emphasis added)

[Community action is the ability] to organize efforts to diagnose and take action to meet social needs which could include the need for people to be effective. Social action is *political action* and they are accountable. (Boston, ABCD, emphasis added)

The clarity of the Cleveland and Boston verbal pronouncements on the characteristics, implication, and significance of an effective community action program is ironic seen in the light of the fact that the actual program in Cleveland has been dominated by political and social agency vested interests and that the Boston program has been totally dominated by the political structure of that city. This paradox dramatizes the irony and another dimension of the pathos of the poor: that a clear verbal definition of community action does not necessarily mean that such definitions will be actually implemented or that there will be serious attempts at organizing the poor for protest and mobilizing their power to obtain "institutional, social and political change." Of all of the cities studied in depth for this report, Cleveland and Boston are among the cities with the least effective community action programs, as effectiveness is defined by their own documents and by the pronouncements of their top officials, and as it is defined for the purposes of this study.

D. *Resistance to Definition.* Some program directors are noticeably impatient with the search for definitions and assume that precision of statement may, in fact, be an impediment to action:

I am not really concerned about it [definitions]. I'm rather concerned about what needs to be done and how and what is the best way to do it. You get into a whole battle of semantics. I can't differentiate between social action and community action. . . . I think that when it comes right down to a definition it depends on the problem you are engaged in at the time. (San Francisco, Hunters Point)

I don't know, I'm really not an expert in definitions like that. . . . Social action is something the group would do to find a way of solving the problems it has. Change some social conditions that are not in the best interests. . . . You can't immediately aim at the top. You've got to change welfare, you've got to have pickets against the Board of Education, you've got to fight. This is our major goal say some of the organizations, but this is not our major goal, our major goal is neighborhood groups. We have always to remember that, because moving in this direction we become change agents ourselves. (Washington, D.C., UPO)

We avoid using this term [community organization] because of its historically limited use. . . . We tend to refer to neighborhood organization or community development to indicate the generating of self-help and social action groups. (Los Angeles, Director, YOB)

[Community organization and social action are to be] viewed as an organic whole. This is one of these academic questions that rapidly becomes obsolete when one gets in an All Systems Go state of mind. (Visalia, California)

Other program proposals emphasize the listing of particular concrete goals, *e.g.*, the suppressing of juvenile delinquency, and avoid stating general definitions of community action.

3. Implications of Stated Goals

A. *Ambiguity of Stated Goals*

The problem of the ambiguity and variety of definitions of what is meant by community action in the various anti-poverty programs has to be understood in terms of the following facts:

(1) The initial anti-poverty programs, while verbally demanding a new approach to the solutions of the problems of the poor, were still influenced by the traditional social services approach to the poor.

(2) It was easier to describe a novel approach to the problems of the poor verbally than to develop appropriate new programs compatible with the new statements of theory, rationale, purposes, and goals.

(3) There are probably conscious or unconscious anxieties concerning the risks inherent in an activist definition of community action—a definition which would make overt the conflict of vested interests, the political and social service cluster of power in the community—and which might directly or in-

directly incite the oppressed to forms of action which would not be easy to control.

(4) Ambiguous definitions might also reflect a deliberate attempt to provide the operators of such programs with a flexibility and an opportunity for maneuvering within which they could explore and experiment with different methods, techniques, and programs of community action.

(5) Probably the most important determinant of ambiguity of definitions is the extent to which a clear, definite, concrete, and activist definition of community action would make starkly clear the essential dilemma of governmental financing of such programs; namely, is it realistic to assume that federal or local government can finance and become accessories to serious attempts on the part of the poor to confront constituted political and governmental agencies and officials to demand actions on the part of these agencies which were previously denied and to engage in activities the consequences of which would be the disruption or major change in the existing political system?

B. *Community Action Programs as Mediators*

The need for communication between the poor and others is a persistent theme that runs throughout the statements of intent and the structures of the programs of the community action plans. For example, the Chicago Committee on Urban Opportunity (CCUO) aimed, according to Deton Brooks, its executive director, *"to bring the poor back within the communication network of the city* through massive doses of education and manpower training in addition to health care, family service, recreation-cultural experiences and environmental help" (emphasis added). A number of community action programs see themselves as serving a positive role of *mediation* between the alienated poor and the society at large. One finds constant references in the data to the gap between the federal government and the poor, between the local government and the poor, between churches and social agencies and the poor, and implications of the mediating role between federal and local programs and public and private agency programs.

The Commission on Youth Welfare in Chicago, for example, expects its area and neighborhood organizations to serve in a mediating role between neighborhood leadership and community-wide leadership (business, schools, the police, etc.). The goals of the Neighborhood Extension Service described in the proposal are: (1) development of local leadership; (2) development of social links between neighbors; (3) the integration of newcomer families into the life of the community; (4) development of specific self-help projects; and (5) strengthening participation for the street and block level in major area-wide programs and organizations.

The core of the Crusade for Opportunity program in Syracuse was the Neighborhood Advancement Center, a model of a multi-service center adapted to the needs of the community. Such centers were to form a coherent design for the implementation of services, and were to act as *intercessors* with bureaucracies. Residents could come for assistance with problems. Through the centers residents could communicate with each other, existing agency services could be coordinated, programs could be redirected for more effective service, and the residents could themselves participate in programs for (1) information and referral, (2) action area planning, (3) legal program, (4) recreation, (5) youth workers, and (6) homemakers.

The New Haven proposal, which defines community action as requiring "activity at the neighborhood level which suggests change for community betterment," states that this activity would be carried on initially by community organizers who would seek to strengthen the program through *interpretation to target area residents* who would encourage residents to act effectively and responsibly; and direct all community action programs carried out on the neighborhood level.

Such programs are essentially integrative ones, coordinating in place and in program the services normally provided separately by public and private social agencies. They could be described as in some sense analogous to the older settlement houses, which provided coordination in program and referrals for the community, or to district or ward political clubs, which, in past years, dominated the urban political structure. These centers provided a central meeting place in local neighborhoods, served as a source of help on such problems as job placement and legal difficulties, and as a focus of social communication and recreation. Such programs are essentially service-oriented rather than action-oriented and represent the imposition, or provision, of services from the outside world to the community of need. They are not essentially indigenous in terms of the initiators of the services; they are indigenous only in terms of the recipients of services.

An eloquent argument in support of the mediation and intergroup communication emphasis in community action activities was stated by the director of the University Neighborhood Councils of Washington, D.C.:

> There's been dialogue between people who have official responsibility and certain influential people, but there hasn't been much dialogue traditionally between people and the people in Washington —where people of different economic, social, and religious groups get together to try to talk about the community. One of the things that we started out with was the concept which we call total community. This includes the black, the white, the young, the poor, the rich, the haves, the have nots, the old and every other separate group, because we think it takes all kinds of people to make a community and they have to have some sense of community. *A sense of relatedness.* And there need not be rigid lines of separation by economics. And I think part of the difficulty growing out of the way that the economic opportunity is being administered all over the country is that we're making such a big issue of the difference and that the poverty is the responsibility of the poor, and the government, rather than poverty being the responsibility of the people. I'm saying this is to say, it's quite right for the government to step in, but it's also quite right for private citizens and citizen groups to step in. Both have an opportunity to step in, because the government's money is the people's money. (Emphasis added)

New York City's Mobilization for Youth, which stressed the need for "participation by adults in decision-making" in matters that affect their interests, also emphasized a desire to develop in the poor a "sense of identification with the community and the larger social order." In a number of projects there was a similar view of decision-making and participatory democracy as a means of mediating or communicating between the minority and the majority cultures. The question of the degree of consistency between the desire for independent participation of the poor and the desire for effective mediation and communication between the poor and others is not raised. These definitions assume that these goals are in fact compatible—or that it is necessary that they be made compatible in a dynamic community action program.

In spite of the strong belief of some observers of and staff participants in these programs that there is a need for communication and mediation between the poor and other groups in the larger community, problems arise in the attempt to develop effective machinery for these purposes. These problems are more likely to be recognized and neutralized by those staff members who have the specific responsibilities of organizing the poor, of preparing them for participation and communication with others, and of operating the mediation apparatus. The problem is seen essentially as one of liaison between the dominant middle-class culture and the alienated lower-class:

So this has been a problem, because you've got a neighborhood worker who has to stay in *the good graces of this middle-class organization,* but yet and still you've got to work more with these poor people to get them organized. (Neighborhood worker, Washington, D.C., UPO, emphasis added)

I had pretty much the same experience, in that there was an organization in my area and the people who participated were more middle-class. UPO is geared towards helping the poor, and it was a struggle for us. *The middle-class didn't understand the problems of the poor. They felt that they wanted the poor people to be able to do what they could do.* (Neighborhood worker, Washington, D.C., UPO, emphasis added)

A middle-aged woman from Georgia, an indigenous community organizer, referred to

. . . the hidden people, the people that have never been involved. They are people that want to belong, but never had a chance. . . . You almost have to drag some out, but those who have already been in there, going, it is not hard to organize them, but the people that you actually want you have to stay with a little longer.

It isn't hard to organize if you've lived in it, because I'm poor myself. *But to go among the middle-class on one side and the poor people on the other, that is rather hard. In fact, it's kind of hard to get them together.* But I've managed to do that on two streets. What they're interested in is the yards. The poor people didn't see any need at first to fix up their yards, but after I came along, we had different activities concerning these matters and they came over. So, in order to get the middle-class and the lower-class group together, you don't have the poor people go over to the middle-class. You have the middle-class meet at the little people's house.

The dilemma of communication of mediation across class lines is complicated in the anti-poverty program by the factor of race. In Washington, for example, where there is a comparatively high percentage of middle-class Negroes and a large number of poor Negroes, the usual class barriers are not made easier to breach by the fact of racial homogeneity. A community organizer for the UPO organization in the Cardoza project hinted at some of these problems as he identified the major dilemma in his account of attempts at organizing a Citizens' Advisory Committee:

. . . a dynamic force in which it can rally maybe 10,000 people around a cause and hit that seat of power, and maybe try to change it. The Citizens' Advisory Committee is a group of, well, it's a cross-section actually of people in this community. You have well-to-do people right on down to poor people and their aim is to have poor people control this and treat it as their own. But I think we must recognize that a lot of times poor people don't have these skills or the contacts to bring about the necessary change they want. Like I would like to see the middle-class people who have these skills, and who recognize their problems, and have some feelings for it, come in and actually work with these people. Not for them, but work with them, and attempt to impart some of their skills to them, so that the poor people could lose their dependency on these types of people. And this is very difficult to do.

Some community action projects recognize that the problem of mediation and communication is a two-way problem. The Chicago Urban Training Center, for example, experimented with a program designed specifically to train the members of the majority culture to understand the poor. The training center, for clergy and laymen, attempted to bridge the gap between church and the community by employing a dramatic initiation method for its recruits, called "The Plunge." Any person who came to the center was given a minimal amount of money and was told to function in the city for three to four days. He was required to live on this small amount of money as many of the poorer residents of any large city themselves have to do. After "the plunge," he came back to the training center and was assigned to various areas. This style implies a cultivation of instant empathy by shock treatment.

The poor have in a real sense been shut out of the culture. Even in the more effective of the mediating programs, where some attempts are being made to relate the majority culture to the poor, the relationship achieved seems to be one of negotiation between two alien groups, somewhat analogous to the relationship in diplomacy, in which separate nations set up channels through which to communicate with each other. One finds this attitude revealed on the one hand in the psychological orientation of those professional workers who enter the ghettos, who fear to travel except in pairs or by special bus, unable even to cross the language barrier to the "culturally disadvantaged," retreating at night to the safer "country"; and on the other in the orientation of black power advocates, whose anti-white stance makes it increasingly difficult to consider a bi-racial relationship except in terms of mutual exploitation.

C. *Community Action Programs as Forces for Social Cohesion and Harmony*

Closely related to the mediation and communication goals of community action programs is the goal of participatory democracy, stimulating a sense of *community harmony* and *social cohesion* among the poor. Such concern for social order, which is an explicit or implicit rationale for all these proposals and programs, seems particularly ironic in view of the charges against Mobilization for Youth and other community action programs as radical or socially disruptive in their intent and operation and in view of congressional and local political resistance to such programs. Among instances of such interest in conservative social values are these:

The Syracuse Action for Youth document gives as one of the goals of decision-making by action area residents the increasing of 'social cohesion . . . through effective organization.'

The Commission on Youth Welfare in Chicago sees *'greater community harmony'* and *'cooperative action'* as one of the goals of neighborhood organization. (Emphasis added)

The Joint Youth Development Committee in Chicago, among its specific program objectives, includes the development of 'attitudes *of respect for law and order* in the community.' (Emphasis added.)

The Hunters Point Youth Opportunities Center in San Francisco planned to 'discover and develop indigenous leadership in the Bay-view District which will operate for the good of all people across social, religious and nationality lines.' It sought to help the people of the district 'fulfill their *citizenship responsibilities* to one another and the whole community through effective patterns of individual and group action.' (Emphasis added)

The purpose of the Community Development program of the Syracuse Action for Youth project is 'to develop the competence of action area residents to deal with the problems of their neighborhood and community; to provide a mechanism enabling action area residents to deal with the problems of their neighborhoods and to make decisions regarding their solution; to *increase the social cohesion of action area neighborhoods* through effective organization; to overcome feelings of alienation and powerlessness among action area residents by increasing their ability to handle their problems themselves; and to provide a mechanism which will enable action area residents who have special talents and abilities to assume key roles in promoting *the social cohesion of their neighborhoods.*' (Emphasis added)

Related to this emphasis on social cohesion is the fact that the programs themselves arose out of conditions of social chaos: the President's Committee on Juvenile Delinquency out of public concern for the rising delinquency and crime wave that followed World War II; the anti-poverty program in response to the rising concern about the state of the alienated poor in an affluent society and their resistance to programs for urban renewal; and the condition of the Negro poor, in particular, among whom pressures for racial and economic justice have led to organized demonstrations and unorganized violence. The community action programs must therefore be seen, in part, as directed by political goals of quieting unrest. In such perspective the citizens' advisory committees and neighborhood boards of the poor play a role of helping the poor adjust to the inevitabilities of social change, as in urban renewal; or of ameliorating the conditions of misery that might lead, as they did in the summer riots of 1964, 1965, and 1966, to social chaos. In several cities also, in the hot summer of 1967, CAP workers from ghetto communities helped to cool the incendiary community mood.

D. *The Role of Community Action Programs as Molders of Individual Behavior*

A number of the program definitions emphasize the need for modifying the behavior of individual poor:

One of the major strategies to be employed in this program is based on the assumption that disadvantaged youth and adults will respond with a greater measure of *conformity to society's expectations when rewards which have meaning for them are made accessible to them* . . . and when an individual's expectations, based on his experience, are contingent with the expectations of the control system, the result will be conforming behavior achieved with little stress or strain. . . . This project, in fact, is concerned with a major imperfection in the operation of the system: the failure or inability of considerable numbers of youth to conform to the behavior that society has defined as law abiding. (Boston, ABCD)

The essence of the approach to prevention, rehabilitation and social control in the field of juvenile delinquency is as follows: in order to reduce the incidence of delinquent behavior or to rehabilitate persons who are already enmeshed in delinquent patterns, *we must provide the social and psychological resources that make conformity possible.* This is based upon the belief that much delinquency behavior is engendered because opportunities for conformity are limited. (New York, MFY, emphasis added)

Through the educational process involving the schools and the neighborhood agencies, our Target Area children, youth and adults develop the skills needed for the fulfillment of these basic ingredients of *acceptable human behavior:* 1. Observance of the law; 2. Preparedness for employment; 3. Preparedness for participation in government. (Minneapolis, emphasis added)

Various methods will be used to generate the motives and interests necessary to the development of skills, the maximum use of supporting services, and the eventual elimination of the conditions of poverty. Some will demonstrate that desired conditions of life are accessible and appropriate; others will supply the energy to learn and use required skills. These techniques include: using indigenous personnel *to make behavior change acceptable because acceptable people encourage and practice it.* (Washington, D.C., UPO, emphasis added)

The goals of the program of the Hunters Point Youth Opportunities Center in San Francisco, like a number of other programs, emphasize improvement of the appearance and morale of the district through educational programs, clean-up drives and beautification campaigns and 'effective programs of social service' designed to 'enrich' individual lives and 'improve their social relationships.' (San Francisco, HP)

These concerns with social order and individual "responsibilities" seems to have influenced the thinking and approach of the operational staff of some of these programs. The member of the staff of the UPO program in Washington, D.C., who was working with school drop-outs stated:

We have some kids working here in the office, to train them in office procedure. We have fellows that are going out doing odd jobs, like maybe cutting grass and washing windows, just anything to earn money, and to be independent, and not depending on anybody else. *This is to give them responsibility, to know how it is to have to report to work every morning and to be responsible on a job.*

I think the biggest problem is self-respect. We've for years been underdogged I think, and we've really or had really gotten to the point where we didn't care anymore, until some of these poverty programs did start up. And the main purpose is to acquire some *self-respect and sense of responsibility.* (Emphasis added)

There are numerous references elsewhere in interviews and documents to "socially responsible" programs. The unstated assumption seems to be that there are certain activities that can objectively be described as "responsible," as contrasted with other activities that can properly be described as "irresponsible," and further that such distinction can be made with some ease and presumably more readily by outside leadership than by the poor themselves. The fact is that others not themselves poor make the initial decision as to what is "responsible" and what is "irresponsible" behavior.

This probably unavoidable note of social conservatism, in the sense of the elimination of chaos and the concern with behavior, is reflected further in the appeal to social responsibility as a characteristic not only to be inculcated in the poor themselves, but also as the determinant of the objective programs and actions in which the poor are to be encouraged to participate. CATC in Syracuse, for example, urged help to enable the poor to become "leaders in a successful community effort to *do the socially useful work* which needs to be done." (Emphasis added)

F. *The Role of Community Action Programs as Agents for Self-Help*

The community-cleanliness and the individual-improvement approaches, like the community-cohesion and social-responsibility goals of community action programs must involve some judgment of the conditions of the poor in terms of the standards of the middle class and sometimes involves the assumption that the individual poor is in some way responsible for his failure to improve his living conditions—to remove the dirt, drabness, and ugliness of his environment and the shabbiness of his own life. The pathos of the poor is again demonstrated by the fact that a number of them express this same conviction to interviewers, as indeed do many black nationalists. Cleveland's CAY's belief that "if we can motivate people to the point where a change is affected in their values and behavior, this will result in a reduction of social problems confronting the residents of the community" can be supported not only as a middle-class perspective but also as a point of view or aspiration shared by many of the more articulate poor. There remains, however, the question of whether there is any independent or realistic evidence to support the assumptions on which this perspective is based. Values and standards of behavior as defined and accepted by the middle class may be worth having and are saleable in the larger society, which is dominated by the middle class. Up to the present, however, there is no evidence that they, in themselves, reduce the social problems confronting the poor.

While the many self-help community action programs make clear explicitly or implicitly that the problems of the poor stem directly from the realities and dynamics of poverty and the related blockages in opportunity and lack of power, they nonetheless place the primary burden for resolving these problems on the poor themselves. The rationale for this may be the pragmatic conclusion that the conditions under which the poor are required to live reflects the reality of the neglect, indifference, insensitivity or callous exploitativeness of others and that if their conditions are to be improved, they must struggle to amend them themselves. If the human damage—and powerlessness—associated with poverty should make it impossible for the poor to improve their condition primarily through their own efforts, is the larger society, by the same rationale, absolved of responsibility? It is one of the dangers inherent in the black nationalists' almost Puritanical assumption of responsibility that the majority community will accept the rationale themselves.

In these self-help programs, there seems to be little plan and provision for involving middle- and upper-class individuals directly in the organizations and the actual operation of programs designed to seek remedies for poverty and the redress of long-standing social inequities. Possible exceptions to this general observation is the role of the professionals who direct and operate these programs and of the federal and local officials who administer and monitor them, and leaders of churches and other institutions that involve themselves in such community programs as Chicago's Woodlawn Organization and Syracuse's Citizens Crusade Against Poverty. These individuals who are representatives of the non-poor are not only not directly involved in the activities of the poor—they tend to see themselves at best as catalysts or primers or at worst as detached observers or analysts—but may also act as surrogates of the middle and upper classes directing and containing the extent and range of action permitted the poor. The middle class is not encouraged to view the problems of the poor as having direct consequences on their own condition.

The responsibiity or obligation of the non-poor to become involved in the actual machinery for changing the conditions of the poor in terms of its own self-interest has not been established.

These questions raise other interesting questions implicit in the self-help doctrine. American democracy of course is based upon the fundamental belief in the importance of participatory democracy. The responsibility of a person for his own welfare is not a *necessary* inference from that democratic principle, but, in American tradition, reflected in the free enterprise system and the American system of morality with its emphasis on thrift and individual responsibility, participatory democracy has more often than not been identified with the responsibility of the individual for what happens to him. A further extension of this ideology led to the melting pot phenomenon, through which immigrants were helped to pull themselves up by their own bootstraps to join the majority culture. Some have concluded that if the individual is unsuccessful in moving into the middle-class culture, he has in some way failed to take appropriate action. So, for example, in a middle-class community the individual homeowner is blamed if he does not protest bad lighting on his street and win over city hall. But these assumptions rest on the fact that proper lighting is regarded as his right. It is assumed that if he complains, something will be done. These assumptions are not valid in relation to the non-middle-class poor, particularly the Negro, whose prior complaints have seldom been effective because the rights are not granted even in principle and who have retreated, therefore, into further apathy, losing faith that their own efforts can achieve anything positive.

The anti-poverty programs' introduction into such communities of the middle-class participatory democracy theory, through neighborhood boards and forums structured after the model of the town meeting, will in itself introduce these people to the middle-class means of democratic action. (These are not incidentally, *upper-class* means of achieving ends. For the upper classes, individual influence at the seat of power, rather than public meetings designed to reach the ear of power, is more effective.) The assumption that such means will work for the poor must be confirmed in practice. The failure of organized action to produce results will further frustrate and alienate the poor. Aware that they are the victims of social conditions that they have not brought about, they will sense the irrelevance of the self-help theory to such conditions, realizing intuitively either that the majority culture does not understand the depth of the problem or that it does not wish to accept the conclusion that the society at large, and not the community of the poor alone, must take responsibility for remedial action. Of course, the very fact that the means of middle-class protest have been introduced into these areas may lead the poor to expect middle-class consequences, leading them to a dissatisfaction with their condition that will compel majority action. But it is a real question how effective such organized political activity by the poor can be.

III
Community Action Programs and Attempts at Implementation

1. Classification of Community Action Programs

The Community Action programs may and do differ from their stated purposes in a variety of ways. The verbal definition may, for example, be action-oriented while the programs are essentially service-oriented, or vice versa. Or the definitions may be oriented toward community action while the programs are content with a community organization emphasis. If one views the matter of service—opportunities—organization—action on a continuum, the data tend to show a movement in one of two directions in the progression from proposal to program. Some move toward action, in response to unanticipated pressures, usually internal to the programs or identified with the program; others move away from action, also in response to pressures, usually external to the program or internal sources identified with external interests, usually political. Wherever there is a shift that leads to inconsistency between purpose and implementation, it seems to be in reaction to such specific stimuli.

In general, the data seem to show a movement from either extreme toward the "center," that is, away from a narrow service emphasis toward opportunity, or back from an action emphasis to organization/opportunity. Other programs are totally consistent with their stated goals. The purposes and definitions must be considered *in relation* to their implementation; only in relationship are they relevant to the lives of people they exist to serve. Should they promise more than they fulfill, they may ease the anxiety of vested interests threatened by social change but they will increase the disillusionment of the poor.

There is a real question as to the relationship between lucid and rationally structured and articulated proposals submitted as requisite for federal or foundation funds and the actual programs that have followed. Program officials may not intend genuine implementation, but even if they *do,* the skills necessary for preparation of good documents may not be the relevant or primary ones necessary for the implementation of programs.

One may even speculate that good proposals and commitments of funds serve the same purpose that demonstrations do for the oppressed, or conventions and structured organization for the middle-class—a form of therapy that serves as a substitute for action, obscuring irrelevance in terms of achievement of the stated desired goals.

An analysis of the program descriptions of fifty-one (51) "community action" projects (see Chart 1), not including the twelve major cities studied, indicated that projects could be classified in terms of nine categories, seven of which were service-opportunity oriented. There were forty types of programs operated or planned under the general heading of community action programs. (See Tables 1 and 2.)

Head Start or some form of pre-school program was the most frequently mentioned program; 41 of the 51, four out of five, projects operated this type of program. The next most frequent were the compensatory education programs operated by 32 of the 51 projects (three out of five). Twenty or more projects operated health services programs and group work and recreational services as "community action" programs. Twenty-three projects mentioned the employment of indigenous staff, generally in the multi-service or neighborhood centers, as aides or liaison workers. Only five projects operated programs which were specifically described in terms of "organization for community social action."

The major finding of the tabulation was that, despite the

designation of *community action,* programs seem to be functioning primarily in terms of *services.* There seems to be little relationship between the theory, rationale, or definition of social action presented in the proposals and interviews and these programs. In these 51 projects examined (not including the twelve major cities studied in depth), educational services and social services accounted for the bulk, as we have seen. The most frequently mentioned of these programs were classified under *educational services*—116 were mentioned (many projects have multiple programs). The next most frequently mentioned were *social service programs* (103). When health, housing, and delinquency are added to the more traditional casework and group work services, the majority of references are, in fact, to services which could be operated without regard either to the "opportunity" theory (2,C,(2)) of anti-poverty programs, and without regard to power theory (2,C,(4)).

If it is true, as past experience would seem to argue, that mere provision of services for the poor will not significantly affect the conditions of the poor or change their predicament, and if, as the HARYOU document suggests, an anti-poverty program built around services will increase the sense of dependency of the poor, then most current programs fail to reflect the more recent innovative approach to the problems of the poor and serve rather as a continuation of the traditional social service approach. Since the social service technique has not been particularly effective in providing any positive solution to the problems of the poor in the past, one would conclude that the request for an increase of such services as a way of attacking the problems of the present and the future does not reflect a serious determination to abolish poverty. While many programs hold verbally to opportunity-power theory, few implement such theory. It is, of course, easier to implement a social service approach; the structure of social agencies has already been built and the temptation is to strengthen existing structures rather than to replace or compete with them. In cities like Cleveland the agencies have, in fact, dominated the community action program. They have extended the existing model even when verbalizing a different intent. Another factor in the continuation of the service emphasis is the actual need for educational and social services. The problem, however, has been complicated by the inadequacies of the context within which the services were provided. Professionals provide tutoring, group work, recrea-

Chart 1: Tabulated Sample of 51 Community Action Programs by Region and State

Region	*State*	*City*
North Eastern	Connecticut	Hartford
		Bridgeport
		Stamford
	New Jersey	Asbury Park
	New York	New Rochelle
	Massachusetts	New Bedford
		Springfield
	Pennsylvania	Pittsburgh
Border States	Kentucky	Louisville
		Whitesburgh (r)*
		Harlan (r)
		Wolfe City (r)
		Hyden (r)
		Barbourville (r)
	Maryland	Baltimore
	West Virginia	Keyser (r)
		Welch (r)
South Atlantic and South Central	Florida	Dade County (Miami)
	Georgia	Baxley (r)
		Athens (r)
		Gainesville (r)
		LaGrange (r)
		Savannah
	Louisiana	Lafayette (r)
	Mississippi	Corinth (r)
	North Carolina	Durham

Chart 1 (*Continued*)

Region	*State*	*City*
		New Bern (r)
	Tennessee	Chattanooga
Midwest	Michigan	Detroit
		Detroit Metropolitan Fund
		Lansing
		Eloise (r)
	Minnestota	Leech Lake Reservation (r)
	Missouri	St. Louis
		Columbia (r)
		Ripley (r)
	Nebraska	Omaha
	Ohio	Cincinnati
	Wisconsin	Milwaukee
Southwest and Mountain	Arizona	Navaho Tribe (r)
		Gila River Indians (r)
	Colorado	Denver
	Texas	Corpus Christi
	New Mexico	Zuni Tribe (r)
Pacific and Far West	Alaska	Juneau
	California	Oakland
		Riverside
		Sacramento
		Santa Clara County (r)
		Visalia (r)
	Washington	Tacoma

* (r) = rural area

Table 1: Classification of 51 Community Action Programs in Terms of Services

(1) *Educational Services*

41	Head Start
32	Compensatory, enrichment programs
10	"Cultural deprivation" programs
12	Adult education programs
8	Teacher training programs
7	Educational counseling and guidance
6	Work study programs
116	= Total of programs offered

(2) *Social Services*

23	Group work and recreation programs
16	Multi-service centers, comprehensive school centers, or umbrella programs
16	Homemaker services, including consumer education
13	Day care
10	Casework services
9	Family planning programs for unwed mothers
8	Arts and culture programs
6	Welfare services
2	Mental health programs
103	= Total of programs offered

(3) *Specific Delinquency Prevention and Control Services*
4 = Total

(4) *Health Services* (No narcotics programs mentioned)
23 = Total

(5) *Housing Services*
10 = Total

(6) *Legal Aid Services*
8 = Total

(7) *Job Training and Placement Services*

11	Job counseling
9	Job training
8	Economic self-help, programs for small business

6 Work study programs (also included under (1))
6 Skills development and vocational training
5 Adult employment, upgrading, experience
3 OJT programs
3 General upgrading of skills
1 Youth work experience

52 = Total

(8) *Community Organization Programs*

15 Organization for program involvement
12 Organization in neighborhood centers
7 Traditional social welfare-settlement house style organizations

34 =Total

(9) *Community Action*

23 Use of indigenous staff
12 Use of indigenous community groups
10 Indigenous leadership training
5 Organization for action
5 Indigenous community representation on boards

55 = Total

SUMMARY

Services		*Community Organization*		*Community Action*	
1. Educational	116	All forms of community organization	34	Leadership training	10
2. Social services	103			Indigenous participation	40
3. Job training and self-help	52			Organization for action	5
4. Health services	23				
5. Housing	10				
6. Legal aid	8				
7. Delinquency	5				
Total = 317		Total = 34		Total = 55	

Table 2: Inventory of Community Action Program Descriptions of 51 Programs in Terms of Services and Frequency of Mention

Program	*Number of times mentioned*	*Classification*
1. Head Start or pre-school	41	Educational services
2. Compensatory or educational enrichment	32	Educational services
3. Health services	23	Health services
4. Group work and recreation	23	Social services
5. Use of indigenous staff	23	Community action
6. Multi-service center programs	16	Social services
7. Homemaker services	16	Social services
8. Community organization for purposes of program	15	Community organization
9. Day care	13	Social services
10. Use of indigenous community groups	12	Community action
11. Adult education	12	Educational services
12. Neighborhood centers	12	Community organization
13. Job counseling and placement	11	Job training
14. Casework services	10	Social services
15. Housing programs	10	Housing services
16. Indigenous leadership training	10	Community action
17. "Cultural deprivation" programs	10	Educational services
18. Family planning, unwed mothers	9	Social services
19. Vista (Not Title II)	9	Social services
20. Job training	9	Job training
21. Teacher training	8	Educational services
22. Small business	8	Economic self-help
23. Arts and culture	8	Social services
24. Legal aid	8	Legal aid
25. Educational counseling and guidance	7	Educational services
26. Comprehensive school centers	7	Social services
27. Work study programs	6	Educational services and job training

28. Skills or vocational training	6	Job training
29. Welfare services	6	Social services
30. Adult employment, upgrading	5	Job training
31. Social welfare approach to community organization	7	Community organization
32. Community representation on boards	5	Community action
33. Organization for action	5	Community action
34. Organization for citizen participation	5	Community organization
35. Juvenile delinquency	4	Delinquency control
36. On the job training	3	Job training
37. Upgrading of skills	3	Job training
38. Mental health services	2	Social services
39. Youth work experience	1	Job training
40. Narcotics and control	0	Delinquency

tion, homemaker programs, and the like, in traditional ways. There is no evidence that they are more relevant for being given a new name, such as "community action programs," or for being subsumed under the anti-poverty "umbrella." The fact that these services are incorporated under a new umbrella has suggested a disaffection with them as given and an awareness of the lack of direct relevance of the social service approach. Mere incorporation has not significantly altered the services themselves.

Social services do not change the predicament of the poor in any basic way; their intent is to *ameliorate* the condition, and their success is no greater than the intent. They may, in fact, add to the poor's sense of dependency—a concrete demonstration of the powerlessness of the person. To intensify such dependency is not consistent with social change. The procedure may be perpetuated for its own sake while failing to lessen the sense of hopelessness of the poor.

A possible exception to the charge that social services do not open up opportunities for change is the provision of educational services and job training. But even educational services, tutoring, remediation, and programs for the "culturally deprived" are compensatory only and do not attack the basic problem of educational inefficiency in schools. Even where effective, such services tend to obscure the problem and divert potential energy from more effective protest and action directed toward the goal of more efficient education for lower-status children. In certain cities, such as Boston, Cleveland, and Chicago, the boards of education have sought to immunize themselves against effective protest by seeking to influence the anti-poverty apparatus. In this regard, it is of interest that the first open conflict in MFY came when organized parents on the Lower East Side confronted the district superintendent of schools on the issue of efficiency of neighborhood schools.

The issue is not whether social services should or should not be provided, but rather the conditions under which they are provided. It is quite possible that social services must be an integral part of any effective community action program and that the new approach of the opportunity-power theory to the predicament of the poor will have to recognize, as the MFY and HARYOU program documents do, that social services cannot be ignored, for among the things from which the poor have suffered is deprivation of services under conditions that humanize. The poor have been short-changed in services customarily provided by government or purchased in middle-class society, *e.g.*, legal, health, and educational services. The poor must be helped to develop the machinery to obtain services, but to monitor them in terms of quality, so that services are seen as rights and not as *largesse* reinforcing inferior status, a sense of humiliation and dependency, and a conviction of powerlessness. Services have traditionally often been provided in such a way as to perpetuate the pathology of the poor and, what is more, as to diminish will and the motivation to change their fundamental status. But services need not be paternalistic in character. Regarded as rights, they tend to strengthen rather than weaken a sense of status.

Thirty-four programs tabulated were concerned primarily with *community organization* among the poor. More than half of these seem primarily concerned with community organization for its own sake, that is, in relationship to services in a "settlement house" as the basis of organizing the community. Twelve of these programs seem to be moving toward an approach to community organization that establishes neighborhood centers which could in fact be effective vehicles for community action and protest programs. These twelve have been classified here under community organization rather than community action only because respondents did not state specifically that the goal of the neighborhood centers was to obtain community action.

Fifty-five programs contained some element of *community action.* Fifty were so classified because they stated as a primary program objective the involvement of indigenous staff and the training of indigenous leadership—it was assumed that any program which referred specifically to a concern for involvement of indigenous individuals or groups at any level other than as beneficiaries of services was closer to the definition of community action programs, as used as a basis for this study, than were social service or community organization programs as such. It is significant, however, that only five out of the fifty-five stated a social action goal as the basis for their program.

One can only speculate concerning the meaning of the fact that of a total of 406 programs mentioned by these projects, 317, or roughly three out of four, were concerned primarily with traditional services and not directly with community organization or community action. One possible explanation is that the social service interpretation is possible not only because of the ambiguity of the last Economic Opportunity Act but because it reflects an easier, less disturbing, less risky, and more traditional approach to the poor and their problems. Specifically, this approach fails to bring with it the risk of serious confrontation and conflict. It maintains the traditional relationship between middle-class professionals and social workers, educators, students, counselors, and specialists in health, housing, and the law, and the poor as the recipients of their skills and beneficiaries. The extent of any meaningful change in the relative status of the poor can, therefore, be controlled by the degree of effective identification and empathy of the professional who provides services for the poor. The psychological risk of direct involvement and potential conflict can be avoided by continuing to provide the poor with a type of service determined by professionals not themselves poor.

Such services could be meaningful in attaining the goals of serious improvement in the predicament of the poor if they did, in fact, provide the poor with the skills and resources necessary to improve their status. There is no evidence, however, that they did so in the past and there is no evidence that they are doing so in the present. The fact that such services are funded and operating under the "community action" segment of the anti-poverty program is an indication of ambiguity. It is another ironic example of the pathos of the poor. It is certainly not based on any evidence that these services are specifically or directly related to community action programs themselves, or to any theory of opportunity or power as a basis for a major breakthrough in the war on poverty, or that they are in any way relevant to the securing of observable changes in the condition of the poor.

The community organization programs can be viewed as a possible transition between the traditional services approach to the problems of the poor and, hopefully, a more effective community action approach wherein the poor are organized to deal directly and effectively with the problem of the relationship among opportunity, power, and services. If not, the community organization approach can be viewed and operated merely as another way to release the frustrations and contain the energies of the poor. This would be consistent with the traditional attitude which encouraged the poor to organize to function more efficiently in community centers and settlement houses where older people participated in therapeutic discussion groups or were encouraged to weave baskets or play checkers, while teenagers danced, played Ping-Pong or basketball as a release for energies which otherwise might have been expended in ways that seemed inappropriate to the more stable middle-class society.

It is possible that, given the new verbalizations, and the new fashion of discussing community action programs, it might be a little more difficult for community organization programs to be contained within the traditional framework and goals. It may be that, once the poor are organized and brought together in groups and clubs, the more articulate and restless members will insist upon moving the group toward real problems, toward confrontation and conflict, and therefore toward some form of serious community action.

2. Changing Professional Attitudes Toward Social Welfare

The changing attitudes toward social welfare are reflected in the following selected comments from officials in some of the most effective community action programs:

The opportunity programs are an addition, really, to what I called before the cornucopia. Up until they came along you had various services that were geared towards helping people adjust or accommodate to a life of poverty, through whatever technology was available; as far as school counseling and all of that. 'We're going to suspend you Buddy, so adjust to it.' 'We'll give you a home bound teacher, or we won't, depending on whether we have it, but you know our intentions are good. See, don't you understand what we're trying to do Buddy,' etc. Understand all of this, you know peace through understanding. Health through understanding. So you have opportunity programs now. I think they're wonderful, and necessary, they're great. But first of all they're not coming through in the massive quantities needed, and secondly the whole thing is dependent upon the locality. By this I mean the people in power, the way it's shaped up; the Mayor, the power structure exercising the option to ask for funds, and how do you apply leverage and stimulation.

I think it has some national significance in that it may be an answer to some of the national disenchantment which we see with social services themselves. I think the nation has been on a kick of opportunity orientation. Forgetting that many of the casualties of the last 50 or 100 years are in serious shape and you can't just whistle to them like a horse that's starving, and say here's oats . . . or here's opportunities, eat. We know that when someone is frostbitten or on a starvation diet you have to adjust them to these new goodies slowly and there has to be a medical watch on this. So what I'm getting at is I think the head of the exclusively opportunity oriented people are becoming aware, that is if they skim off the cream of the disadvantaged groups, the racially contained groups, and begin to skim them off through employment opportunities and other things, they're getting down to a population level that has suffered, that is distrustful, that needs more patient, longer term preparation. And here is where re-tooled, re-oriented social work and other technologies can be very useful. I think that this has begun to happen here. It's happening there. Mobilization for Youth knew this all along, obviously, in the way that its structure was set up.

We started with an almost simplistic orientation to opportunities, and maybe this was because the race for grantsmanship—to get grants—made it an advantage to profess a different philosophy that was different from others, because this would interest the people who were giving grants, who were interested in putting their chips on different horses.

The existing agencies, and I think we have a good complex of good agencies in this community, were not too well related to serving this population, and in the neighborhoods. So subtle efforts were made to try to involve the existing agencies in serving this inner-city population.

Effort was made to try to get a coordinator of social services to get more involvement of existing social services, but it came to be increasingly evident that there was an additional input of services needed as well as connecting up with the existing agencies.

Social workers in our district office aren't in close contact with the client. If they don't want to see a client, all they have to do is tell the switchboard people or the receptionist. Clients just can't come right in and hear them. With us it's different, we have these little apartments, the client can come in and besides, we go around and we see them. The point is we're closer to them. And that's why I guess it's all become real.

I think some of the agencies are taking a fresh look at their way of serving a community, and this is no secret, whether it be in New Haven or Hartford, or New York. The middle class can do a better job in suburbia than they can in the city. Now Boy Scouts are trying to make a real major effort to do an inner-city job. And we're getting reasonably tough with them. Saying if they really want to do this job, make the commitment. The commitment is some real staff time. To become part of our team.

Some of the representative groups, Boy Scouts, 4H, Girl Scouts, are now beginning to change their direction, and want in. You see there's a certain amount of status that's coming from beginning to work in the inner city. The pressure is on the national Boy Scout organizations, the National Girl Scout organizations, and 4H on the national level. You know, get into the urban picture, because you're losing out in the rural area anyhow.

We're not social workers. What we try to do is to connect up the individual with the agency which can help. The problem is that the agency is over its head itself nine times out of ten. Most of the agencies operate at poverty level themselves. They don't have staff; they don't have the expertise; they don't have the resources, so what's the agency going to do? Agencies in the beginning had a tendency to dump their problems on this great big super agency because it had plenty of money and high-powered staff, was new in the community. It was our responsibility to solve all the problems. And we soon found out that our role is catalytic, our role was to stimulate institutional change.

Our role was to get agencies to do things differently than they had done things previously. We would provide certain resources, but they would have to provide different techniques, different ways of doing things to meet the modern responsibility. We made it clear from the very beginning that our workers were not there to solve the problem, but rather to identify gaps in service, to get people to the proper agency, and to relate people to those opportunity programs that would help lift them out of this morass of poverty.

This is a coalition type of program, a program of negotiation, mediation and getting together with people to create things rather than lining up against somebody. We have a political system here that has been ahead of social work in what it wants to do for people. The goals of the political system are consistent with the goals of what I would consider a progressive social welfare system.

We have students from the School of Social Work but we have no training program. I have my own ideas. . . . I spoke before a group of fund raisers just before I went on my vacation and my conception of what constituted social planning flabbergasted them. My interpretation of what I included in health and welfare they didn't believe should be in there because it didn't have a label on it. The whole matter of getting into the issue of racial tension and compensatory education were too far out they felt. We are involved in urban re-development. We are concerned about anything which tends to impinge upon the health and welfare of people, whatever the changes. Whether physical changes or interpersonal relationship, we have a role. This is a broadened role. If you are going to be at all effective you must get into social action.

I think one of the major contributions our organization has made to change—institutional change—is working with the Public Welfare Department during the past year. There's been a change in the leadership of the Public Welfare Commission where the Chairman of the Commission has been very active with our organization for a number of years, as well as other organizations in the community. He brought a willingness—a desire to make some changes in the way in which services were being offered by Welfare and particularly a greater emphasis on giving services to people and changing some policies which were on the rigid side. Our organization worked very closely with the Public Welfare Commission in supporting and suggesting certain changes. We didn't take leadership but we worked with other organizations and informed citizens.

They [the Public Welfare Department] are providing for increased professional staff. They are providing for increased clerical staff to relieve professional staff of some of the chores. They are interested in liberalizing payment of checks, and the budget and policies of eligibility so that there will be less of the cutting out someone because you don't technically quite come within the procedures that probably the law can be liberally interpreted more now than in the past. Working with other agencies in the community, working with citizens on the program so that citizens can have some knowledge and some motivation about these services. These are some of the things.

On the other hand, a position paper of the board of directors of the National Association for Community Development ("The Community Action Agency and Resident Participation"), speaks frankly and aggrievedly about the criticism addressed to service organizations questioning the political initiative of the poor and the effectiveness of the new participatory model to achieve genuine social change:

We have another concern which relates to the *Workbook* of the OEO. The section on Resident Participation is based upon the assumption that the various service organizations 'tend to become separated from the poor,' and 'are oriented toward the interests of the politically effective sectors of the society.' Believing that most community agencies do not care about the poor, OEO staff adopt a crusading spirit to save the poor by seeing that they 'acquire political effectiveness.' This is to be achieved by 'developing autonomous and self-managed organizations which are competent to exert political influence on behalf of their own self-interest.' It is also to be achieved through board membership by representatives of the poor. OEO is the champion of the poor against all local agencies, using its power to withhold needed funds to force communities to adopt its methods for involvement.

It is false to imply that all community service organizations are oriented only toward the interests of the politically effective sectors of society. To be sure, some may tend in that direction, but many others do not. While the presence of poverty in an affluent society suggests institutional failure, it is not simply a matter of who is and who is not politically effective.

It happens that most of the community action programs that started before the passage of the Economic Opportunity Act were initiated by local governments and related voluntary agencies who were concerned about the problems of poverty. When the Act made available new Federal sources to do something about poverty, the political and agency leadership in hundreds of communities responded by seeking financial assistance from OEO. Our impression is that most community agency programs have been initiated by this leadership, sometimes spurred to action by such groups as civil rights organizations, but rarely in response to an uprising by the 'politically ineffective.' Thousands and thousands of community leaders care and have started community action programs in good faith.

When OEO challenges the good faith of community leadership, it tends to *build resistance* from community agencies. Thus it obstructs the opportunity for meaningful dialogue and mutual searching for ways to achieve meaningful resident participation. But even more crucial it fails to appreciate the dynamics of community action and the evolutionary process that is required to increase resident participation.

. . . We are concerned that the model chosen by OEO may not be able to effectively mobilize resources in every community. Although this may prove to be a workable approach in some locales, there is already experience that shows it does not work very well in other places. By and large, a large board of many interests tends to follow the practice of health and welfare councils, which usually include representatives of agencies and of special interest groups, including labor, business, religion, and minority. A few even include persons who live in low-income neighborhoods, usually not the poor, though. Health and welfare councils, however, have not been very effective in *bringing about major community change, and this is one of the most needed tasks in many communities.*

A confederation of interests tends to balance one interest against another. The result may be closer to the lowest common denominator rather than leadership toward significant change. While this may be a suitable way to divide up the new Federal funds, it will mean playing down the role of catalyst and change agent.

The position paper went on to say, however, that resident participation "helps to further the ideals of representative democracy. It counteracts the tendency of welfare paternalism on the part of some, although not all, agencies which serve the poor." It accepts an analysis presented at the House Subcommittee hearings by Dr. Charles I. Shottland, who testified for the National Association of Social Workers:

. . . In one-to-one personal services we recognize that a helping service does not begin until the individual wants it and participates actively in the helping process. We know, similarly, that programs directed toward groups of people achieve a much more significant level of participation if the members have an important role in the creation and administration of such programs.

The tendency on the part of these programs to regress to the social service approach or to stagnate has been counteracted directly in some instances by confrontation and conflict. Other attempts to counteract this tendency are indirect. The community action approach has had some effect, for example, on the traditional social service agencies and on the training of social workers. There is some evidence that the social welfare establishment is moving slowly away from the more sterile "helping" casework or group work approach to "clients" toward a recognition of a more action-oriented professional relationship with "citizens." There is evidence further that the antipoverty program has had some effect on the thinking of those responsible for planning curricula and social work training.

Social workers already in the field have felt the impact of the verbalizations of action and of some of the programs. They have also had to react to the fact that these programs have brought in other professionals not previously involved with problems of the poor, such as lawyers, artists, school teachers, labor organizers, and that the programs, therefore, have not been able to depend on professional social workers alone. It is significant, in this regard, that the direction of these programs is not for the most part controlled by professional social workers. Leaders have come via the political route, via government or labor union experience, and untrained lay workers have been brought in to various sub-professional positions. There is no evidence so far that their level of effectiveness is significantly different from that of professional social workers, though in a supervisory role professionals appear to be more effective than do indigenous staff workers.

The field of social work is to some extent moving in the direction of greater relevance to the day-to-day lives and aspirations and needs of the poor. In fact, the anti-poverty program has forced the field to reexamine its professionalism in terms of its prevalent psychiatric model; and to seek to establish a newer base in social action, returning to the Jane Addams–Lillian Wald model, which emphasized social action and change as the core of social work. So, too, it encourages a move toward subjective involvement with the poor and away from the hitherto more approved technique of impersonal objective counseling at an emotional distance form the client. In the long run, this may prove to be a significant contribution to changing the predicament of the poor. In the short run, it may aid attempts to make the anti-poverty program more viable.

3. Community Organization and Action

The transition from social service to community organization can be seen as essentially one of emphasis, reinforcing the status quo, or it can herald a movement toward actual social change. The community organization approach can, from the first orientation, continue to emphasize social service and make the machinery an instrumentality for benevolence.

The Crusade for Opportunity in Syracuse had Neighborhood Boards largely social service oriented—health, jobs, recreation, etc. The purpose of the Neighborhood Boards is to 'decentralize to a neighborhood level the planning and implementation of programs for meaningful participation.' The Crusade is complying with 'maximum feasible participation of the poor' by electing local residents through the Neighborhood Boards to the Crusade Board.

On the other hand, it can focus on the preparation for community action, as Syracuse's other program, CATC, did; that is, voter registration, identification of problems, determination of methods to solve the problems. This latter perspective is a first step toward programs based on a power rationale, which demands a change in the predicament of the poor.

Ambiguity and confusion can arise out of the inability to be clear as to which of these emphases is to be followed. One can be verbalized and another implemented. Power may be verbalized and yet the actual program prove to be essentially service.

Another basis for confusion can be the adoption of a statement of a community action program prematurely without adequate preparation. New York City's HARYOU is a good example of such premature verbalization with an attempt to implement without basic preparation. There, the plans for Neighborhood Boards and the community action goals of the boards had been so clearly spelled out in the document that the political threat implications became apparent to Adam Powell before any organization to resist his attempt at control could be set up. Powell, in terms of his own interests, moved in to take the program over. Powell was the first local politician to see the political implications of the new approach to community organization. Later, Mayor Daley in Chicago, Mayor Walsh in Syracuse, Mayor Collins in Boston, and Mayor Wagner in New York, in the case of MFY, saw the implications for themselves. It is of interest that a challenge to City Hall control of community action programs came from Adam Powell, who, when still chairman of the House Education and Labor Committee, asserted (April, 1966) that he would fight to block the attempts of mayors to take over control of anti-poverty programs. Not being the mayor but himself then a competitive political force whose bid for control of HARYOU had met some resistance, even though relatively ineffectual, from City Hall, Powell assumed for himself the role of champion of the people.

Some of the community action programs attempted to solve the problems caused by lack of opportunity and by powerlessness by emphasizing the problem of power primarily, and, therefore, encouraged the organization of the poor to seek redress of their perceived grievances. Most of these programs, however, remained dependent upon a parent organization or other sponsors who exert some measure of control over the opportunities available. They have been discouraged from seeking independence; attempts at achieving such freedom have often been thwarted.

Mobilization for Youth, New York's active program of citizen participation, voter registration drives, and rent strikes, was tempered after a noisy investigation and charges and countercharges from August, 1964 to March, 1965. It retreated, on the whole, from an emphasis on attempts to win power for the poor to an emphasis on provision of services and opportunities. The verbal definition of the MFY program remained the same as the original document, but there was some evidence that the actual program would be modified, in response to public controversy, away from the more conflict-producing activities. There is evidence, however, that MFY is returning to an effective form of community action through the organization of welfare recipients and similar action programs for the poor.

Community Progress, Inc., of New Haven attempts to bridge service, opportunities, community organization, and community social action. It offers its opportunities for education, employment and other programs through door-to-door canvassing and visits to pool rooms, churches, and laundromats. It organizes and develops block associations or neighborhood councils to build leadership and "to get people together around common problems." But beyond that it seeks to stimulate institutional change through community reform. The Citizen Participation

Committee, however, has been "generally an advisory board . . . it is not policy making." It provides criticism, suggestions for modifications of programs and proposes new programs. The New Haven program is concerned with power and the need for effective social change, but the major instrumentality for such change is the city government itself, not the organized poor.

Some community action programs assume that the predicament of the poor is due *primarily* to the fact that they are powerless in all situations affecting their lives. To bring an end to poverty and powerlessness, the poor must therefore gain power. People who are victims of long-standing injustices must be organized to identify their problems; to determine methods to alleviate the perceived problem (and often pathological conditions); to develop and sustain the type of organization for collective action which can survive when confronted with internal or external conflicts; to state their goals in terms of observable community change or change in the predicament of their lives; and to address the collective action itself to the achievement of these goals.

Paterson, New Jersey's Task Force for Community Action, the Community Action Training Center of Syracuse, New York, and the United Community Corporation of Newark, New Jersey have been examples of such programs.

Such programs differed in important ways from community organization plans that gather representatives of the poor on boards and in neighborhood groups to offer extension of services and opportunities and to provide some review of such programs. The power and action-oriented plans try to mobilize the energies of the poor to make them count on the scales of influence in their community by organized political and economic activities.

In several cities, the program began with a social action emphasis and was altered either by accommodation to external conflict, as in the case of MFY in New York; by decay in an atmosphere of controversy over internal control, as in the case of HARYOU; or by defeat by counterattack, as in the case of the shift of federal support in Syracuse from the action-oriented SCDA program to the social service-establishment program of CFO.

The Syracuse program SCDA, in particular, is deserving of examination despite the later dissipation of effort, as a model of what can be done and how in the organizing of the poor to fight for their own rights.

A. *The Community Action Training Center and the Syracuse Community Development Association*

The President's Committee on Juvenile Delinquency funded the Syracuse Action for Youth program, controlled by the Mayor. The SAY proposal stated among its concerns that a Community Development program be organized "to develop the competence of action area residents to deal with the problems of their neighborhood and community" through "effective organization," thereby overcoming "feelings of alienation and powerlessness among action area residents by increasing their ability to handle their problems themselves."

It proposed to work for change in an evolutionary pattern of several stages: In Stage One, the Mayor's Commission for Youth would appoint an advisory committee broadly representative of the action area. The advisory committee would select a director; the director would select three professional community organizers to be assigned to the action area neighborhoods (one to each area); the organizer, director, and advisory committee would select an appropriate facility to open a Neighborhood Development Center; and the advisory committee together with its professional staff would begin to work in the neighborhood to identify the problems, potential leaders, and activities which are of mutual concern.

In Stage Two, neighborhood leaders would be engaged by the Mayor's Commission as Neighborhood Workers. The worker would become familiar with the problems of his area, aid in the organization of groups, develop solutions and plans of action, and assist in formation of a Neighborhood Council, an on-going group to consider and develop solutions to neighborhood problems.

Stage Three would include the establishment of the Neighborhood Councils as *autonomous units,* legally incorporated and assuming the employment of the director and the staff of the Center. The advisory committee would continue to act as liaison between the Commission and the Association.

When SAY became Crusade for Opportunity and was supported by OEO funds, its Community Development component was relinquished (a) for research and training to the Syracuse University Community Action Training Center and (b) for action to the autonomous non-profit corporation, the Syracuse Community Development Association.

CATC had gained experience in a special program in social action begun at Syracuse University's School of Social Work two years earlier. Starting with two students in 1963, it expanded into a Community Action Training Center in 1965.

CATC received funds in February, 1965 from OEO under the Demonstration, Research and Training component of Title II A of the Economic Opportunity Act of 1964. The funds covered an eleven-month period, but OEO agreed to fund the project for a two-year span if the project showed promise. At first, both action and research had been directly sponsored by Syracuse University. Then, as one Syracuse official put it, "The University was getting a lot of questions about its role as an action organization, and sort of a divorce of convenience took place, in which the action phase of the program was separated out from research and training so that the University could justify its research and training as a normal thing for a University to do." So SCDA was formed, a non-profit corporation separately funded from OEO. CATC provided courses, seminars and lectures. SCDA was the instrument to operationalize the concepts and the basic philosophy of CATC and served as a placement agency for the students (candidates for Masters of Social Work and other non-degree students) enrolled in Syracuse University's School of Social Work. SCDA and CATC worked rather closely together.

Nine councils were organized in poverty areas by the Syracuse Community Development Association. The councils were designed to be independent from Syracuse University, from local political factions, social institutions, and agencies, and to establish their own leadership. They were to determine the problems of the community and decide how to solve them. In each organization there were approximately 30 to 65 people who were fairly regular active council members and approximately 200 peripheral members.

The nine councils functioned independently of each other. Some groups were involved in voter registration, others concentrated on providing better welfare services. However, a Joint Action Committee, comprised of representatives from the nine councils, planned over-all strategy when residents considered that a massive attack would be more advantageous to the poor of Syracuse. The nine councils joined forces, for example, during the Mayoralty election to protest against Mayor Walsh, his political cohorts, and the problems of Syracuse which perpetuated the cyclic pattern of poverty.

In each area there was a neighborhood organizer; many areas also had block captains. Neighborhood organizers started out by visiting respected individuals or institutions in their area, then held meetings in homes. Since many of the people had never been in formal organizations before, the organizer first had to prove that organizations had relevance to their needs. He encouraged them at the house meetings to discuss their needs—garbage collection, police protection, and the like. One such meeting led to another.

After six to eight weeks of house meetings, a central meeting would be announced and leaflets announcing it were distributed throughout the neighborhood. In a neighborhood of four hundred to four thousand families, between 70 and 130 people might show up. Temporary officers and a Constitution and By-Laws Committee would be elected; the organization had begun.

The organizers themselves were not members and could not vote, but might intervene to rescue a situation, appealing to "self-interest, building anger" and then "duck back out quickly and remain inconspicuous." The organizer helped with knowledge about the ways of governmental agencies which the group wished to approach with a complaint—perhaps using role-playing techniques with the neighborhood people taking the part of, for example, the Housing Authority. The director noted: "It's usually quite a shock to a housing director to experience" the confrontation with persons fresh from such a rehearsal.

The councils faced the typical problems of democratic groups —competition of leadership, different "styles of action," with different age groups "pushing their own problems—the aged asking for more police protection, the young people wanting less." When apathy or conflict occurred in a neighborhood organization, as in one case when two strong leaders were at odds, the organizer stepped in to help resolve the crisis. A stable neighborhood nucleus took months to develop. "In the early months the organizer is the crucial person who tries to make sure that all the disasters that plague the organization can be avoided," Warren Haggstrom, the executive director, noted in an interview.

The regular organizations in the community were often disinterested or even negative to the new ferment. Some ministers expressed sympathy with CATC's program in Syracuse, but, as a staff member put it: "Some of our organizations are composed mostly of welfare clients because this is a low-income area, and most of the population is on welfare. Many of the churches have considerable status concerns and not all of the ministers feel that they would want to go to a meeting in which they are rank and file members with low-status persons present." Unlike the Woodlawn Organization in Chicago, which began not with the poor but with a coalition of neighborhood organizations, among them churches, SCDA was not such a coalition but rather—with support from the University and CATC—an organization of the poor themselves.

"We have no power," Haggstrom said. "The neighborhood organizations have gotten some power from their own point of view—and that's not *our* point of view." SCDA-CATC has been committed to the need for an independent role for the neighborhood organization. Its leadership offered "certain kinds of restraints (like its own non-partisanship) which have nothing to do with bounds . . . but we will not set a restriction on the organization's becoming controversial or moving along their own lines in their own way to resolve their own problems." SCDA was unwilling to accept control over the neighborhood organizations as a condition for the receipt of funds. Should such a condition be asked, "It would not be a legitimate program any longer. It would just be another respectable service. . . . CATC was started before there were any funds from the federal government, and will continue without any more funds from the federal government."

With 30 to 65 persons in each organization active in each of nine communities, and roughly two hundred somewhat involved, families of thousands of members were represented in an area of 40,000 population. In comparison with other large-scale organizations this is a high level of participation.

But the organization had its frustrations, for the staff as well as for the people. As one official said:

I don't say that it doesn't crop up every once in a while, because this is a difficult thing. People that have been leaders have come into this program as trainees and it's very much quite a temptation to jump in there and seize that leadership and keep that thing going faster—because everybody gets very impatient when you are sitting with a group and you are waiting for them to come out with the ideas, and trying to stimulate those ideas and maybe an hour goes by before they come around with them; but they finally do, almost inevitably; but if they don't, well then they make a suggestion but they don't take over the meeting saying this is the way I would do it and knock-bang-bang 1234 and that's the end of the meeting. Now let us go out and put it into effect, and you will have to go out there and do it.

The organizer is taking too much of a responsibility. Pushing, pushing, pushing. You have to wait for the people. At the same time the organizer is contronted with this unless this is done now, all of this is going down the drain. The same thing happens when an organizer is at a meeting, for example, where a meeting is bogging down, and the chairman up there leaving all kinds of things dangling or making speeches when the people are the ones that want to be doing the talking and that organizer knows that very quickly they are going to start to walk out of that meeting and will not be coming back, and he has got to make up his mind as to—well, am I going to talk to them about this after the meeting or shall I step in now in the interest of saving this organization, all those people that I got to come to this meeting that I know are never going to come back unless something is done right now and they go away from here feeling either a sense of accomplishment, which they are never going to get the way he is doing it, so then at that point they step in. But somebody that believes in the old school of group dynamics believes that he has no business stepping in—they should let the chairman make all those mistakes and drive all the people out and then start over again. Nobody could do that in his right mind.

CATC sought to fulfill the needs of research and study as well as of action, the only community action program with private sponsorship by a university:

We are interested in a social change kind of model which has never or rarely been researched in this kind of way. We are interested in building organizational theory not based on the old bureaucratic model or organization theory but based much more on these organizations . . . we are dealing with. For example, most organization theory seems to come from people who have studied the late stages of organization—highly bureaucratic kinds of things—without much dynamic left and they make some sort of assumptions of what took place in the early stages of these organizations by getting some of the history of it. We have a unique opportunity to watch these organizations grow over time and have detailed information as time goes on, and natural information.

Can the organized poor really be autonomous? Even the director of SCDA, with its commitment to the independence of the poor, thinks that they need professional guidance:

There are people who are doing a beautiful job out there, and a lot of leadership is being developed; but what I think is even if you have the most highly developed leadership you could imagine out there—without a skilled person—say that person is one of the people from these organizations who are paid daily—it couldn't survive. In my opinion I don't know of any. I would be happy to hear about any surviving for a length of time without a paid staff.

But another official said that the members must see themselves as acting on their own initiative.

Crusade for Opportunity, set up by the Mayor as an umbrella organization to handle anti-poverty funds for Syracuse, also attempted community action but, through neighborhood boards and elected representatives to the CFO Board, it resembled the traditional community organization plan to build a service-opportunities liaison between the poor and the majority who provide the services. It was planned originally that on the CFO Board no more than one-third of the members would represent traditional institutions and no less than a third would represent the poor.

What happened to Syracuse when the CATC-SCDA program alarmed the Establishment is described in IV.

4. The Participation of the Poor

The organization of the community of the poor is not merely a matter of permitting the poor to organize. Many are reluctant—or unable—to participate effectively in the anti-poverty programs despite the apparent eagerness of the government to have them do so.

A. *Unfamiliarity with Organization and Suspicion of Organization*

One of the problems blocking effective participation by the poor is their lack of experience with organizations and their suspicion of all organizational procedures.

You don't start out with poor people and expect them to come to you organized. I think they have to be reached out to and brought into the normal organizational forms of community. . . . *Organization as we generally know it is not a normal everyday way of life for poor people. They don't have time for organization.* Organization requires a lot of time. It requires reading time, meeting time, and poor people are generally too concerned with the basics of life, food, clothing and shelter and looking after the screaming children. So that they don't have the spare time to go out to meetings, generally, so unless this is introduced as a meaningful, helpful way of improving their lives and their lot, they don't get into it.

My theory is that you have to begin in improving the community where people are. You have to take those who have an inclination to an organization, and spread the work and involve these poor people, and make it possible for them to become members of organizations, and become organizationally oriented. . . . The whole business of communication is an important thing in organization. Formal organization means to most of us meetings, but there was mobilizing and getting support through communication from information. If people who are unable to come out because of their ties in the house can be informed on what's going on, they will find time, from time to time, to get into meetings.

And they, also, when they find that the meetings have some direct bearing on their situation, make the time. And then when people are working together as neighbors, they can alternate in attending meetings, so that the whole message gets spread faster. (University Neighborhood Council, Washington, D.C., private agency, emphasis added)

We're talking about people who had never been to meet as a group for anything. Or the few times they met as a group, nothing happened. So they don't have any confidence in me or the program they are afraid to survey. This is particularly true in Washington, because of the housing situation. . . . We have to learn to work at it at their pace. *This program is particularly slow, because it's designed to come from the bottom up.*

Mothers have no one to leave their children with, have to arrange one person in the house to take care of, have meetings in the neighborhood so don't have to dress up, nearby so that older child with younger can come for directions, etc.

This man out here on the street doesn't want to know what's going to happen two years from now by his meeting, he wants to know what's going to happen right there and now, as a result of this meeting. Now when you get into what they call middle-class organizations, yes, people are used to working together and pulling together and they can accept a long-range goal. You've got five children and a wife pregnant, you're making forty bucks a week, in the first place you're not listening to anything long-range, getting the food, paying the bills, and this kind of thing. Getting along with the boss. So I think until such time we can take care of these very basic things, then you don't get anybody to listen. They just hear you but they don't listen. . . . *It took a year before people would start to listen.* I was saying the same things I had been saying all along. They heard me, but they weren't listening. (Neighborhood development worker, Washington, D.C., emphasis added)

When you first go into these blocks, *some of these people have never been in any kind of organization.* Well, you find the general consensus of the block to find out what the problems of the block are. After you have talked to a certain number of people you try to set up a meeting in one of the houses and in doing so you bring together those people around this one particular problem. After you're there you might involve them into the other problems that they are involved with in the block—high rents, bad conditions of housing, sub-standard housing, employment and unemployment, school drop-outs, inadequate schools, etc. Meet two to four times a month. They have involved themselves in a cleanup campaign—which are small, very small things to get them involved in—I think in order for them to start working on the big problems they first have to have some successful wins with these small problems. They gain momentum in their working with these small problems and are now attacking the larger problems. (Neighborhood organizer, Washington, D.C. emphasis added)

Personal problems often take precedence, many families have 12 children and they have their own problems and they're often too busy or too confused to get involved with groups. . . . So we've been working slowly and gradually towards this becoming a truly representative group of poor people. I think it started with maybe 80% middle-class oriented people, and now it's about down to 40% of those people and 60% are poor. (Washington, D.C., UPO)

One is forced to speculate as to the implications of the transference of a middle-class, meeting-oriented voluntary-organization style of life from the community of the majority to the community of the poor. Middle-class duties are increasingly being asked of the poor, partly, it seems, as a sign that the poor are being accepted as part of the characteristic Amercan culture, partly as a sign that those who ask to be accepted must pay the price of responsibility. But to ask of the poor that they take on the added burden of middle-class obligations without the social and economic assets and resources of the middle class is to bring a certain illogic into the situation, an illogic many of the poor seem to appreciate. It may also serve to increase the frustration of the poor when the time and energy required for organizational structure do not lead to prompt observable change. The middle-class tolerance of slow change may be directly related to the generally satisfactory conditions of their lives and the corresponding lack of a sense of urgency for change.

B. *The Search for the Indigenous*

Central to all the discussion of community organization and "participation of the poor" is the discovery of and use of indigenous individuals. No one has studied systematically who the indigenous *are,* what is involved in the selection of indigenous leaders, what is the nature of their involvement, what is the relationship of an indigenous leader to an effective community action program, what is involved in sustaining concern or commitment of indigenous leaders, what are effective roles for the indigenous? So far, discussion of the indigenous seems to be characterized more by sentimentality and condescension than by realistic appraisal.

The need for indigenous involvement is a rationale found in both the self-help-opportunity approach and the power approach to community action.

(1) *Definition*

What is an indigenous leader? The study's questionnaire brought a variety of responses to this question. Among them were:

Someone who represents a group of persons who reside within a target area and does not have a college degree or equivalent. (Detroit, Mayor's Committee, Total Action Against Poverty)

A person who lives in a target area and who has demonstrated leadership by actual positions he has held within his area. This category is limited to the non-professional and excludes ministers, teachers, social workers, etc. (Cincinnati, Community Action Commission of the Cincinnati Area)

The natural neighborhood leader, usually from poverty group. A long time resident of the community. (San Antonio, Oneida-Scott County Community Action Program)

Person who exercises significant influence over a segment or segments of low-income community; person who typifies characteristics of low-income community and is intimately involved with low-income problems. Identification may also include factors such as: articulation, leadership in community organizations, etc., but this presumes developed local structure. (Visalia, California, Tulare County Community Action Agency)

An indigenous sub-professional leader is a sub-professional, who lives in a target neighborhood and who possesses status and position from which he derives influence above that enjoyed by the average citizen. (New Haven, CPI)

'A local resident who has a following of persons concerned with community problems.' The project, however, has used indigenous non-professionals who do not come equipped with support: 'However, we hope they will be able to develop such a following.' (Los Angeles, EYOA)

C. *The Role and Effectiveness of the Indigenous*

Indigenous staff and indigenous volunteers are generally incorporated into the service-opportunities function of the community action program. They participate as employees supervised by non-indigenous middle-class professionals. Rarely do they appear in any positions involving policy and planning. Their role is to facilitate the *mediation, social cohesion,* and *individual improvement* goals of the programs, to serve as a link between the intervening culture of the educated affluent and the undereducated poor, to promote harmony and rehabilitation in the neighborhoods. As New Haven's CPI pointed out:

The use of indigenous professional aides in Neighborhood Services has important advantages. In recruiting candidates for a skill training program, for example, one of these workers can move at ease around the pool rooms and other neighborhood hangouts. A stranger to the neighborhood would have difficulty going into some places. The same principle applies in the case of home visitations.

Such workers generally operate within a neighborhood context rather than serve in a downtown central agency. In example:

Los Angeles' Economic and Youth Opportunities agency uses subprofessionals in various roles including 'house to house visits to ascertain needs of the communities, give information, services and referral, organize community groups.'

The Youth Opportunities Board in Los Angeles set up Information and Complaints Outposts through which workers operate as 'trouble shooters' or neighborhood advocators working with individuals and families on a 'first-aid' basis providing a link among services and identifying gaps and barriers in services. The Los Angeles Board also provides Citizen Organizations for Civic Action which range from autonomous neighborhood improvement groups to citizen advisory groups of service projects; and Self-Help and Mutual Help Organizations from child care cooperatives to credit unions. Indigenous community aides are paid; indigenous volunteers are also involved in the program. The program is designed 'to stimulate the organization of poverty area residents into community action programs for the satisfaction of their own felt needs, and the fulfillment of their basic rights as citizens.'

Neighborhood workers will work informally throughout the neighborhood, serving as a bridge between residents and service agencies. They will get to know adults and children, the elderly, and the sick by visiting in homes, on the street, in stores and taverns, at churches, and in jail. They will be persons to turn to in time of trouble. With the guidance of the neighborhood services coordinator, they will know what resources are available. Above all, their presence will be tangible evidence of community concern for people and their problems.

The main qualifications of a neighborhood worker are to be emphathetic with neighborhood residents, to speak their language, and to be accepted without reservation. He, therefore, might well be indigenous, and need not have professional education. He will receive training and daily supervision from the neighborhood services coordinator, whom he in turn will serve as eyes, ears, hands, and heart. (CPI, New Haven, "Opening Opportunities," April, 1962)

The Action for Boston Community Development program provides interrelated services and programs including a Neighborhood Service Corps of indigenous sub-professionals to assist in implementation in Neighborhood Action Centers for such programs as adult literacy, day care, and tutoring.

The Chicago Commission of Youth Welfare proposal describes the training of volunteers for leadership in local neighborhood offices. Neighborhood leadership groups were to be related to each other 'with the object of greater community harmony and for cooperative action' with a Social Adjustment Division providing services, and Neighborhood leadership was to be related to community-wide leadership, *i.e.*, business, district schools, police, industry, political groups.

The Cleveland Action for Youth provides Neighborhood Centers which operate a neighborhood extension program. Professional community workers, neighborhood aides, homemakers, and the like, work with residents, street clubs, and tenant groups. The city of Cleveland provides personnel for the neighborhood extension units.

Through the program of the United Planning organization of Washington, D.C., eight Neighborhood Development Programs were established throughout the district. These programs were related to existing voluntary or public community facilities and were expected to coordinate a wide range of new services to be introduced into the neighborhoods of poverty.

The Commission on Youth Welfare in Chicago encourages residents to act upon their perceived problems in the community, but the function of CYW itself is to identify gaps in services and to extend and provide the services which are lacking.

A secondary function of the indigenous worker is to move the participants out of the role of indigenous poor altogether. With more income, a leadership status, increase in pride and self-image, and identification with the majority culture, such workers may make the leap into the periphery of the middle class. This transition of *upward mobility* is revealed in some of the interviews conducted by the study in the Washington area:

Through talking—and the more you talk the more you can feel that this person is capable of being a leader. For instance, in this block I have found a man who works for the Bureau of Standards and he had at some time more knowledge than I had of this Freeway thing and he knows how to talk to people, how to reach the people. They respect him. They look to him for leadership. That's one of the sort of things you sort of look for. Sometimes you think you find it and you find yourself to be wrong after a while, but you have to keep looking. (Former laundress)

You have to be a versatile type of person. You have to talk with everybody, anybody, even the men sitting out that have just finished a bottle of wine, that type of thing. You can't go in a home and have them think that maybe you think a chair is dirty, and you have to be dressed in a casual way, in fact, we all are poor ourselves, so naturally we don't have the type of swanky clothing that maybe a person that have worked for the government for years might have. So we are a member of that community, so therefore, you can be a part of these people. Just like their next door neighbor like yourself.

The children become attached to you, the adults become attached to you, and in fact many of them that don't come out to the block clubs they yell for you when you pass the street and want you to stop in and talk to them and they will support you in what you are doing. You do find a few die-hards who are determined not to be a part. It has given me a better outlook on life. It certainly helped me in many ways. *The financial part of it has helped an awful lot, and the learning and training that I've gotten from this program would help me and I feel like it has prepared me to do many different things, work with people, how to work with people and most of all how to get out and try to help myself.* (Woman, neighborhood organizer, emphasis added)

In our program we are beginning to make headway. You'd be surprised at how difficult it is to help people to help themselves and our people are so used to somebody doing things for them and that's what they still look for. *We are beginning to get them to understand the importance of doing things for themselves and getting that feeling of self-accomplishment.* And it's beginning to respond. Here in the urban renewal area it is very difficult to get them to respond because there is no hope. They just seem to have lost hope.

My day, when I am not having a block club meeting, is knocking on doors, talking to the people, trying to get them out to the meetings, trying to get them interested in civic matters concerning community problems, offering assistance, directing them to services. I just go, knock on doors, talk to people, something of this nature. I direct them to our legal service. Maybe it's a domestic problem and I recommend them to the welfare and family services. . . . It is an eight-hour day's work. You are steadily on the go when you're not making out reports. (Man, 35 years old with record of 12-year reformatory sentence for drug addiction, furniture refinisher by trade, worker for Washington Urban League, emphasis added)

In the beginning, I found that many people were shamed on the block. They felt that they weren't getting services due them from the Sanitation Department. Their alleys weren't being swept. Their streets weren't being cleaned and they were ashamed of the way their houses looked. After the block was cleaned and there was cooperation from most of the people in the block—the houses and yard that were vacant other people cleaned them up, and then people came home in the afternoon and saw this clean block. It made quite a difference. On Hanover Place, another street, a man who lived on the block was chairman of the advisory council. There had been plenty of crime, plenty of crap games in the street in the day. Mr. Kenton with his ability to lead and with the respect that he had from the people on the block, they combined together, and really did a remarkable job on the street and they didn't stop there at the one clean-up. Every morning they would get up at 6 o'clock in the morning to clean up their street. It was a thing where the people—it just brought them close. One would knock on your door at 6 o'clock in the morning. O.K., let's go with the brooms. They would look forward to that. Somebody would poke a pot of coffee out the back door and that type of thing. So it was really a wonderful program. Mr. Kenton got sick but the people went on. The crap games moved in the back, no longer going on out front, drinking beer, shooting crap. After looking around they said 'We can't do that here any more' and they moved to the back. Then they found out they couldn't do it there anymore—I don't know whether it was the stares and glances or what they were getting but they moved someplace else. I don't know whether they are inside or just what happened. They got trash containers for the street. They use the trash containers now instead of seeing beer cans and everything up and down the street you see a clean street. So when people speak of Hanover Place now, they speak of it in a different tone than they used to. (Woman, neighborhood organizer)

Evidently I must have learned a lot about stretching a dollar myself. The things I've used throughout my life are some of the things that I am demonstrating to people now, how to shop around, how to get the most for their money, I'm studying now on budgeting. [If program stops] I think where some people's courage have been built up, if we don't continue with the program they are just going to continue to say as they always have said—everything is for the white man. This is what they have always said, nobody is in our corner because we are black. . . . Those that really want to fight on perhaps they will go on. But the ones that we really have been trying to reach, if we really don't continue on we've lost those people completely. (Woman, 41, school dropout, mother of five, now Consumer Aide)

Many of the people that are on public assistance are trying hard to get off public assistance, and many are getting involved in other community activity as a result of these block clubs. Things such as the Neighborhood Development Center. *There is a new awakening as I stated once before of the group . . . this type of program has given a lot of hope to people.* [It was hard to get people together at first, didn't believe it would work, but now] the block club has brought some togetherness on these blocks where the people didn't know each other too well or really didn't bother themselves too much about their neighborhood. Now when you find that there is a sick person on the block there is somebody there to help them or bring them some dinner or any little thing that they can—maybe wash a few clothes. It has brought about a closeness. (Woman, neighborhood organizer)

The National Association for Community Development, in its position paper cited above, says:

Through such leadership OEO has made a particularly significant contribution by encouraging (although not requiring) the hiring of indigenous staff in nonprofessional roles in the community action program. As the (OEO) *Workbook* points out, this helps to overcome staff shortages, to provide staff who can do things and reach people in a way that middle-class professionals cannot do as easily, to achieve resident participation in the actual conduct of the program, and to lead the way to the creation of more job opportunities for persons without professional training. As of March 31, 1965, nearly 90 communities had made commitments to hire a total of 4,454 such workers, and others have joined this list since then. Already this is one of the more noteworthy accomplishments achieved through the leadership of OEO.

Such programs reach only a minute fraction of the poor and succeed in altering the life styles of a very few. Further, a number of the indigenous workers are not serving in a leadership capacity at all but are, in effect, hired for chore duty in neighborhood offices on a make-work basis. Few programs provide, as New Haven does, for the progression of neighborhood workers to higher level jobs through training and graduated responsibility. New Haven plans a deliberate movement up the ladder:

There will be a substantial expansion of professional aides as the New Haven community action programs expands under the Economic Opportunity Act. Most of these will be indigenous to the inner-city. Moreover, through promotions from the present staff it is expected indigenous workers will begin to move into supervisory positions.

Under Title I B of the Economic Opportunity Act of 1964, CPI is proposing to place up to 400 inner-city youth in professional aide activities in support for the community action program. Local public and private nonprofit agencies have already drawn lists of useful work these youth can perform, in new service occupations such as recreation aides, community school aides, family aides, clerical aides, social worker aides, neighborhood worker aides, family relocation aides, etc. Agencies requesting youth under this program intend to use them to relieve professional people of the more routine tasks which are inconsistent with their training. Furthermore, the agencies' activities in the community action program can be strengthened and expanded with the use of professional aides. About 25 professionals who are already regularly employed in community service agencies will provide the supervision of these 400 youth.

This Title I B program seeks not only to provide work experience for youth and to enable the service agencies to expand their operations, but also to create permanent new job categories in the service occupations. This is one way to ease the strain on a limited supply of professionals in the service occupations. Hopefully, youth who perform successfully in the work-experience program will be hired on a permanent basis after the special program is completed.

The other programs that will use indigenous workers as professional aides include the expansion of Neighborhood Services, particularly aimed at greater resident involvement; the Unified Social Service Unit as case aides; the Day Care Program as teacher aides; the Tutoring Program; Elm Haven Family Services; the Elderly Program Development Study.

The I B work training program will use indigenous work supervisors. The College Work Study Program under Title I C will enable a sizable number of inner-city youth to work as professional aides on a part-time basis. Expanded Adult Education Program under

Title II B will make extensive use of neighborhood residents as part-time teachers and as volunteer tutors.

Under the expanded program indigenous staff will be promoted to the positions of Assistant Coordinators of Neighborhood Services and field supervisors in the work-training program. These positions will generally parallel the degree of responsibility and salary of entry positions in the professional service field.

As the attached table indicates, of the new positions as full-time staff, part-time staff, and volunteers, approximately 60% will be indigenous. This will raise the total of indigenous workers from 35% to 46%. Of particular significance is the fact that at the professional worker and middle-management level, excluding teachers, about one out of five of the staff will be indigenous. Professional aides will outnumber the senior staff, teachers, professional workers and middle-management personnel, and four out of the five professional aides will come from the inner-city.

Staff of the New Haven Community Action Program

Category	*Present* (November 1964) Total	*Indigenous*[a] No.	%	*Proposed Additions* Total	*Indigenous* No.	%	*Total* Total	*Indigenous* No.	%
Senior Staff ($9,500 & over)	21	1	5	17	1	6	38	2	5
Teachers	56	2	4	33	4	12	89	6	7
Professional[b] and Middle Management ($6,000–$9,499)	55	10	18	28	6	21	83	16	19
Professional Aides ($5,999 & less)	76	40	53	333	293	88	409	333	81
Clerical	59	14	24	43	26	60	102	40	39
Part-time	187	95	51	393	235	60	580	330	57
Volunteers[c]	955	330	35	247	87	35	1202	417	35
TOTAL	1409	492	35	1094	652	60	2503	1144	46

(a) Indigenous: Persons who come from and reside in the inner-city.
(b) Professional: Positions requiring specialized training that is generally obtained with a college degree.
(c) Numbers are estimated.

The rise of the indigenous may serve to alienate him from his former peers and thereby diminish the effectiveness of the role of mediation he is to play. So a private agency director in New York City reported about an indigenous teenager who had been hired to work with her:

It grew into a vicious circle, because the people are hostile, and envious of the larger society, so to speak, so the minute that these people become identified with them, this causes them to get hostile at them, too. I hope I'm making it clear, because it's very clear to me.

You can see this process in Byron. Byron, right away, was quick to pick up on things. I gave him brown envelopes, etc., to take around. He was very quick to raise up, and stand up tall, and carry his folder in the neighborhood. When he gained status, then the people were quite proud to see him walking around with his folder. And then he decided to go to college. And then this completely removed him from the people on the block. Completely isolated him from the people in the neighborhood. They were—'resentful' isn't the word—'angry' is the word, and it comes out sometimes like hostility. Fear is just anger, the people . . . don't know what they want, and they are negative to everything. (From "Resident Participation in New Haven's Community Action Program," CPI, January, 1965)

Not all indigenous staff are pleased with their role. One observer in Syracuse's CATC program revealed suspicion and resentment in an interview:

The way the organizers work is that they really don't let the people think for themselves. They make the decisions and with their little tricky ways they make the people believe that the ideas come from them. Now, the people are beginning to wake up. They find that they are not making the decisions. The decisions that they made, like tonight, the organizers will go back to a strategy meeting among themselves and everything the people want is changed. Some of these people aren't as stupid as they [the organizers] think they are. They want to know why you are going to tell us to do things and then turn back around and do it a different way. Just because 'I' wasn't there to tell what is going on, you tell me that the people want it changed. It's bad.

Query: Do you think that they are just using people?
That's right. Just using, baby.
Query: For what?
Guinea pigs.

The use of an indigenous staff can most realistically be seen as a more positive step away from welfare. It is the beginning of an increase in the pride of the individual, priming his mobility. But, to expect of him in the initial stages the same level of competitive perspective or values toward work, reliability or concern with the task as that expected of the middle-class worker flies in the face of the realities of his prior social and economic condition.

Of the two field investigators with whom this study worked directly, one indigenous worker proved upwardly mobile, and task-oriented. The other brought verbal dedication and articulateness to the task, but also inconsistency of productivity and the tendency to "hustle." The one who was verbally committed but inconsistent in production wanted certain advantages from his job but with a minimum amount of work. He gave many excuses for uncompleted tasks. His articulateness had led his middle-class supervisor to believe that he was serious, but he did not have the ability to disguise his inadequacies; they quickly became easily apparent and his verbal fluency proved a transparent disguise. He gave the same alibis repeatedly, and this repetition of familiar explanations was suspect; he did not have the middle-class facility for persuasive alibi. The middle-class/upper-middle-class person who sees his job as a hustle, and is somewhat cynical or expedient in his attitude, gives more sophisticated alibis for inefficiency.

There is some evidence, also, that the indigenous worker who begins to move away from that status in perspective and in job is likely to be quite severe in his judgment of the remaining indigenous, likely to express more intolerance, and to reject the possibility of their effectiveness. These individuals who share some characteristics of the indigenous can be rejecting toward the other indigenous and probably should not be put in a supervisory position over them, unless, as the New Haven experience may demonstrate, this severity can be ameliorated by training and experience.

The indigenous worker does bring certain positives to the role. He has an identification and rapport with the poor and can associate with them with ease. He knows the level of information which the poor have and what the poor, therefore, need to know. He may be able to organize and operate a relevant type of community or neighborhood action program. So far, however, the programs the indigenous workers have been asked to operate have, almost entirely, been designed by the non-indigenous. Generally the indigenous worker is used as a mediator, and has not been permitted to function as initiator. He is seldom permitted to select his own allies—such as numbers runners—but must follow certain rules of propriety. If he breaks these rules, he does so surreptitiously. The genuine involvement of persons at the submarginal level of our society is more the exception than the rule. Total involvement would bring risks which the middle-class operators of programs are not prepared to take.

It may be possible, furthermore, that the new fashion of "involvement" of indigenous workers is the new form of the "flight from the client"—once more removed—which afflicts many social work professionals. The use of the indigenous as mediating links makes necessary less contact between the poor and the professional. The positive side would be that a mediating link is better than no link at all.

Some basic questions still need to be asked about the indigenous:

(1) Who are they?

(2) How long do they remain indigenous if they work for community action programs?

(3) What is the role of the indigenous and how do they fulfill this role?

(4) Can indigenous representation and staff facilitate the basic goals of indigenous persons or has such involvement of the poor, in effect, become a substitute for serious change in the predicament of the poor?

One private agency director summed up the problem in an interview:

Articulate is not the word I would use. I would use the word helplessness or helpless.

Query: Would that mean that they [the indigenous] *could say what they want or what the problem is, but they have no concept of how to go about changing the situation. Is that what you're saying?*

Almost that. They can see and they can talk about their anger much better than they can talk about just what's making them angry, and then take the steps necessary to do something about it. But more sophisticated people have to help them. They cannot make it without the help of more sophisticated people. And you couldn't in any sense, just take a neighborhood like this [Harlem] and say well here, where's your indigenous leadership, we have $100,000 for you, take it and help yourself. The people could not do it. I think that they cannot attend to their own destinies. I think they can only help other people to know what it is that they have to do. Whatever you do has to be something constructive. Whatever you do has to be something that's going to benefit them. I think they have an advisory capacity in indicating to you what it is that really will benefit them. And even so, you have to interpret this.

Has the term "indigenous" itself become a shibboleth, seeming verbally to be an extension of democracy, congenial with the American position of liberalism and egalitarianism, but actually characterized by sentimentality and naïve optimism unrelated to actual social change? Does it free the individual who accepts the theory uncritically—the indigenous worker and the middle-class person—of any sense of real responsibility to abolish the conditions of poverty? There is indeed a strong possibility that this is an effective way of avoiding responsibility.

A story in the *New York Times* of February 20, 1966 is relevant to these questions. It said, in part:

The 'condescension and contempt' of many social workers toward the poor is denying the social worker a useful role in the drive against poverty, a report based on a four-year study of low-income families here said today.

The report, published by the Health and Welfare Council of the National Capital Area, a non-profit social welfare agency, attacked a view it said was held by many professional social workers that 'the poor are a culture apart' with 'a special language' who must be 'dealt with by indigenous leaders.'

The report appeared to lay responsibility for the popularization of the 'new stereotype of the poor' as an unapproachable 'caste' on both Federal anti-poverty program and on the 'old line' social welfare structure, of which the council here is a part.

The report thus underlined and sought to reconcile a major point of tension in the program—between social work professionals and the 'new wave' of antipoverty workers, many of them from the ranks of the poor.

In many cities, established social welfare agencies have been bitterly attacked by new organizations of poor persons financed by the antipoverty program.

While strongly supporting the Federal program, particularly its statutory requirement for 'maximum feasible participation' by poor persons in planning and executing its work locally, the report cautioned against the idea that the poor can communicate only with the poor.

Such 'new stereotypes' it declared, 'have the practical effect of keeping Negroes from gaining full acceptance and from becoming full participants in American society.' The stereotypes, it continued, burden poor Negroes with the prejudicial disadvantages not only of being Negroes but also of being poor.

'The jobs of professionals—teachers, social workers, policemen, and probation officers—demand that they categorize poor families under various labels,' the report said.

'Thus,' it declared, 'the poor are seen as "problems"—as school dropouts, as neglected children, as welfare cheaters, as family deserters, as felons, parolees, and probationers' with non-middle-class values.

'Poor families have a high regard for professional knowhow but resent the condescension and contempt that too many social workers, teachers and law officers demonstrate in "dealing" with the poor,' the report said.

'By this rationale,' it went on, 'the Negro poor are supposed to be particularly "hard to reach" both by whites and by middle-class Negroes; social workers, teachers and other professionals, the theory goes, must find "indigenous leaders" or people-to-people workers among the ranks of the Negro poor . . . [who] speak the same language. . . .'

In fact, the report declared, there is no 'culture' or even 'community' of the poor. It said that projects based on the assumption that 'since low-income families live in the same neighborhood they can be organized into a viable community' were bound to fail.

The study of 55 low-income families, all but eight of them Negro, disclosed that 'contrary to popular belief' the lives and goals of poor families 'are as diverse as human nature itself.'

'Within the ranks of the poor,' the report said, 'there are some who are lazy, others ambitious; some strait-laced, others sinful; some wasteful, others thrifty.'

The four-year study of low-income child rearing practices here was financed by a grant from the National Institute of Mental Health.

D. *"Maximum Feasible Participation of the Poor"*

In addition to the involvement of the poor in staff positions, the community action programs have, usually under prodding from the OEO, sought to increase participation of the poor at the level of advisory councils, which review, with varying degrees of responsibility, the choice and implementation of programs.

Most concentrate on representation of the poor on neighborhood boards or block organizations that meet at stated intervals to discuss area problems and to plan activities of one kind or another, usually oriented toward self-help projects such as vacant lot clean-up drives. In certain cities, the poor are also appointed or elected to advisory boards with some responsibility for guiding and criticizing over-all programs. In such situations, the poor are seldom *numerically* in a dominant position (as they came to be in San Francisco after a period of conflict with the Mayor), serving rather as a minority among representatives of the community of affluence, such as political leaders, community chest directors, lawyers, labor union executives, ministers, and the like. And never are they in a dominant position in terms of *actual power and influence.*

It is, at the least, oversimplification to say as a California community action program director does: "Community organization is the basic thrust in which professional activity is directed. Social action is when the indigenous leadership takes over."

The OEO *Workbook* describes two methods for stimulating resident participation. The first is to put the poor in positions within the community action agency "that permit the poor to influence the objectives, policies, actions, and services of the organization." "The second approach seeks to assist the poor in developing *autonomous* and *self-managed* organizations which are competent to exert political influence on behalf of their own self-interest." (Emphasis added)

The *Workbook,* an advisory manual says:

> . . . It is required that every Community Action Agency give priority attention to resident participation, that is, to increasing the capability of the client populations to gain representation and influence community affairs. . . .

Insuring that the client population shares authority for the development and management of Community Action Programs is a federal requirement. Involving the poor at the administrative level of CAA's is a condition of funding. This condition cannot be satisfied by a mere symbolic act of placing a member, or members of the client population in the policy group of the organization. It is required that the poor and the advocates of the poor occupy positions of evident influence.

The National Association for Community Development, in its position paper quoted earlier, presented the following continuum to show the wide range of possible choices for resident involvement, arranged from those programs which are mainly public relations and least controversial at one extreme to those that are most direct-action-oriented and potentially most controversial on the other:

Press releases
Newsletters
Opinion surveys by professional staff
Officials meeting with citizens upon request
Hiring indigenous staff as professional aides
Opinion surveys by indigenous staff
Public hearings, open but not promoted
Advisory committee appointed by CAA
Meetings with neighborhood leaders
Meetings with existing neighborhood organizations
Planning committee of CAA staff and residents appointed by CAA
Planning committee of CAA staff and residents selected by neighborhood organization
Public hearings, following serious efforts to publicize and develop neighborhood testimony
Appointment of neighborhood leaders to CAA board
CAA assisting formation of neighborhood organizations
Autonomous community agency assisting formation of neighborhood organizations
Neighborhood organization selecting representatives to CAA board
Self-managed, indigenous organization carrying out programs
Neighborhood residents electing representatives of CAA board

Neighborhood organization endorsing political candidates nominated by a political party
Neighborhood organization running its own candidates for public office (local government, State legislature, or the Congress)
Neighborhood organization picketing public officials or voluntary community service agencies
Neighborhood organization sponsoring mass demonstrations
Neighborhood organization sponsoring sit-ins
Neighborhood organization sponsoring civil disobedience

A very few of the community action organizations express real intentions to encourage independence for the organizations of the poor. One of these is in Trenton, New Jersey. The Trenton anti-poverty program, United Progress, Inc., gave as one of its goals:

To develop with the help of Federal funds and indigenous organizers, strong and representative Neighborhood Councils in each of the target areas. The success of these Councils will be basic to the success of the entire anti-poverty effort as it is presently conceived. *Strong* and *independent* [emphasis added] Neighborhood Councils will be a major assurance that the program is being conducted democratically, and that individual projects and priorities are consonant with the wishes of the poor people who are supposed to be helped. Most importantly, the Councils will provide a convenient communications channel through which the poor people will be able to voice their objections or criticisms of UPI, its programs, the social agencies, and the policies of the city government, and through which they will be able to make known their program preferences and suggest new and more realistic courses of action.

For the Councils to be effective, it is essential that a fairly large number of neighborhood people participate in the election of Council leaders, that the Councils develop a large number of action committees involving as many neighborhood people as possible, that Council representatives be on the policy-making bodies of all anti-poverty projects, and that active, vocal, neighborhood organizations be developed on the sub-council level, preferably on the block level. Finally, it is essential that the complete independence of the Councils from UPI or any other city agency be made absolutely plain to any agency or person who might be affected by the Council's actions.

So far, the leadership bodies of the Neighborhood Councils have been elected in East Trenton and South Trenton. Organization for an election in North Trenton is now under way. Plans are being made for cutting the Councils free of any dependence or formal relationship with UPI. Organization on the sub-council level has not yet begun. (May 25, 1965)

The precise *form* of organization seemed to at least one official of New Haven's CPI to be less important than the *fact* and *purpose* of organization.

I don't think that the structure makes a continental difference; if the group feels that this is the kind of way they want to operate, fine. Many of them, at least at the outset, are not ready to have a president or vice-president. They don't even know their next door neighbor. But ultimately, most of them wind up with a structure. The structure is unimportant, in my opinion. It's the purpose for which they get together, and how they use themselves that is important. In helping them to develop an understanding of political process, the socialization of the individuals involved so that they speak a common language, they address themselves to the needs and problems of their community, and they draw some strength from their organization. This is what I see as the ultimate good of the group.

The National Urban League has undertaken a program to discover, identify, and train a self-conscious political Negro community leadership. Under a Rockefeller Foundation grant, ten urban community assemblies will be held to turn up at least 1,000 future leaders to form the core of neighborhood projects and for membership on boards of community organizations. It is then intended to see that they get on the boards of various organizations.

(1) *Elections of the Poor*

In some cities much has been made of the election of the

poor, a recognition of the political dimension of the community action program. It may be instructive to present an example of one city's election program—Philadelphia's—to show how one city, which believed its method successful, implemented this plan. The analysis that follows is excerpted and digested from a paper, "Promoting Participation of the Poor: Philadelphia's Unique Anti-Poverty Program" by Arthur B. Shostak of the sociology department of the University of Pennsylvania.

In only one city in America do the poor elect their own representatives to the city's anti-poverty governing board. The general pattern is the time-honored one of political appointment; the Mayors of Chicago and Pittsburgh, for example, pick all the members of their anti-poverty boards, while the Mayors of Los Angeles and New York appoint the majority of their cities' board members (anti-poverty neighborhood groups designate the others, or 7 of 25 and 16 of 62). Philadelphia alone meets the Federal requirement of the 'maximum feasible participation' of the poor by having the poor elect representatives to the Philadelphia Anti-Poverty Action Committee, or PAAC. Philadelphia remains alone [Los Angeles held such an election in March, 1966] to this day because the concept of involving the poor themselves has turned out to be the most unique—and certainly the most controversial aspect of the entire anti-poverty effort.

This essay will review the background of PAAC, the problems of including direct representatives of the poor, the character of the Town Meetings held to rally public support, the significance of the anti-poverty election returns, and the four-month old record of the new representatives of the poor. Particular attention will be paid in closing to insights available into four national race-related controversies: the debate over the alleged homogeneity of the Negro poor, the rift between the Negro poor and the professional social workers, the rivalry among factions in Negro slum neighborhoods, and the uncertainty of the Negro poor's preference for racial separatism or integration.

Background. In February, 1965, the Mayor of Philadelphia established a new command group (PAAC) for the local War on

Poverty. In keeping with the history of two short-lived predecessors, the Mayor staffed PAAC with seven representatives of the city and accepted the nomination of ten delegates representing private welfare agencies, religious bodies, organized labor, the business community, and the three leading civil rights groups (NAACP, CORE and the Urban League). Contrariwise, in a sharp break with previous history, and at the vigorous urging of Shriver's Office of Economic Opportunity, the Mayor instructed the 19-member PAAC to expand to include a dozen direct representatives of the poor.

Three difficult questions were apparent from the start: Who in the community could be said to speak directly for the poor? How could spokesmen be chosen to serve on PAAC? And in what ways could public support be secured for the entire endeavor?

PAAC decided that only Philadelphia adults living under the level of the original Federal 'poverty line' of $3,000 gross annual income for a family could qualify as spokesmen for the poor (a $500 allowance was permitted for each family dependent up to a $6,000 maximum). PAAC contended that long-term users of public and private welfare agencies could provide unique insight into the effectiveness of social services, could best define the needs of their poor neighbors and suggest ways of meeting them, and could help overcome long-established 'colonialism' in the social welfare field. . . .

PAAC next decided that spokesmen for the poor would be chosen by direct election rather than by nomination by neighborhood anti-poverty groups. PAAC contended that many able poor declined membership in existing neighborhood groups, and deserved a chance to run in an open contest for representative spokesmen.

PAAC resolved the third difficult question—that of securing public support for the May election—by deciding to employ large-scale Town Meetings. Accordingly, under the very intense pressure of a June 30th deadline set by the OEO for summer financial aid requests, PAAC in late March set a date of April 28th for the holding of the Town Meetings.

Town Meeting Analysis. [Some 8,100 came to the twelve Meetings. A University research team found at six randomly selected meetings, however, that whites and Puerto Ricans did not attend in proportion to their representation among the poor. PAAC claimed 30 percent white attendance; it should have been 55 percent.] Women, especially Negro women, made up the vast majority of the audiences; the absence of males, a reflection of the matriarchal manner of the poor. . . . The younger, better educated members (24 to 40 years old) refused to accept the PAAC Program in part or in whole. The older less well-off members endorsed the program in part or in whole. The third group, the majority who sat, were undecided and admittedly confused. The 'Angry Young Men' [feared political domination of the Council and the greater effectiveness of the non-poor members, and feared that the low income criterion] 'was a clever device to insure inadequate spokesmen for the poor, and thereby continue the dominance of the Mayor, the Ministry, and the social welfare professionals.'

[Charged that the failure of PAAC to promise salaries to elected Council members, was] foolish and hypocritical; some alleged it was likely to insure that certain spokesmen for the poor would accept graft. . . . The shortness of time between the March announcements of Meetings in April, the May formation of local PAAC Councils, the early June formation of a 31-member over-Council, and the June 30 deadline for OEO applications was judged unfair and insulting; some alleged the Program was being 'rammed down their throats.' The rigid instructions to Meeting Chairmen to avoid debate, refer doubtful questions to PAAC headquarters, and stress only the election procedures was judged officious, high-handed, and anti-democratic. . . .

[The supporters of the program were less conspicuous, vociferous, and influential.]

Over and above all, the sentiment of the loyal supporters was captured in the impatient cry of a woman who declared: 'We need less talk and more action. There's been plenty of talk.' She echoed here the popular advice tendered earlier at various Meetings by visiting PAAC director, Attorney Charles W. Bowser: 'Don't let people get you tangled up by little arguments. They'll get you tangled up and you'll still go home to a dump.'

Election Analysis. 13,493 Philadelphians voted. There were 144 open positions and twelve members were to be elected to twelve Community Action Councils; twelve thus were to join 19 non-indigenous on a 31-member Philadelphia Anti-Poverty Action Committee. 347 appeared on the twelve community ballots (an additional seven were disqualified for political or ministerial ties).

[Women outnumbered men as candidates (222 to 125), as winners (92 to 52), and as Community Council representatives to PAAC (8 to 4).] Negro candidates appeared to outnumber whites by a very high margin, as did also Negro voters. Possibly 10 of the 144 winners were white, as was one of the 12 Council delegates to PAAC. The smallest turnouts recorded were in the communities with the highest white population rates.

Contrary to the misgivings of some of the poor, the well-off did not take advantage of their eligibility to swamp the ballot-box; with rare exceptions only the poor went to the polls. Nor did the welfare agencies, the anti-poverty neighborhood groups, or the Philadelphia Archdiocese, the community organizations or the civil rights groups seriously attempt to seize control through the use of puppet candidates. While organized slates backed by settlement houses, the NAACP, and local political clubs appeared in a few communities (and were rumored in several more), they frequently checked one another and seldom succeeded in electing a majority of the candidates as the community's twelve Council members.

PAAC Meeting Analysis. While PAAC has only met on eight occasions at the time of this writing, the representatives of the poor have already established certain practices hinted at in the Meetings and the election. For one, the twelve generally vote as a bloc, frequently picking up support from CORE and certain denominational representatives. In a 'showdown,' the minority of twelve can expect at least fifteen of PAAC's thirty available votes, a situation possibly unforeseen by the designers of PAAC (with its 12 to 19 nominal vote distribution). Second, the twelve do not appear 'overwhelmed' by the professional qualifications of the other 19 PAAC members. On the contrary, the twelve clearly value their own insight into poverty, and challenge the views of the nineteen others with no apparent hesitation. Third, the twelve make a unique contribution to the PAAC deliberations with their regular resort to anecdotal case histories as illustrations of more general problems (a spokesman for the poor will typically illustrate the need to improve the welfare program with moving accounts of neighborhood suffering). Finally, the twelve differ somewhat among themselves in their basic trust of PAAC, their confidence in the venture's ultimate success, and their vision of what success really means. Reflecting differences common among the city's 350,000 poor, the twelve representatives are variously suspicious, hopeful, and utopian, their division finding full reflection among PAAC's nineteen other members.

General Analysis. The Philadelphia experiment, from Town Meetings through the Elections to the performance of the twelve representatives on PAAC, challenges four popular conceptions about the Negro poor: In certain quarters the Negro poor are perceived as a defeated, disorganized, homogeneous mass. Their dependency on professional social agencies is taken for granted. Their leadership by one or two self-appointed (and press-accepted) spokesmen is taken for granted. And finally, their commitment to an anti-poverty effort of an integrated character is also taken for granted. These four conceptions are all *mis*conceptions, to judge from insights suggested by the Philadelphia data.

Looking beyond the apathetic many, one large group of critics among the poor concentrates on the painful inadequacy of allowances and the debilitating character of petty rules and regulations, while another, the latest to appear and the group most clearly connected with the liberating spirit of the 'War,' rejects the welfare system in its entirety. This new group loudly and emotionally indicts the 'half-fare' system of permitting people to turn into listless, passive 'vegetables.' The controversy goes deep, the very presence on PAAC of the twelve poor Philadelphians challenges the historic claim of welfare professionals to exclusively represent their 'wards.' . . .

Leadership builds on heterogeneity, and generally divides into four types: a few leaders counsel suspicion and withdrawal, these men preferring separatist self-reliance schemes (as for example, the Muslims, other Black Nationalists, etc.). A few leaders at the other extreme counsel dependency and gratitude, these people—generally religious, family-raising elderly women—preferring reliance on better-educated, professional Negro and Caucasion 'do-gooders' with years of experience. In between are two other Negro leadership types, the one differing from the other in preferring trust to mistrust, patience to impatience, and non-violent protest to aggressive and possibly violent community action.

Finally, the Philadelphia experiment challenges the idea that the pro-integration orientation of the Negro poor can be taken for granted. To be sure, a rights-conscious Negro poor constitute the leadership vanguard in the anti-poverty effort (only 60,000 of Philadelphia's 142,000 poor families are Negro, while 11 of the 12 PAAC spokesmen are Negro). And participation in the anti-poverty effort is participation in an effort as integrated (and as white-dominated) as social welfare efforts generally are. Nevertheless, the bulk of the Negro poor waver between apathetic neutrality regarding the Philadelphia anti-poverty effort and emotional support of more Negro-dominated programs. Influenced by "Angry Young Men" who distrust PAAC, by older people who are resigned to apathy, by outspoken critics of existing welfare schemes, and by Black Nationalists who advocate separatism, the Negro poor remain undecided about trusting their pride and hope to an anti-poverty effort that is also interracial and pro-integration. They recognize Negroes among PAAC's decision-makers, but distrust these men as middle-class professionals; they have elected their own neighbors to PAAC, but wait warily to see if their spokesmen will have any real power or if election will alienate their spokesmen from them. And they remain especially attentive at this time to their white-distrusting, time-impatient, action-oriented younger leaders who demand better schools now for Negroes (rejecting bussing), more jobs now for Negroes (rejecting merit), and more power now for 'indigenous' Negroes active in the anti-poverty effort (rejecting interracial equity).

Whatever the statements of purpose, what counts is the consequences. The Philadelphia program worked in the neighborhoods after the election in the following way: The twelve-member Community Council on Poverty Pocket G, for example, was made up of three whites and nine Negroes. They were responsible for selecting workers, including social work professionals, for the projects in their area. They met at least once a week, sometimes more often.

In between they are like political precinct committeemen in that the poor in their bailiwicks come to them for aid, advice and referrals.

'I feel more at ease talking to Mrs. Mendoza, telling her my problems, asking her for help,' said a young mother with a small army of offspring tugging at her skirts. 'It's different than going into these formal places. It's cold there. With Mrs. Mendoza it's warm. It's personal,' added the young mother. 'Besides she knows what I need most and what I can best do to help myself.'

It costs Mrs. Mendoza about $20 a month out of her limited income to be a poverty councilor. The money goes for a baby sitter for Carlos, Jr., carfare, and an occasional meal out made necessary by long agendas. All the councilmen serve without pay.

G District Office is administered by a council assistant at $5,000; a secretary at $4,000, a social service worker at $4,000 and three clerk aides at $3,900 each. All were picked by the council, all live in the district.

On blackboards in the G office are lists of jobs available, both clerical and factory. The office has a census under way in the district with aides going from door to door gathering correct statistics on the area's poor and leaving at each home an invitation to come to the office for guidance and help.

'This way we'll reach every poor person,' said John B. Archer, 59, former grocer, real estate man, long time civic, welfare figure in G area. Temple University has honored him for his welfare work. The office is now open until 10 P.M.

'We can weed out the phonies among the poor, the frauds who don't want to work or help themselves,' said Mr. Archer. 'We know of them or hear about them quickly.' (New York *Herald Tribune*, December 5, 1965)

Nearly all the 2,000 men and women who had found jobs through the twelve area offices had been on relief.

The *Herald Tribune* reporter Robert T. Moriarty comments as follows:

The representatives of the poor have had to dash many false hopes on what the anti-poverty program would mean and do. A Fishtown representative said that when the program was announced, many had visions of immediately increased relief grants. In South Philadelphia's Ramcat district, a woman representative said some of her poor assumed they would have new jobs and new homes within weeks.

The big job of the leaders of the poor was to convince their fellow poor that the anti-poverty war was one in which they would have to help themselves; that they were not just going to stand on a corner and have the Great Society's funds handed to them without them doing anything.

One observes in the Philadelphia story the high degree of suspicion and alienation with which the poor greeted the anti-poverty program, the relative unwillingness of whites and men to participate in the community action program, and the emphasis of the elected councils, despite a frequent verbal militance, on patterning themselves, or being patterned after, the social services-opportunity orientation of the settlement house–political club facility of the past. One may speculate on the extent to which the representatives of the poor are inadvertently being used by the majority culture to sell its concept of self-help to the poor and even to tamp down the expectations and aspirations of the poor. To the extent that this *is* the consequence, such programs fail to lead to effective social change and indeed may serve as a positive inpediment to change.

There is a real question, despite the enthusiastic response to the Philadelphia experiment of the observer quoted and the New York *Herald Tribune* reporter, whether the elected poor have been able to be effective in representation of the poor in Philadelphia or elsewhere.

Trenton was the first city in the country to organize elections for neighborhood councils and the Trenton anti-poverty program seems to have been more effective than many, but the elections themselves were hasty and the councils neither strong nor democratic enough to give strength to its members. The strength of the Trenton program seems to come rather from the clarity and candor of official leadership.

In Los Angeles, an election was held on March 1, 1966 to choose seven members for the board of the Economic and Youth Opportunities Agency. Out of an estimated 300,000 eligible families, only 2659 persons voted. Unlike Philadelphia, where only the candidates had to prove impoverishment, the voters in Los Angeles did also, and may have been reluctant to do so. Furthermore, the election was held, deliberately so many of the poor thought, on the day when relief checks were due; recipients, fearing theft, customarily refused to leave home that day. In addition, the public transportation available in a city where the middle and upper class all have cars is notoriously meager, and no arrangement was made to reimburse voters for travel expense to the polls. A number of polling places were in middle-class neighborhoods inconvenient for the poor to reach. The political, religious, business, and other power groups in the community apparently did not regard the election as significant enough to command their real support. It seems clear that the election, which Mayor Yorty described as "a costly farce" (*New York Times,* March 4, 1966), mirrored what earlier observers had noted as a climate of alienation between the poor and the community-at-large. Yet, after the 1965 summer riots, Los Angeles leaders were widely quoted as astonished that the potential for violence had been smoldering in the Negro ghetto.

Only 1500 voted in Syracuse's elections for neighborhood council board membership (pre-registration was required); 2659 in Los Angeles—less than one percent; 13,000 in Philadelphia—only 2.7 percent of eligible voters.

All the elections were conducted by officials in the anti-poverty programs; in none, apparently, were the poor themselves asked for suggestions as to procedures. The agencies publicized the elections but seem to have contributed no funds for the candidates, who were on their own. One cannot help but question in the first place whether the election of the poor is regarded seriously either by the leaders of the community or by the poor themselves. The failure of power groups to seek to influence the Philadelphia elections was a case in point.

The pressure of the OEO for "maximum feasible participation" of the poor has led to the elections. But there is no evidence that the elections have led, in turn, to the poor gaining "influence" over community affairs or developing the "autonomous and self-managed organizations which are competent to exert political influence on behalf of their own self-interest."

Disturbed by the fact that there was no correlation between the amount of money it spent on elections and the voter turnout (in Los Angeles, $61,000 was spent, in Philadelphia, $34,000), OEO changed the rules on elections of the poor and suggested alternatives such as an "assembly of interested citizens" in poor neighborhoods to select representatives. It would fund no more elections until a city proved it could not get poor people involved in any way, according to a story in the *New York Times* (April 22, 1966).

The results of elections among the poor, which generally show a small percentage of eligible voters participating, suggest a number of possible explanations:

a. That the poor consider the process of elections itself meaningless;

b. that the poor sense that the meaninglessness of elections is part of a deliberate charade to present the appearance of power without the actuality of power;

c. and that the stagnation of poverty depresses individuals psychologically and robs them of energy and the will to act, even in their own behalf.

(2) *Assessment of Indigenous Leadership*

The participation of the poor on boards has created problems both for the community of affluence and for the community of need. In San Francisco, for example, the Mayor had resisted the attempts by the poor to control the anti-poverty program, but, after intervention by OEO, the poor won control in the summer of 1965.

The following telegram was sent to San Francisco's Economic Opportunity Program on August 25, 1965:

The Regional Office of Economic Opportunity continues to look with great concern at the difficulties of San Francisco's community action program. This telegram is addressed to all of those individuals representing the four target neighborhoods, for in your hands rests the opportunity to give San Francisco's program a chance to prove its strengths and weaknesses. The strengths of the program, as we see it, are:

1. The giving of authority to neighborhood boards to veto the establishment of any community action program in their neighborhoods;
2. The fact that you, as the neighborhood representatives, are in absolute majority of the executive committee and it is this committee which must screen program ideas which are presented to the larger council for approval;
3. The fact that neighborhood representatives and those who represent organized minority groups compose almost fifty percent of the larger council. Congressional opinion has spoken of a '3-legged stool' on community action agency boards. In San Francisco, by any test, the groups in areas to be served clearly hold at least one leg of that stool. Given the above three points, this office has gone on record in citing the San Francisco program as the boldest and most creative governing structure known to our regional office.

You may wish to compare it to the recently announced Los Angeles plan and note the great differences.

The major potential weakness of the San Francisco plan is that the neighborhood boards can say 'no' to program, but they have only a minority vote when it comes to saying 'yes.' We know that beginning evidence of bloc voting by non-neighborhood representatives on the council has led to the current stalemate. We ask that neighborhood representatives return to participate on the council and the executive committee. If, in the next six months, there is continued evidence of bloc voting against the neighborhoods, and if neighborhood boards are always put in the position of vetoing program, we shall ask the mayor and the chairman of the council to reexamine the structure and composition of the community action agency.

We are further recommending an extension of program review time until October first for those neighborhoods which have not completed their review. Upon the council's request we will move to seek immediate release of funds for those neighborhood programs already approved, as well as those programs which pertain to the city as a whole, rather than any particular area. If by October first, neighborhood boards have still not approved of programs, we shall seek the release of program funds pending the following conditions:

(A) Such release is requested by the council;

(B) The delegate agency for the program which was concerned with problems of poverty prior to August, 1964, and this agency agree to establish policy advisory groups composed of program participants and/or their parents.

In closing, we want to repeat that this office must, by virtue of its legislation, always remain sensitive to those groups who have been shut out of full participation in our society. When we stop being this kind of office, we ought to disappear. We are always ready to meet with you, and work with you toward realizing the goals of the Economic Opportunity Act in San Francisco.

Melvin B. Mogulof, Representative in Charge, Community Action Program

By January, 1966, however, the *New York Times* reported as follows:

San Francisco, Jan. 15—Ghetto leaders who wrested control of the local antipoverty program from City Hall six months ago are still struggling to put the program into effect.

Delay and dissension boiled up this week at a City Hall conference called at the request of unidentified members of the Economic Opportunity Council who wanted to dismiss the executive director, Everett P. Brandon, while he was on vacation.

Mayor John F. Shelley said he had just listened. *The Mayor, whose appointees are in the minority on the opportunity council, was standing by in case he was needed to pick up the pieces.*

'I'm beginning to get rumbles and grumbles that there is no program,' the Mayor said with no evidence of pain. 'There was a program, but they set it aside. There is feuding.

'What comes of it I don't know. I lost and I am just going to sit back and wait and see. *We have given them the rein and the wagon hasn't moved. In fact, the wheels haven't even spun.*'

The spokesmen for the poor here, while militant and articulate, appear to be short on the technical skills needed to hire a staff, sort out reams of official paperwork and get a project rolling. Washington gave the opportunity council a $1.8 million grant last July, but few projects have got off the ground and applications for new funds will not be filed until April.

The delays mean a probable forfeit of millions of dollars in antipoverty money for the city. They also tend to weaken the argument of the organized poor that they know their needs best and can shape their own environment, given a chance. . . . (Emphasis added)

The position paper of the National Association for Community Development referred to earlier commented as follows on the problem of participation of the poor on boards:

Nevertheless, if OEO persists upon making a large board of interests a mandatory requirement, there are probably some gains and certainly no harm in neighborhood residents being represented. *However, board representation may truly be symbolic rather than having a real sense of influence,* as the *Workbook* points out at one point. *Most poor persons will not have experience in the communications process of a board meeting, and if they are selected, instead of nonpoor neighborhood residents, their participation in board discussion is likely to be limited.* (Emphasis added)

Similar comments came from persons involved in CAP programs in three of the cities studied:

If you have highly educated and articulate people with a very small group of uneducated and inarticulate people, and the educated people are sophisticated in terms of manipulation, in terms of other people, and power, *it seems to me to be a little nonsensical to expect that the uneducated, unsophisticated person can compete effectively with them. If they could they wouldn't be poor. They wouldn't be powerless.*

From my observations of the interaction between board members, our board members and representatives from the poverty community lead me to believe they responded in one of two ways. They're either silent or they're vocal, and when they're vocal they are in an attempt to be just like any other member of the board. Which means that *the maximum feasible participation of the poverty-stricken people doesn't exist, and their inclusion on boards makes no difference at all.* They can be manipulated, they can be out-voted and then non-represented. What interest can they represent? Suppose they disagree on a tack or a direction that the board embarks upon. First of all, they're inarticulate, for the most part, which means that they cannot get their points across. Secondly, they're outnumbered. And that business of including them on the boards is a blind. It's another way of hiding. What they should be doing is turning over cars, and beating policemen. I just don't think that it makes any difference in having them on the board. (Washington, D.C., emphasis added)

First, let's talk about the 39 (members of the board). First off, seven of these people are named by the mayor. The mayor himself is one of the seven, and then we have people like the health officer, superintendent of schools, and director of the planning board, officials of that type. So that's seven right away. Then the others mainly represent: (a) the social welfare agencies; (b) civil rights organizations; (c) what you might call ethnic considerations. Right now, I would say that of the 39 there are between eight and ten authentically poor people. But I would say roughly a third.

Query: And what power do they have?

Well, that's the rub you see. Because now you have to talk about naming poor people to a board. The point was made that many of these poor people, after they fight so valiantly and heatedly to sit on these governing boards, have a kind of deep sense of frustration because of the fact that they don't have all the facilities they need to really wheel and deal on this level. That's not true, but what I'm saying is a number of these people more or less just sit silently, but not really participating. I'm sure that there is all kinds of caucusing going on, and they may not be saying anything, but when the issue comes to a vote . . . there are all kinds of cross currents at the board meeting. What I'm saying is that some of these people who don't say anything at the debate, you can see who they are listening to by the way they vote. I'm not completely negating the influence that these people can have, but they have to be prepared in many ways to enter into the overt dialogue. We have a limited extent of that now. (Newark, New Jersey)

On the other question of leaving Mayors and local communities determintion of structure and so forth, there again OEO is calling the shots. There is no one way of achieving citizen participation. To have members on your board as the requirement is much too rigid a determination. You could have a board of all citizens and still have a highly paternalistic situation and have a board with no citizens and have a non-paternalistic operation. Each situation should be judged on its own merits—there should be no rigid criteria—and OEO has been sending out rigid criteria. They started out by saying that there are 20 different ways in which residents can participate. So look at 20 different ways and not say the test is whether they are on your board and how many are on your board. I look at Philadelphia where they had this election and there are four on the board and it is really of no great significance as far as program is concerned. (New Haven)

The indigenous people are often acutely aware of "the participation of the poor" as a kind of charade. They know that they are not really equipped to represent the poor on boards, that they cannot talk as persuasively as persons whose business it is to talk. They are aware that those people who are alleged to be indigenous leaders are accepted as such principally because they are more articulate than others. When the really indigenous function in the role of "leaders of the poor," it is because they are verbal; they usually have had some kind of leadership experience prior to their identification as "indigenous" for these purposes. Or they are persons who are not really indigenous but have, in some way, chosen to assume that role, although they are, in fact, of higher education-income status. In South Harlem, a woman who is considered an "indigenous" leader and who gets grants from foundations and the anti-poverty program is actually not an indigenous leader in the sense that she does not come out of the group she is leading. She lives there, it is true, but she is more sophisticated than the neighborhood. If an apparent indigenous leader has appeared to function as such over a sustained period of time either it is *not* leadership in a *sustained* form, or it is temporary verbal involvement on a particular issue, or if it *is* sustained, the individual leader does not personally share all the following empirical requirements of the "indigenous" and, in fact, differs from the persons he purports to lead in that he has:

—a higher level of education, or

—a higher income or standard of living, or

—more sophistication in organizational ability and in serving as communication link between grass roots and sources of power and funds.

These individuals may have had their original roots in the group, but, in general, have moved away from it in present status.

"Indigenous" characterizes a way of life that is on its face undesirable and dominated by deprivation. Anyone with capacity, ability, power, luck, or any talent to help him escape would do so at the first opportunity. Yet, by definition, leadership itself implies such positive characteristics; it implies that the individual has something about him which he can use to change his own situation. It would seem to follow that if a person *has* these characteristics he will have used them to change. The indigenous leader is concerned to lead himself out of context of being indigenous; that is his primary goal, even though unconsciously held.

The poor themselves recognize that "indigenous" as OEO uses it, may not apply to their own neighbor, that it implies more than where one lives. It implies an attitude and identification. In New York City, a professional put it this way describing a Harlem street:

> The people who are potentially leaders, they are already gone. They're not in the district by the time they become a leader. Now you know there are two very important people on the block,——and ——, and the role that these two people can play we're not too sure of. Because, again, they're not indigenous. They're really quite isolated. People talk about them as if they were living downtown.

Who stays in the indigenous community? In general, those who can't, for a number of reasons, get out. This lack of personal power is inconsistent with effective leadership.

Who comes back to the indigenous community? Some come for purposes of exploitation: to dominate, to take advantage of a situation in which people are more easily exploitable than more privileged peoples. Some, it is true, come to help, but, in general, those who come into the neighborhood are those who never lived there or persons who were never stigmatized by poverty themselves.

What is the possibility of training indigenous leaders? There is no evidence to demonstrate or suggest that there has been any sustained success in identifying and training such leaders or in getting such individuals to assume the primary or exclusive leader's role in organizing people of poverty to identify their problems or to undertake a sustained effort of program until change is achieved.

This seems to be equally true of Saul Alinsky's program. Those leaders he offers seem not to be themselves indigenous, nor is there evidence, for example, that the institutional activity in the Woodlawn Organization in Chicago, which does involve the community itself, has resulted in *fundamental* change, in the schools and in housing, to take two important areas in desperate need of change.

The assumption that the indigenous, by definition, are rock-like and independent may well be sentimental. To project into this group all manner of virtue and strengths, and the capacity to resist demagoguery, is, in theory, questionable. It also may reflect a romantic form of class or racial condescension. Nor, in terms of the evidence, is this projection sound.

The "involvement of the poor" has become a major criterion of the success of a community action project of the anti-poverty program. These requirements point up the proper beneficiaries of the program—the poor and not the political patronage system. But it has tended to cause the government and others to overlook the fact that involvement of the poor was intended to be a means to an end—the abolishing of poverty. To the extent that involvement would lead to social change it could be useful. But an over-concern for the means could prove a temporary palliative, obscuring without effecting change at all.

5. Empathic Professionals as Surrogates

It may be more relevant and forthright for a community action program to concentrate on the empathic relationship of professionals who will serve as surrogates to the poor and who have the training and skills to identify with and to help the poor. When labor needed to organize it depended on trained organizers who could serve as spokesmen from the vantage point of independence supported by national union backing. The poor need similar support. Of primary importance is the freedom of such surrogates from loyalty to any ideology or organization that would exploit the poor in its own interests.

In a program that utilizes such professionals, special skills would be needed, given the facts of the conditions of the poor:

a. The ability to operate without a condescension which contributes to powerlessness and dependency;

b. the ability to maximize whatever power does reside within the people; and

c. the ability to define as accurately as possible what power is really there.

The ultimate skill of the leader is demonstrated by the extent to which he is no longer required. There is latent power in the poor—not merely the power of life, but a level of energy that is really harnessable—and the leader must mobilize these energies and sustain them until change is effected. If there is sufficient energy among the poor such mobilization would require not just organization of the poor, but certain kinds of observable external changes coincident with the harnessing of energy. The experience of the past has indicated that the community of poverty is debilitating and that those who can mobilize the energy to escape do so. This natural process will continue. Therefore it follows that realistic organization of the community of poverty cannot be achieved with static continuation of the community of poverty itself. There must be concomitant evidence of changes in the conditions that have been debilitating. The failure to produce such evidence is the rock on which anti-poverty programs fail.

IV
The Control of the Poor and Attempts to Protect the Interests of the Poor

1. The Control of the Poor: Political Power

The definitions of purpose and the projects in the community action component of the anti-poverty program have been described. But, beyond that, it is essential to survey the attempts to control these programs, as for example: *the efforts of political leadership, or social agency leadership, to guide and contain the programs; and the counter-attempts to compensate for containment or for ineffectiveness through parallel programs designed to protect the interests of the poor, supported by churches or civil rights groups or national citizens groups.*

Perhaps primary among the forces encouraging (and sometimes discouraging) organization of the poor are *political* forces. These can be seen as deriving from three central sources: (a) the federal government's intervention through the OEO, allocation of funds, and other means; (b) the initiative of the local government, either alone or in cooperation with the federal government; (c) intervention by partisan political personalities or political parties.

In some cities the community action programs are directly related to political action. This has been regarded in some cities, such as Syracuse, Chicago, Newark, San Francisco, Cleveland, Minneapolis, Paterson, and New York as a threat; in others, such as New Haven, as a promise.

In the community action programs that consider political relationship as a boon, it is assumed that both powerlessness and lack of opportunity are responsible for the predicament of the poor, but primary priority is given to lack of power as a derivative of lack of opportunity. This type of program, therefore, holds that more opportunities must be made available to the poor but that these opportunities can be better extended and taken advantage of if the poor have access to power. The poor may gain power by organization around their common community and personal problems, taking action to seek redress of their perceived grievances. Or they may depend largely on surrogates. However, even in their own organization, they are encouraged to activity through the vehicle of the parent body; and since the parent organization has some control over opportunities, any organization formed is to some extent dependent upon, and therefore an arm of the parent body. The organization may or may not be intended to become fully independent of the parent body or of the political structure. In no city studied, however, has this been achieved.

A. *Coalition of Political Leadership and CAP Organization in Behalf of Positive Change*

(1) *New Haven: Community Progress, Inc.*

New Haven's program is the best example studied of integrated effective coordination, more accurately a coalition, between the community action program and the local political leadership.

Begun in the wake of an enthusiastic, widely acclaimed citywide renaissance, CPI has benefited as the heir of success. It was based on experience of citizen participation in a long-range urban renewal program that sought rehabilitation of what had been a decaying city. Urban renewal, its supporters who are many say, has led to social renewal. In each of the neighborhoods where renewal or rehabilitation of housing is underway an active neighborhood organization was set up; upon its support the success of renewal itself depended. In some communities whites who had moved out of central city areas moved back in and shared housing with Negroes.

Like most community action programs which derive from the

initiative of forces in the majority culture, New Haven's appears to be task-oriented, with neighborhood groups assigned certain responsibilities and their effectiveness judged by the extent of their fulfillment of these responsibilities. The groups have been as useful to the city as to the poor, and possibly more so. But in general the interests of the poor and the city appeared to coincide.

CPI was devoted from the beginning to the achievement of basic institutional change in the city. While it provided access to services, it was not primarily service-oriented. Its documents and proposals show social sensitivity toward the predicament of the poor. Its leadership has apparently consistently had a high degree of zeal, intelligence, social indignation and political shrewdness—a combination of characteristics that the political leadership of the city appeared to share. The two have been allies in what is perceived as a common cause.

The local political leadership in New Haven under Mayor Lee has been identified with the community action program. CPI's director saw the rationale of CPI as balanced between the traditional view of community action as the provision of services and opportunities, and the newer, more radical view of action as participatory democracy on the part of the poor themselves, in response to their perception of their condition of powerlessness. "I'm for both. If you go off too hard on the opportunity kick," Mitchell Svirdoff said, "you'll get a paternalistic kind of operation which will not yield the results that you believe ought to take place. If you go off too far on the other kick [powerlessness] the same thing is going to happen and it might even be another kind of paternalism." In essence, it is "the competence of the capability of blending these two theories so that you are not overwhelmed on the one hand by paternalism, and on the other hand by the kind of participatory democracy which adds up to chaos and more frustration because it doesn't lead anywhere."

The New Haven emphasis on political orientation reflects also the tension between the older social agency approach and the approach of politics to observed social need. This tension is confirmed in the observation that the only groups that apparently opposed the New Haven program are social agency and other professionals, such as teachers, whose own training and psychology are more closely identified with the social work approach than with the direct action political approach, and certain militant activist groups. (In a number of other cities, for example Boston and Chicago, it was pointed out often in interviews that a similar resistance to programs involving the poor was found among school officials and personnel.)

As one of the New Haven CPI officials said, the service-opportunities program is not adequate for persons "so frustrated, so angry": "It isn't enough to come around with your goodies, your little ice cream wagon of opportunities."

To give the poor the evidence of genuine change in their lives seems to be one of the concerns of CPI, as staff personnel affirmed:

I think what we're saying, we have a certain amount of enthusiasm for what's going on here, we have the feeling that we have a City Hall that's trying to face up to this problem, and really do something about it. And we think it's manageable. *We think people are moving from poverty into middle class.* Your best example is CPI. They look for leadership and people volunteered in our program, and all of a sudden they went along with the poverty group. They're working for CPI. (Emphasis added)

What's happening is, with the opportunities coming through in terms of employment in the last couple of years, you have *an increasing Negro middle class.* You also have kids in the neighborhood youth corps who are coming through what we call a work crew. And this is a pretty good program. Kids who are . . . had been given individualized as well as group attention, who have had a chance to flex their muscles and most of all their minds, and have also, with their own particular perceptiveness, have been watching the system. These kids are growing up to voting age. And you've got parents. (Emphasis added)

The New Haven CPI staff believes its enthusiasm for the program is shared by the people:

I think the residents, by and large, a great majority of residents think the CPI (program) is a great asset. A tremendous asset. The people who see us as interlopers, as meddlers, are the school personnel, the lower echelon, the Goldwater Republicans and that ilk. I think that if we were put to popular vote tomorrow, we'd probably get 90% of the popular vote in favor of CPI. I strongly believe this.

New Haven, incidentally, was the only city studied where officials encouraged interviewers to talk directly to the community residents. In several other cities, including one whose program was far more strongly oriented toward participatory democracy than New Haven's, there was evident anxiety about such interviewing among CAP officials.

The question of "participation" in New Haven is complex. There is this eloquent testimony of a normally hard-boiled official:

I wandered in and listened to six neighborhood residents giving a class in Neighborhood Services to Neighborhood Services people from other communities. They were explaining in their own way their own experience and what this process has meant to them. I must confess, I'm not a sentimental person, but I was almost moved to tears. I had a Congressman with me and I wanted him to hear, otherwise I wouldn't have walked in.

As we have seen earlier, New Haven has an extensive program for involving the indigenous as staff and of helping them move up the ladder into the middle class. CPI also has a program of neighborhood organization and a Citizen Participation Committee, formed in the summer of 1965 after many months of considering the best methods of involving the poor more concretely in planning. It was decided to apply no means test, since this was a condescending way of separating people. Similarly, "the poor" was rejected in favor of "Inner-City Residents" as a designation of the people served by CPI. The Committee was proposed not as a "rubber stamp" committee but as an official body. Two residents would be selected from each of the seven neighborhoods and two or three of these

Advisory Committee members would be elected by the committee to the CPI Board of Directors. The residents were to be chosen at neighborhood conferences by methods to vary depending on the wishes of the neighborhood, with CPI neighborhood staff assigned the task of insuring that the poor were involved in the conferences. CORE was pushing for a majority of "poor" on the CPI Board and CPI held meetings with CORE and NAACP to gain their support of the advisory committee plan.

CPI's directors took an unromantic view of participation of the poor:

> The other thing that troubles me about this business of participation is that there are people who think that there's such a thing as *instant participation.* There's not—this is a slow and sometimes frustrating and sometimes torturous process. And there's not just one way of doing it. It doesn't have to be a protest movement—sometimes it has to be but it doesn't always have to be. And it doesn't always have to have loud and ringing slogans. It expresses itself around all kinds of issues—schools, housing, cleanup, fixup, social affairs—there are dozens, maybe hundreds of different ways. I said this is one area where New Haven had been weak. I don't think we are weak any longer. We started back before there was much thought given to this in '61 and '62. But it's starting to make itself felt now. But it's best to talk to the people on whose life this is making an impact.

On the other hand, the Citizen Participation Committee was not a governing body. It "is generally an advisory board . . . it is not policy making." The seven neighborhood representatives sat on a policy making board. "The process will be that of giving us criticisms, suggesting modifications of programs, new programs, expansion of programs. Programs that don't emanate from out there will be reviewed by them."

CPI's leadership has been impatient with many of the plans for participation of the poor in other cities: "You could have the perfect structure and the perfect methodology according to their design and still have nothing of substance."

New Haven's poor are by no means in charge of their

program. Yet the program itself is social-action oriented, not fearful of change. This apparent paradox seems to owe its explanation to the reform-committed mayor of the city and the corps of pragmatic dedicated tough young men he has gathered around him. Though the city's charter is a "weak mayor" charter, the mayor is strong and exerts leadership despite the structure:

Everybody says we have very special conditions. We have a Mayor who is apparently enlightened and is an activist, a small community, a community council—all interested, concerned, enlightened.

Query: But is this true?

Yes. The question is how do you get this kind of situation, this combination, in the average American community.

A similar concept of realistic leadership dominates CPI, one of whose officials responds to a question:

Query: But it still, as far as I can see, comes down to the individual who is running the city.

It also comes down to the individual who is running the community program and what that community action policy is. Let me put that community action man in one of those more difficult, more typical situations. That community action man is going to be spending a lot of time with the city administration in the role of mediator. He can't as some people suggest—he can't be totally independent, therefore, as some people would have it—of city hall or of the city administration.

New Haven's community action leadership, as we see, has conceived of its role as mediator and as partner with city hall. But it does not describe the origin of this alliance as dependent on luck alone, rather upon its own skill and astuteness:

The power structure of this city was very uneasy about us because we started playing this role from the start—we overstepped the line a few times and they had the right to be uneasy on that count, but even when we weren't overstepping the line they were very uneasy.

So it became our function—the community action agency has to play a mediating role—it became our function then to try to educate the city leadership to the importance of social action and to the fact that social action can have positive and constructive results, can help the local situation. We frequently intervene in these situations working on the one hand with the people and on the other with the administration, saying to the administration—you've got to meet with these people, you've got to hear them out and you've got to have an open mind on this one. You may not agree with them but you've got to hear them out. And as a matter of fact we may even express the view that these grievances are very serious and very sound and ought to be dealt with. [The relationship with the mayor] had to be cultivated. There was a time even in the development of this organization when the Mayor was so mad at us that he was ready to throw the whole thing down the drain. And we had to bring the situation along. We had to keep our heads. We had to keep the thing in perspective. We had to bring the situation along. And above all we had to demonstrate to him too that there were solutions to the social problems of the city in a community action program and that social action needn't lead necessarily to a chaotic situation. That there was a way for an administration to respond to social action in such a way that the results would be positive not only for the people but for the administration also. But this didn't happen over night. This was a painful process.

Both the political and CPI's leadership has been self-confident and self-assured. One could speculate that a shrewd mayor might well wish to encourage the belief that his support had been won, not bestowed. Both, however, recognize the fact that political strength must have roots in genuine popular support:

This doesn't mean that you can't have varying degrees of community organization associated with social action. In New Haven we do put a greater stress on the role of the executive, the role of the bureaucrat, the role of the leader. Though we put more emphasis here, we recognize that the effectiveness of the bureaucrat, the executive, depends on community support. He can't get too far out ahead of the community. Although he is vital to the process of social change, he cannot affect social change without engaging in community organization—without involving himself in community—it might be community organization through a political organization, through civil rights organizations, through PTA's or whatever, but the two vital ingredients of social change are I think, effective executive bureaucratic leadership combined with effective community organization.

But leadership can guide the community, as New Haven's did in one "reverse bussing" dispute, when it was proposed to transport white pupils into predominantly Negro schools. There had been pressure from Negro groups to improve the quality of their schools. Many of the white children assumed they were coming to an inferior school; the Negro children, in turn, resented this. And yet the opposition, in this instance, was apparently dissipated. Given as an explanation by one CPI official was the city's quality of leadership:

The important thing here was that the board become committed to it. To a bussing policy. They did have a series of public hearings before the board inaugurated it. In the public hearings there were tremendous feelings expressed. The board teetered momentarily, but then held firm with the bussing program. There was a modification of the program, because my area, for example, was left out of this piece because of the violent opposition to bussing. But modified bussing programs went in. It was a 100% success, but the thing that made it was that the board was responsive to the Mayor, they agreed to hold firm. If they had agreed to disintegrate then we wouldn't have had a bussing program, regardless of all education and everything else that went on.

The key to CPI seems primarily to be shrewd politics, politics in the style of reform, but depending on time-tested experience in old-line techniques. Politics, in New Haven, is considered to be nothing to be ashamed of. As several CPI officials put it:

Then let's get involved. Let's have a new attitude toward politics. Let's stop looking at politics as a dirty business as the social work profession has been looking at it for so long—which is one of the reasons they are now out of the mainstream. Let's look at it rather as the life's blood of social change. Let's get into it. Let's not look down our nose at people who are in politics. Let's make it respectable. Prestigious. And above all let's make working at the local level respectable and prestigious. Otherwise, you know what we're going to have? We're going to have federal programs because we have to have programs, we're going to have them run out of Washington and run at the local level out of Washington, by Washington civil servants, the way we run our employment system today, the way we run vocational education, the way we run social security. That's what's going to happen. If you say this other approach is naive and hopeless, maybe it is, but the minute we say that it can't be done we might as well get the hell out of this at the local level and let the federal government do it. It's a very difficult thing. We've got to do a lot of things. For example, let me give you an idea of what I think the foundations ought to do. Foundations give great big prestigious fellowships to people to go abroad to go into foreign aid, to write. Why don't they give great big prestigious fellowships to people who'll go to work as assistants to Superintendents of Schools, as assistants to Mayors, as assistants to community action directors? Put a few in here, who can then go out of here into other cities, as we are now sending a lot of staff we've trained into other cities. Put them in Detroit with Jerry Cavanagh. Put them with Carl Marburger in Detroit. One of the real comers in our educational system. Put them in these hopeful places in fairly large numbers and give it prestige and take people out of the universities and even out of the business community and let's start elevating the . . . why do you laugh at that? You see it's all right to do it with the universities with the federal government and so on, but nobody's ever thought about doing this at the local levels where the battle is going to be won or lost. With the local machinery. . . .

I mentioned the foundations as just one of the things that can be done. The foundations have a lot to do with values and policy. Where the foundations put their money has a very marked influence on values and social policy. Where the federal government puts its money has a very marked influence on values and social policy—so I'm not saying only foundations. I'm saying the federal government, the universities—you know there is no university in the country today that's training community action directors—they wouldn't know where to begin. There is no school of public administration that's training administrators to take leadership in this very critical area of social policy. They train them to be good technicians.

Most of us as social workers or as labor people will go into a community and expect that we have to do battle with city hall, and many of the neighborhood coordinators who came in here started with that orientation. They had a little bit of difficulty here until things were understood. It isn't that city hall is perfect. But you get more and more accomplished here through this coalition, and through putting the pressures in ways that can accomplish it with city hall, than necessarily coming and beating the Mayor over the head. You can beat him over the head, but by and large CPI social action is more in the direction of helping the neighborhood people to find ways and means of getting action on these things and apprising them of the appropriate ways that this can be done.

I think social action to be effective has to be political action, ultimately. In one form or another it's social action. Social actionists are going to press political leaders, they're going to press political institutions. They will press them most effectively if they know how to deal with political process, which means that ultimately they're going to have to get involved with political process. And that means that ultimately they will have to start making compromises. And the social actionist who can't do that, after a while will become a voice in the wilderness. I'm an ex-labor leader, and I came through the '30's and I saw the social actionists of that day so pure that they could not engage in the process of collective bargaining, because this meant compromising. They got lost ultimately. They faded away. They made a lot of noise and they were vital to the movement, but ultimately someone had to come along and pick up the pieces, and make the process work.

Yet political control of CPI does not seem rigid. The three persons the mayor appointed to CPI's board were not office holders or civil servants, but laymen:

As a matter of fact, there was a conflict of view on this one. There were some people who felt that the Superintendent of Schools should be on the board, the head of the Redevelopment Agency should be on the board and that the Mayor ought to be on the board. It was the Mayor's feeling, and my feeling . . . that the board would have a great deal more independence and flexibility if it did not have on it as members the office holders and bureaucrats (not used invidiously). Some felt that these people ought to be on the board so that there would be a greater possibility of effecting change vis-à-vis the institutions they represented, but the Mayor's view carried the day. The Mayor was also somewhat concerned about what would happen if he didn't run again and if an administration unfriendly to the program took over.

Yet the involvement of the mayor in CPI and CPI's involvement with the mayor seems clear. The coincidence of perspective and purpose may have made direct supervision unnecessary. There was doubtless security, too, in the tremendous popular victory the administration increasingly registered at the polls. One hears that CPI has not withdrawn from the political arena in time of election, but has participated in various ways that might be looked upon with disfavor by the opposition. In the event of a Republican victory in New Haven, CPI might have a less happy relationship with city hall and be less sanguine about politics.

In the meantime, up until the disorder of the summer of 1967 the atmosphere had been one of remarkable serenity and, as would be expected in a situation of political alliance, the only real enemy has been the specter of civic chaos. CPI's leadership has a somewhat caustic opinion of the view of many liberals that conflict is *per se* evidence of social progress:

Whenever a review team [from OEO] comes in this is their emphasis. 'Where is the evidence of social action?' 'Where is the hard evidence of resident participation?' What it often adds up to is 'Where is your chaos?' If you don't have chaos something is wrong. Director after director has told me this story. A fella told me what they think they have to do before a review team comes in is to stir up a little chaos in order to get a seal of approval.

The core of CORE comes from the young militant Yale students who deal in conflict. Their whole purpose in life is to create conflict. Those of us who have been in this business many years certainly see the value of conflict, but when you have a Mayor who is more oriented in social reform than any social worker I've ever dealt with in my whole life, and I've been a social worker all of my adult life, I question the value of constant conflict. When you have that kind of a new political structure, that's bending over backwards to work for the good of people and not against people.

Consistent with this dislike of conflict and chaos, some of CPI's leadership expresses firm distaste for Saul Alinsky and his version of participatory democracy and grass roots protest against the Establishment. In New Haven, the Establishment has considered that *it* represents the grass roots, though the events of the summer of 1967 occasioned doubts on this point.

Query: What do you think of Saul Alinsky's approach?

I think it is an over-simplistic notion of community organization and social action. It takes a brush and makes a broad sweep across the nation as if the problems in every city across the nation were the same. My problem with Alinsky is the broad brush stroke. It doesn't take into account differences in local situations. There's a kind of paternalism to it too, that says you're going to do it this way, and like it. I've seen reports about people who have actually been pressured into participating in programs Alinsky style, and in a sense being . . . you've heard the story about the revolutionary who says you're going to eat strawberries and cream, and what is more you're going to like it. Well, there's something of Alinsky in that. The main problem is that there is a neglect in Alinsky, and in too many social actionists, of programs. They don't understand programs. They don't understand the role of public policy. And they are not affecting changes in public policy. They have an impact, and they have a role, but to make of Alinsky an ideology, to make of what he's saying the beginning and the end, is I think a short cut to chaos. . . . Alinsky has made a tactic a dogma. And that's my criticism of SDS. It makes of a tactic a whole philosophy. I go with Bayard Rustin in his article—how do you convert this picket line into better education and employment, and so forth.

It wasn't only my dialogue with Alinsky but Alinsky's dialogue with some four Negro ladies who are working with the Chicago anti-poverty program and who he kept referring to as 'political hacks.' And they took him on. He was somewhat taken aback since they were applauded and he is the only one who is usually applauded. They pointed out that they were not political appointees—that they've never held a decent job in their lives, and that what they were doing now they felt was important and gave them a sense of dignity. And then they described some of the things they were doing and said in effect, 'Tell us what's wrong with this. Why do you call it names, because we're earning four thousand a year and because we are being paid with public funds when at the same time we are doing something very important and very helpful for people who need our help?' And he says, 'Well, the reason I call you political hacks is wait until you start to picket city hall.' So I said at this point, 'That's the trouble with you. You mix functions—you mix roles. It's not their job to picket city hall. Their job is exactly what they described. It's your job to picket city hall. When you start playing Sargent Shriver and Sargent Shriver starts playing Alinsky, that's when you start getting mixed up and in trouble.' That I think is the problem. We haven't really defined the function. The function of social action and social protest is a private function—it's not the function of the government. The government is supposed to be pressed by social actionists. It's not supposed to make its own social action. That's a little like the corporate state. First of all, I don't think it's going to work. It's not working now. When I say this it's like attacking motherhood, because when I say this it's immediately interpreted that I'm against social action. It's not that at all. It's an argument against the government sponsoring and paying for social action. Now making it possible to take place is another story, legitimatizing it. You know what that decision did with collective bargaining in the '30's. Protecting people who engage in it or legislation that establishes an atmosphere in which it can be most effective —voting rights in the South—that's another story. But paying for it, putting money into the organization of social action so Alinsky can say 'wait till you start picketing city hall when you're being paid with public funds' then you're getting into trouble. . . .

The government can even play a role here as it does in voter registration. It is legitimate, I think, to train people, educate people, give them the kind of education that will help to make them effective leaders. . . .

I think social action against housing authorities, welfare agencies, is certainly possible. We consider it completely legitimate to use public funds to help organizations become more effective in terms of carrying on this kind of social action. We can help them in the training of their leadership, we give them advice. But here's what we don't do—we don't carry the picket signs. We don't say to them, 'The only way is to picket the housing authority tomorrow morning.' We say, there are a number of alternatives. You can write a letter asking for a meeting. You can issue a press release. You can picket. You can wait. You can have a meeting. There are a dozen different things to do. They have to learn to find the alternatives and make a choice between alternatives. This is a legitimate role for us.

Query: If the housing authority is approached by hitherto unvocal people and they are tied up with the Mayor and they know that part of the training that made it possible for these people to become vocal came from the federally sponsored poverty program, will not there be the same sort of reaction to the poverty program from city hall and its appendages that you would find if you were to give money and say—'Go picket these people.'?

Yes. There would be some of this but it would be manageable. If it was in terms of what I described a minute ago—technical assistance, basic education, exploration of alternatives. There will be some cities that would be very upset over it. But not all cities, which is what you're getting now where you start doing it Alinsky style. Syracuse, for example, where it's hardly the case of exploring alternative approaches to problems. It starts out with the ideological conviction that you can't work it out with the city. You can't bargain with the city machine—you have to fight it. That might be true, but that's one of the alternatives. It oughtn't to be the only way of doing it. What I'm saying is that if you give technical assistance which really left it to people to make choices instead of telling them there's only one way of doing it and that one way is fighting city hall, you'll have some problems in some cities, but you won't guarantee the mobilization of all the major cities against the program.

I'm not saying that you shouldn't be doing this. I think this is a legitimate role for government—we've played this before with the farm community, the business community. We ought to play it with the poor community too. We ought to help them develop leadership. We ought to help them develop viable effective organizations. But we ought not to say that the only way you can do it is by dumping garbage on the steps of city hall. That may be one way of doing it. But when you are dealing with Alinsky you're saying that the only way of doing it is by declaring war on city hall. First of all, I think it's wrong to say that that's the only way. And secondly, a policy like that can't survive politically.

If you want your voices to be heard you have to be organized and you have to act. Now there are a number of different ways to act. Now they have been fighting the city and we are with them, but we don't carry the signs. We don't lead the parade down to city hall. We don't speak for them. And when Alinsky does it the other way, Alinsky is being a paternalist. He's telling them there's only one way to do it—here's the way to do it, and he even speaks for them very often.

Query: This goes back to the old question of whether you can have meaningful social action if the people who are involved in social action are receiving funds from the government and are protesting against the government.

I go back to the labor movement. We had legislation in the 30's which legitimatized collective bargaining, made unions legal. Made collective bargaining a matter of national policy and stimulated a lot of social action—but it never provided the unions with the money to organize. That was a private responsibility. The law set forth a national policy and stimulated a lot of movement but never provided the money. Our tradition is a separation of functions, and I think we are getting all mixed up with this one now. Even if you can make a good philosophical case with this one, I don't think you can make a good political case with it. I don't think you can have a national program lasting very long if it will cause—if one of its effects will be to mobilize a powerful opposition to it, an opposition which will frustrate it, namely, the Mayors. You can't have a national program which stimulates a powerful political opposition survive very long. I just can't see it.

Just how much, if at all, CPI's effectiveness is weakened as an agent for the poor by its political ties is unclear. One official said that practical political education for the young people would be "too radical for New Haven. . . . I think in a quiet way this is being done. I think in New Haven it has to be bootlegged."

Far more disturbing as a symptom of trouble was one case reported by S. M. Miller and Morton Fein in "The Demonstration as a Strategy of Change."*

In New Haven when a Negro was accused of raping a white girl, CPI's neighborhood lawyer came to know the case through his local contact with the family. He uncovered new evidence to support the claim that the accused youth and the girl had been seen together before the alleged rape incident. The public defender did not want to use this information. The lawyer became convinced that the public defender was handling the case badly. He claimed that Connecticut like the South offered no justice for the Negro. The neighborhood lawyer was not permitted to become actively involved in the case in court, because an open fight on this issue might weaken CPI's community support by embarrassing the Mayor. CPI succumbed. One question is raised by this incident. Can the community in the future count on CPI's support when the interests of the neighborhood residents and political forces conflict?

The New Haven program, despite its involvement of the poor at numerous levels of organization and its own sense of empathy from the top down toward the poor, is nevertheless paternalistic. The program is highly structured: each step is planned in detail in advance. Few contingencies are overlooked. And despite the reform character of its programs, it has been ameliorative rather than directed to fundamental change in the status of the poor. The program is organized *for* the poor *with* the poor but not, essentially, *by* the poor. The alienation of at least some of the poor was apparent in the summer of 1967. As the

* Paper presented at the Columbia University Mobilization for Youth Training Institute Workshop, April 30, 1964.

mayor himself said at that time, New Haven still has a long way to go.

(2) *Paterson: Task Force for Community Action*

There was a close connection, also, between the political structure and the anti-poverty program in Paterson, New Jersey. Significant was the response of the then executive director to an interview query:

Query: What kind of conflicts do you anticipate?

We don't anticipate any conflicts from the Negro Democratic crowd because they're in this up to their ears, and they really see it as an instrumentality which can be useful to them. But from where I sit, their objectives are basically more or less the same as ours. They want better housing, they want better police. Now in the terms in which Ty is talking it really doesn't matter whether or not they're involved.

Now there's a very strong ward, the fourth ward, in which initially the majority of Negroes were located, and the Negroes who were there for a number of years. More recently there have been other wards developing a newer Negro and Spanish population. But the way we have it set up is that no ward can really dominate.

The director felt that the lack of opposition could be traced to the genuine desire of liberal political forces to organize and develop the areas of poverty: "A politician doesn't necessarily have to be threatened by outspoken people. He very often cooperates."

The Paterson program was organized both from the top and bottom at the same time, with a federation of neighborhood councils, set up before the councils were organized to avoid *ad hoc* neighborhood groups overlapping and competing with each other. At the same time, neighborhood councils were to be developed with neighborhood centers, delayed inadvertently by the failure of the federal government to give the necessary funds. In the meantime, individuals were recruited into the federation. The centers were to be used for the councils and as outposts for services such as legal aid and job referrals, a kind of "para-political" organization, like the early political clubs that arranged for services, to avoid control by traditional outside agencies. The Paterson program looked forward to moving beyond demonstrations and protests to extensive community organization beginning with day care centers, consumers' classes and the like and, as more people were trained, to co-operative business efforts, owning a camp for example, or operating a treatment center for juvenile offenders. The plan called for the development of a disciplined group of neighborhood organizers, community service advisors, and neighborhood aides. A large steering committee was elected from the council areas and planned a city-wide convention to stimulate a sense of identification among the poor to start a training program and to choose representatives to serve on the governing board of the anti-poverty task force. A form of "patronage" was intended to affect a unity between the community organization and available services by encouraging participation by offer of services. With the emphasis on discipline and careful planning, the Paterson program was controlled from the top toward the end of competence and independence for the poor.

One would be less likely to find this kind of balance between opportunities and power in a city like Syracuse where the local political leadership was in opposition to the program, and this expectation was borne out. The experience in New Haven, Paterson, and Syracuse suggests that the involvement or acquiescence of local political leaders, *if it is consistent with the program itself,* may introduce or permit a form of rational systematic guidance of the program, and that political leadership would, in turn, react with frustration and hostility to a random and in its view uncontrolled kind of participatory democracy.

The questions that arise in such a program are (a) whether the poor consider that the city's political leadership, in fact, represents them; (b) whether the genuine needs of the poor are met or rather contained and hidden by the appeal of a progressive city regime; and (c) whether political support for programs endangers those programs when political leadership changes; (d) whether the absence of conflict or ferment among the poor is a sign of community health or stagnation; and (e) whether there is, in such programs, evidence of the potential for sustained long-range social change leading to the abolition of poverty and its attendant ills.

These questions cannot yet be answered.

In other cities, the political structure has considered the community action program a threat to its own power: for example, Syracuse, Chicago, Newark and New York.

(3) *Newark: United Community Corporation*

The Newark program, too, was politically astute but basically independent. It functioned as an open membership corporation, with a number of thousand members, all voting for the board of trustees. Each area had a neighborhood area board representing more than 2,000 members each, serving as a monitor on the city's programs and autonomous and hence, despite the intention that they not endorse candidates as a *board,* it was a potential political force, uncommitted and therefore not to be ignored. The only stipulation was that the area boards of trustees must be members of the Corporation, and ten percent (about 200 persons) of all must be under 21 years old. The area boards' and UCC board's relationship was one of checks and balances, each to counterweight the other.

B. *CAP Threats To Local and Federal Political Control*

(1) *Syracuse: Community Action Training Center*

Syracuse's CATC program, sponsored by the University and, for a time, by OEO, is an instructive example of a relationship between a community action program and city hall that turned into a battle.

One of CATC's first "errors" in strategy was to stimulate a voter registration drive. The poor registered heavily Democratic. Republican Mayor Walsh, who earlier had expressed pride in Washington in the city's program, was agitated. To him, as to many a political figure, community action neighborhood organization had taken on aspects of competitive political base.

Saul Alinsky was brought in as a consultant to CATC and, though CATC is not an Alinsky organization, its techniques have resembled his programs in some ways, particularly the plan for strong neighborhood groups organized by professionals. Neighborhood councils were formed representing the poor. A Joint Action Committee from the councils planned strategy. It was intended to unite the councils in combination with churches and other groups to form an organization of organizations, somewhat after the manner of Chicago's Woodlawn Organization. In the pattern of the participatory democracy groups, the neighborhood councils directed their attention to concrete social need—improvements in public housing and recreation facilities and the like—and achieved a reputation for being controversial and a threat to the Establishment.

Its philosophy, as expressed in its documents and policy statements, has been that

> . . . the central problem of the poor is their dependency, their powerlessness, the fact that their lives are controlled by persons and forces outside themselves, that there are no socially provided structures through which they can exercise control over their own lives. As a result, persons in areas of poverty tend to become apathetic, without long on-going courses of actions central to their lives, without confidence in or hope for themselves. Experience has indicated that through organization, the poor can create social systems which begin to provide an area for action, which motivate the poor to resolution of the tough problems which poverty imposes on their lives, which can make them leaders in a successful community effort to do the socially useful work which needs to be done.

CATC has tried to practice what it preached and what it thought OEO meant by asking for "maximum feasible participation of the poor." Its actions were political in the broadest sense but not narrowly partisan. Yet it could not avoid involvement in a political struggle. It was attacked by the Mayor and the press, and the official city departments reacted. A CATC worker was arrested when the Syracuse Housing Authority protested outside agitators. A group of mothers on relief were arrested and condemned in public statements by the Mayor after confronting the Welfare Department in a sit-in protest. A year before, the Republican Mayor had a good deal of support among these same people. A Republican Negro had been elected to the County Board of Supervisors over a militant Negro Democrat. After the attack on CATC, the views of many changed.

A leader of CATC said, "We are trying to maintain very carefully the fact that we are not partisans. . . . Neither party's happy with the appearance of these organizations in the neighborhoods in which they had only themselves to worry about before."

Mayor Walsh won reelection by a stronger margin nevertheless. OEO refused to refund CATC directly as a demonstration project, though CATC and SCDA thought that their agreement with OEO covered a two-year span. Shriver suggested instead that CATC-SCDA apply for funds through the local city-controlled program Crusade for Opportunity, then later, when the university answered it had a legal right to ask for funds directly, that the training and research part of the program of the university, CATC, would be considered but not SCDA, the neighborhood organizing arm, which could appeal directly to him should Crusade reject it. The explanation was that the experiment was a success and now belonged under the city's umbrella agency. The People's War Council was organized to try to get the decision reversed, and SCDA refused to ask Crusade for funds, in the belief that its independence would be lost, accusing OEO of abandoning its determination that the poor should be helped to build their own organizations. When Crusade held elections for its own neighborhood boards, only about 1,500 persons voted.

The previous summer the U.S. Conference of Mayors urged OEO to support existing or city-hall endorsed local organizations as the official CAP organizations. Mayor Daley of Chicago was named chairman and Syracuse's Mayor Walsh was a member of the committee.

The Crusade program has been much like many other cities' projects—service and opportunities-oriented, with a network of neighborhood groups organized for cooperative service, not for social action. The poor originally comprised one-third of the membership of CFO's board and were elected by the neighborhood boards; the rest of the board represented the majority culture—social agencies, the press, political groups, etc. Crusade was the official and respectable program. As one person at CATC put it: "Among poverty programs there is the good guys and the bad guys. We're the bad guys and Crusade are the good guys."

But to CATC-SCDA, Crusade represented the enemy, and, therefore, to apply to Crusade for funds would be to surrender. CATC-SCDA was prepared to collapse rather than risk emasculation.

The question is whether the political pressure from city halls directed at OEO is great enough so that "independent" programs funded by the federal government will be forced under by local political control, or whether OEO is willing to fund such independent programs should the local agency reject them.

Edward McGuire, director of SCDA, said that the OEO decision "raises a very serious national question—whether OEO is going to fund any independent programs anywhere. If they can't fund an independent program in this city, with the opposition party in control, where can they? This is the only demonstration of its kind, and if it's abandoned here, it means this approach is being abandoned for the whole war on poverty."* Ironically, but predictably, when in 1967 the CFO board

* Edward McGuire, quoted by Jules Witcover and Erwin Knoll, "Politics and the Poor: Shriver's Second Thoughts," *The Reporter,* December 30, 1965.

itself was led by a majority of representatives of the poor it, too, lost financial support from the federal government, which charged irregularities.

(2) *The Political Implications of Participation of the Poor*

The irony is that OEO has been pushing hard for involvement of the poor in areas where city hall has resisted such involvement—in Chicago and Los Angeles, for example. Yet, where the poor had been organized with the help of federal funds, as in Syracuse's CATC-SCDA, and had taken firm action to improve their own conditions in the traditional self-help manner (albeit with some drama), OEO shied away.

Earlier, the federal government and its foundation allies, particularly the Ford Foundation, seemed to consider that it was more effective to organize the community power structure "downtown" than to expect power to reside in the ranks of the poor. Hence their original emphasis was on strong local political and civic support for programs. Later, the focus on participation of the poor led to attempts to put more poor, particularly Negro poor, on neighborhood and city-wide agency boards, and to attempts to foster elections of representatives of the poor.

But as soon as such programs came in conflict with local political and civic leadership, the local and federal governments began to show strong signs of a strategic retreat and began to mollify local Establishment leadership while nevertheless pushing verbally "participation of the poor." If, as seems the case, local government controls even the evaluative process—if, for example, it is able to propose the persons selected to prepare histories of the anti-poverty community action programs in their cities—the chances for objective analysis of the effectiveness of public expenditure seems dim.

The position paper of the National Association for Community Development is revealing on this point:

There is a substantial body of experience with citizen participation in urban renewal planning which indicates that there are limits on the extent to which an official agency can go. Through a long process of interchange between renewal planners and neighborhood residents, it is often possible to achieve a workable plan satisfactory to both. But complete agreement is not always possible, and the urban renewal agency may make a decision that the residents do not support. This can put the community organizer in an untenable position, and in a number of localities the urban renewal agency's community organization operation fell apart on this dilemma.

We believe that OEO would be well advised to recognize the limitations that practical operations impose upon a community action agency. There is no point in promoting unachievable methods. Protest and direct political action fall within this category. They are certainly needed in all communities, but it is not realistic to expect a community action agency to be the vehicle through which they are achieved.

Throughout American history the government of this nation has exercised restraint in financing organizations that relate to belief and to political action. We have a constitutional separation of church and state, although freedom of religious practice and belief has been encouraged. The government has not given financial support to trade unions or to employers' organizations, although the right to organize and to bargain collectively is assured. The government has not financed political parties, in spite of occasional proposals in this direction, although the political party is essential to the way we practice representative democracy. Similarly it seems inappropriate to have government finance protest and nonpartisan political action, although the right of such organizations to act should be protected. Among other problems, there is the unanswerable dilemma that if a protest group favored by those who now control the government is supported, what happens when the government changes hands and another kind of protest group seeks governmental funds.

And, too, there is a tactical reason for deemphasizing "political effectiveness." It is partly semantic. Politics, in the broad sense of the term, relates to anything having to do with the process of public decision making. But many people think of politics only in terms of the selection of public office holders. If OEO goes around the country promoting political action, then mayors, county commissioners, and Congressmen will begin to wonder if rival political machines are being established. This could threaten continued support of community action programs, both locally and by the Congress.

This is not to imply that neighborhood organization is an invalid approach for a community action agency to facilitate. It is an important method for resident participation, and it should be encouraged. But it must be done within a framework that is supportable by the community action agency. Such an effort would focus upon communications, upon the democratic processes related to considering specific issues. Stress would be upon participating in new opportunities in education, employment, and other activities that can lead to self-sufficiency. It may well be that as neighborhood groups gain strength and certainty they will move toward political action. But this they will do on their own and not at the direction or by the stimulation of a staff member of the community action agency. It is the residents speaking and not the community action agency. When it happens this way, the community action agency can more easily handle its relationships with whoever is the target of the political action.

The question raised in New Haven remains unanswered: can the government be expected to finance opposition to its own practices? Can it be expected to encourage unrest and protest or is its role rather one of the maintenance of public order? If it cannot permit and encourage protest, OEO will become the defender of the status quo, and other, non-governmental forces will need to support the voice of discontent.

An official of the moderate CFO in Syracuse said he felt OEO's real policy may be simply to have no standard stance and to react simply to whoever has "the club": "Whoever has the club, that's the policy."

One politically astute director of a large community action program expressed the belief that the federal government will not be able to resist the opposition from local political leadership.

I think that any more concerted pressure by the big city bosses, and they'll back away. There has to be some private trust. Probably what will happen is that the government will really back away from the neighborhood councils, and go more with the programmatic services to people. And it will be increasingly necessary for the council-type operation to be funded by private groups.

The paradox of the community action programs is this: the programs need, and have received support from government, *i.e.,* the established order; yet their very effectiveness depends on challenging that same order and transforming the society itself. The central question to be answered in this regard is: *Can government endure and support financially such challenge against vested interest and the status quo? Or is there an inherent inconsistency between the fact of political control of public funds and the possibility of realistic social action?* But, perhaps even more central is the contrary: Can a wise democratic government afford not to endure—even encourage and foster—such challenge? Is not democratic protest against injustice totally consistent with and the suppression of such protest totally inconsistent with the purposes of democratic government?

It *is* clear, however, that it is naive to overlook the close relationship between community action programs and political power. In at least one community, Washington, D.C., the *lack* of political structure to relate to has given a diffusiveness to the community action program:

The lack of home rule has given this organization an unique opportunity to move ahead on the political action definition of social action and I think we miss that opportunity. The lack of home rule has meant fantastic vacuums in terms of who has power, who makes the decisions, and all talk about power structure in Washington is really a kind of euphemism. There really isn't a power structure as such. There's no Negro leadership that's identifiable in relationship to power. . . . And only recently have there become some instances of rumblings on the part of political organizations trying to move in on these centers, trying to take over, and that's an over-statement; they're just beginning to feel around, when home rule seems imminent. (UPO official, Washington, D.C.)

It seems to be important for the community action programs to have a clear understanding with whoever is at the political helm. The relationship can be positive or negative, depending on the commitment of both to the same goals. Where both are concerned with positive social change, the program proceeds apace, as in New Haven and, earlier, Paterson. Where neither is primarily concerned with basic change, the relationship is static, as in Boston and Cleveland, though not necessarily productive of civic peace, as the rebellion in both those cities demonstrated, Cleveland in the summer of 1966, Boston in the summer of 1967. Where the community action program is committed to progress and the political structure is not and feels threatened by the competitive power, the program faces stalemate or defeat as in Syracuse, San Francisco, and MFY in New York. There is no instance in the study in which the political structure itself is committed and takes the offensive against an ineffective CAP. The poor seem to have found no effective recourse in cities where local power is hostile to basic change. So far, neither the federal government nor private power has risen to a successful defense in such cities.

2. The Control of the Poor: Social Agency Power

The community action programs seem to many private and public social agencies to parallel, to compete, and sometimes to threaten their own programs. It is natural then for agencies in certain cities to be in conflict of an overt or more usually convert nature with the program, and in others to attempt to control it, as though the anti-poverty program were to be seen primarily as a logical extension of traditional social welfare.

A. *Cleveland: Action for Youth*

In Cleveland, the political, educational, and social welfare establishments have seemed united in control of the community action program, Cleveland Action for Youth. In other cities where the agencies are not dominant, they often resent the program. This seems to be the case in New Haven, in New York (MFY) and in Syracuse (CATC). Where social agencies are dominant the programs are service-oriented, and less directly related to the poor than the political structure is related to the poor in cities where *it* is dominant *and* effective. The politically dominated programs that are *positive* are opportunities and action-oriented. In such cities, if the agencies themselves are strong, there is generally tension between the social agencies and the community action program and between the agencies and the political structure.

The social agencies are really the one group that's really mad now, much more than the political establishment . . . because the politicians don't give a damn if the poor are involved as long as they control the process. (Paterson official)

It's the social agencies that would prefer to get their money from a governmental structure, they're less restricted. They don't have to involve the poor. So they're not really anxious to hook up, except that the money has to come out of Title II. . . . And we have strongly suggested at this point, we have not made it mandatory, a condition of contract, that they begin to get poor people from the area boards on their board. Since we are the custodians of the money of the poor, it is the poor people who are bringing this money to you. Therefore, there's no longer an excuse to keep them off your board, because they are your biggest fund raisers. (Newark official)

Like many Mayors he wants control of all the poverty programs. He would like to control us . . . but he does not have it. I think the biggest threat we face is the Health and Welfare establishment. That's the problem here and will be across the country because the traditional Health and Welfare establishment is the middle man. Take a look at those boards. (CFO, Syracuse official)

The document proposal for Cleveland's community action program, Cleveland Action for Youth, established in 1962, emphasized the interrelationship between social welfare agencies and the new program:

Suggesting a multiple form of intervention, with the primary social organizations providing the essential base for the initiation of interaction, is not to suggest a total 'saturation' approach—namely, one in which every community organization would have its operating intensity increased simultaneously. While stressing the role of primary social organizations as the initiating base and framework for much of the anticipated change, it is recognized that there has been a great deal written about the problems of making bureaucratic community organizations with middle-class oriented staff do the job that needs to be done under present conditions.

What is suggested for the Demonstration Program is the use of many existing primary social organizations, in conjunction with newly created programs where there presently is not appropriate sponsorship, with a plan that ultimately the effective pieces of the Demonstration programs would be included within the on-going programs of the existing organizational systems.

The Demonstration Programs must deal, therefore, with the modification of organizational functioning and the interactions among organizations in order to achieve its objectives.

Among the types of change which will need to occur within institutions, if they are to achieve the objectives desired are the following:

1. More and better defined information about the nature of and changes in the problems with which the institutions are concerned.
2. Changes in the attitudes of professional personnel toward the individual personalities of the clients with whom they are working and in recognizing the potentials for change.
3. Modification of administrative structures and policies to make programs relevant to the needs of individuals.

4. Provision for special resources and back-up services for the institution to raise its level of efficiency and competency.

5. Increases in visibility and communication and a decrease in defensiveness growing out of limited achievement under the difficult conditions of the immediate present.

Involved in the original planning for CAY was a constellation of civic leadership: ministers and priests, city planners, lawyers and politicians, public and private social agencies, educators, street club presidents, community council representatives, ward leaders, and area council officers. The program has drawn on support from the Division of Urban Renewal, Department of Health and Sanitation, Department of Housing, and Cleveland Board of Education, and from the private Cleveland Associated Foundations.

The program ran smoothly in a city widely known in social welfare circles for its progressive and pervasive social welfare program. There has been no ferment, no trouble within the program itself. Its identification with the Establishment—social, political, the press—has seemed complete. It had, in fact, successfully contained the frustrations and aspirations of the poor by a service-oriented program, and come to terms with the vested interests and the status quo, or at least it had done so superficially and temporarily. Yet behind the scenes all is not so peaceful.

Before CAY began, the schools, the private agencies, and the local and county government opposed the program as unnecessary, but each voted for it in the apparent belief that the funds required would not be forthcoming from the others. There was early strife between top officials in a struggle by the schools to win influence, a struggle the schools won when the deputy director of schools became executive director of CAY with the planning director and primary figure behind the CAY document in the compromise post of associate director. The associate director resigned about six months later. The executive director was called back to the schools in 1964 and until April, 1965 he served both as CAY director and deputy director of schools.

The schools criticized CAY but were, nevertheless, its chief financial support—in its first year the schools gave far more than the city gave and almost 5/7 of the CAY budget. Ralph Findley, a Negro, director of OEO programs in Cleveland, was on the Cleveland Board of Education. He was considered a conservative, conciliatory personality:

Ralph Findley, former director of Fireside Life Insurance Company, as School Board President four years before had made himself unpopular to many poverty area people when he opposed efforts to gain bussing for double shift classes. Consequently, many had no confidence in him as the willing tool of interests other than those of the poorer neighborhoods. However, middle class Negro organizations give him their support. (Brief submitted to Powell Committee by Rev. Paul A. Younger, Task Officer, Citizens Committee for an Adequate Cleveland Community Action Program)

Civil rights leadership seems to have been brought astutely into the picture. At first not on the Council board, several Negro leaders were appointed to the board after their organizations criticized the Council. Among the new Council members were the presidents of the NAACP and the Urban League:

Poverty area community leaders, residents and poor involved in the Citizens Committee regarded this as a 'sell out' by the middle class Negro leaders. It seemed they had used the Citizens Committee protest as a means of gaining position for themselves without involving the poverty area residents and the poor with them. While good Council members themselves, they could not claim to be poor or residents of the poverty areas. Dr. Clement [Urban League President] has long been an independent voice on the Cleveland scene, but he has an ample income, lives in the Heights and has never seen the issue of representation as important. Clarence Holmes [past NAACP President] also lives in the suburbs and is a lawyer. Hamilton [Businessmen's League] and Jacobs [NAACP President] live in Glenville, an area with limited poverty. Mr. Hamilton's main contribution to the board so far has been to support an unsuccessful move to have Neighborhood Youth Corps wages reduced to $.75 an hour. (Younger brief)

The area boards also were criticized for non-representativeness.

> The area councils in poverty areas, even in the best cases, are dominated by property owning resident organizations, and, therefore, tend not to represent the poor in their areas. They are organized into a city-wide Area Council Association under the Welfare Federation. The Association officers are city-wide leaders who live in the suburbs. . . . Actions of the Association are subject to review by the Welfare Federation board. Controversial involvement or action of the councils tends to get lost or blunted in the arrangement. (Younger brief)

The commitment of the Council for Economic Opportunity to the status quo and its resistance to change was indicated by one revealing incident when the then president of the school board, one of the major incorporators of the Council, refused to accept on the Council board as representatives of the community:

> Anyone on the board who had actively supported the efforts of the previous year to challenge Cleveland's *de facto* school segregation which included a 90% effective school boycott involving almost all Negro community leadership.
>
> Consequently, the only poverty area resident selected was the president of the area council of the all-white near westside, Mr. Morris Matlin. The area council has been dominated by a group with anti-Negro and anti-poor attitudes. The only Negro board members were Charles Lucas, an old-time conservative Republican leader who controls considerable real estate in the poverty areas, and Rev. Fuller, pastor of a large Central Area church who opposed the school demonstrations. The Protestant community was represented by one inner-city pastor, John Bruere, who vocally opposed the large group of Protestant leaders supporting the school demonstrations. His home is in the suburbs. (Younger brief)

The school board president ran for Mayor as an Independent but was defeated, coming in third after Republican Mayor Locher, who was running for re-election, and Carl Stokes, the Negro who in 1967 defeated Locher in the Democratic primary.

The CAY staff itself seemed to be more committed to social action than the city leadership but generally expressed this commitment quietly to avoid overt conflict. It did, however, support the civil rights position in a dispute with the Cleveland public schools and thereby incurred the displeasure of the school system. ("Why are we spending good money to equip our enemy?" some school officials ask.)

All program proposals have been reviewed by the Anti-Poverty Operating Executive Council which consists of executives of Cleveland's various social agencies, including the director of the Cleveland Urban League. The Chairman has been executive director of the Associated Foundations, and apparently a major power in Cleveland.

Criticized for lack of participation by the poor, the Board of Directors of the Anti-Poverty Program planned to add five (out of forty) people from the poverty areas to the board. "They probably will be reasonably frightened, and unable to cope with the articulate people who've had long experience on boards," one executive said. "It is a kind of hoax being perpetrated on the poor."

Whether or not these charges were justified, certain things about the Cleveland program seemed clear even before the 1966 riots lent inflammatory confirmation: (1) that the smoothly running program concealed bitterness and severe tension and a sense of alienation among the Negro poor; (2) that there is considerable social distance, as in Los Angeles and Chicago, between a number of the Negro middle-class leaders and the poor.

But even if there were less power-maneuvering beneath the surface in Cleveland, the Cleveland program might still remain fundamentally ineffective, as this study defines effectiveness. It would remain a traditional social service-oriented program engendering all the dependency and resentment among the poor that such programs classically arouse. Even in community action programs originally designed to foster independence, such as HARYOU, social agency leadership has moved to the fore—most of HARYOU's Cadet Corps is led by the City Mission Society. Where a program is clothed in controversy, the social work profession risks its own reputation by association, but the chance to help or the temptation to avoid the abdication of leadership in the field of service is often too great to be resisted.

In cities where the agencies are closely involved in community action programs the participation of the poor in planning and review has been drastically limited. In cities where social agencies are only peripherally involved, a sense of rivalry between agency and community action leadership has often resulted. The basic question remains whether a social service-oriented community action program is sufficiently relevant to the need in any major American city. Certainly it is inconsistent with the definitions and goals of community action, as described in the federal legislation and guidelines.

3. The Role of Civil Rights Groups

The pattern of involvement of civil rights groups in community action programs shows erratic and inconsistent influence. The civil rights organizations are not centered in the neighborhoods of the poor but tend to be middle class in their orientation and their leadership. In local communities they have sponsored forays in behalf of the Negro poor, but primarily on a racial issue—leading picket lines, for example, as in Cleveland, against school segregation and inferior education. As organizations, however, despite the fact that many of the anti-poverty workers had prior training with civil rights groups, they have not devoted their major energies to the organization of the poor in community action programs for sustained social action. Civil right groups in many areas do not feel related to the community action programs and prefer not to take the risk of too close involvement with the political structure, preferring to concentrate on issues more directly racial in content.

In San Francisco the primary force for social action in the redress of the grievances of the Negro has come from the United Negro Freedom Movement, which parcelled out action assignments to its various member organizations, *i.e.,* to picket in behalf of non-discriminatory hiring. CORE's picketing and harassment of the Bank of America (changing bills into silver and back again) brought an end to discrimination in hiring practices at the San Francisco bank. Also in San Francisco, three thousand persons staged a sit-in for the *Ad Hoc* Students Committee at the Palace Hotel and in one month the beleaguered hotel chain reconsidered its hiring practices. Doubtless civil rights leadership was influential in the ascendancy of the poor in the San Francisco community action program. Yet the anti-poverty program of community action itself in San Francisco appears to be floundering.

In Los Angeles, Negro leaders tend to have ready access to the white power structure and are even included in decision-making. But the rise of individual Negroes into positions of personal acceptance in government, business, industry and civic organization, often neutralizes their commitment to seeking solutions for the predicament of the ghetto Negro, and the Negro poor in Los Angeles are alienated from Negro leadership as well as from the white community. In the Watts ghetto of Los Angeles there was a clear chasm between middle-class Negro leadership and the Negro poor and, despite the Los Angeles United Civil Rights Committee (which included the NAACP, CORE, SCLC, SNCC, the Urban League and others), little had been done to mobilize power to bring about effective social change in depressed Negro areas.

In Cleveland, the NAACP and Urban League joined in the Establishment to guide the poverty program, but according to Paul Younger of the Protestant Ministry Against Poverty, this decision was regarded with some bitterness by the Negro poor who considered it a "sell out." With financial backing from the Ford Foundation in the summer of 1967, CORE undertook a voter registration drive in Cleveland. Martin Luther King's group has also been active in that city but, as with CORE, outside the Community Action Program itself.

In Syracuse, CATC had little association with any of the civil rights groups because the roots of these groups are not in the low-income population with which CATC worked. As in New Haven, where most of the CORE members seem to have come from Yale, Syracuse CORE and Friends of SNCC are based on the Syracuse University campus; the NAACP leadership of Syracuse is also not centered in the poor areas.

In Chicago, the Coordination Council of Community Organizations, headed by Albert Raby, a federation of civil rights organizations, took the lead in demonstrations against *de facto* school segregation and the administration of Superintendent Willis, and drew considerable local and national support for its protests even though its major goals were not achieved. But like most civil rights groups in Northern cities, it has been concerned with the city as a whole and has not been structured around the problems of particular neighborhoods or specifically with the poor. Middle-class leadership tends to be interested in a wide, rather than a narrow base for its operations, and assumes it will be more effective the closer it is to the seat of power, and the seat of power is usually "downtown."

The efforts of Martin Luther King's SCLC to transform the lives of Negroes in the slums of Chicago and Cleveland introduced a new civil rights element in neighborhood organization in Northern cities, but whether King's associates can develop techniques for sustained progress toward effective social change is still to be determined. Except for this venture, the Southern-based civil rights organizations—notably SCLC and SNCC—are not significantly involved in social action programs in Northern cities. SNCC's involvement has, on the whole, been confined to sporadic ventures of personalities like Rap Brown into troubled ghetto areas. The Northern-based organizations, like NAACP and CORE and SDS, are active, but oriented toward specific issues-response and do not have on-going intensive local social action programs or extensive neighborhood organizational structure. The Urban League, for its part, is oriented toward opportunities rather than to community action, according to its traditional philosophy, though it is now moving in the direction of training leaders for community organization.

The Urban League and the NAACP, which have firm relationships with the economic and political power structure, feel that these very liaisons add to, rather than subtract from, their own power. In avoiding involvement with often controversial community action programs they may protect those alliances. But whether independent militancy or more dependent maneuvering—or either one—will prove effective in changing the day-to-day lives of the urban Negro poor in any substantial and observable way has still to be demonstrated. Social action programs may lead to social change; then again, they may present the appearance rather than the reality of change; indeed, in the very energy of their activity, they may offer a psychological substitute for the fact of genuine change.

The community action programs, therefore, represent an approach in terms of organization and goals different from those of the traditional civil rights organizations. Supported by government funds, the programs are more clearly structurally dependent on the local political structure, and are less free to be independent to make alliances or not.

Yet civil rights groups have not used their independence to serve as "watchdogs" for the anti-poverty program. Much of the individual civil rights leadership which might be available for critical review has been absorbed into the poverty program itself. The director of the Cleveland Urban League sat on the Operating Executive Council of the Anti-Poverty Program, which reviews proposals. The NAACP seems to have had some influence in the appointment of the director of the Cleveland anti-poverty program, scarcely a strong advocate of social change. In Minneapolis, the head of the NAACP served on one of the steering committees of one of the city's poverty programs, and the head of the Urban League on the steering committee of the Youth Development Program. Both men, like most of the Negro leadership in that city, have been involved in local civic organizations and their personal leadership is identified primarily with these groups rather than with the civil rights groups themselves.

In New York City, the Urban League became closely involved with HARYOU, contracting to direct its Project Uplift program, but when the fiscal debacle occurred, it was the former Urban League Frank Stanley against whom the HARYOU director, Livingston Wingate, directed much of the blame. In Newark, a number of the members of civil rights organizations have been on the board of the United Community Corporation. Members of CORE affiliates, the Newark Committee to Preserve Racial Peace, the American Negro Association, the Urban League and the NAACP served on Newark's UCC board, though as individual citizens, not as official representatives of their organizations. UCC counted on help from groups like CORE to picket and demonstrate on behalf of its goals.

In response to this study's questionnaire, a number of civil rights groups described their own position in regard to the poverty program in their city. For some, the response was one of endorsement: The Chicago Urban League found the program congenial to its own program; the Detroit Urban League said it worked at all policy and staff levels with the project; the Philadelphia Urban League reports: "We believe in it" and noted that its executive director serves on the local committee; the New York Urban League thought it should play a "watchdog role" for the program. Only one responding group expressed criticism and a sense of distance—SNCC found its "social position" different from that of the program officials and reported that the "poverty program is trying to affect change from the top. We work from the bottom."

In general, then, one can say that civil rights executives and board members are involved at various levels in the anti-poverty program, from the staff to the planning and policy level, but that the organizations themselves stand somewhat apart from the programs whether or not they choose to promote specific social protest. They may feel the programs are already irrelevant. If not, one must ask whether there is not less danger in the loss of independence their involvement would mean than in the default of leadership such independence may cost.

4. The Role of the Churches

In the cities studied for this report, churches played a variety of roles. In some cities religious institutions seemed peripheral, nearly irrelevant as a potent force in the community action programs. In others, churches were involved, primarily through representation of the major faiths on the advisory boards. In others, churches seemed resistant to programs that take social action seriously.

A sampling of the comments about churches taken from interviews in Syracuse and Washington and New Haven shows a pattern of indifference or cynicism about the churches' relevance to the poverty programs:

To some extent the churches have been helpful, but the churches, I've found, in this town are paternalistic bodies, in that instead of helping people to help themselves, they create dependency.

Here and there a minister gets involved. There is a Committee on Religion and Race which is a little nothing.

If you go to a Deacon or Reverend in the block you would find that they want to base everything on a religious basis. This could not be done for a block club because naturally in a block you've got number runners, you've got bootleggers, most anything. If you are only going to center it around the church view of things you will not include these people. In our block clubs, we include everything. The Deacon, the number runner, the bootlegger too. You'd be surprised at how well these people can work together.

One of the biggest problems we've found in Washington is the existing institutions, where community leaders often force the dependence, in perpetuating their own image. They like to say, 'we'll do it for you.' There's a Minister up the street who's great, a very good guy, but he goes out and never helps them develop leadership, or any idea about how they might do something themselves. He goes out and tells them what they should do, how they should do it, and he ends up doing it. He's great, he's wonderful, but he's not helping them.

We have found in some cases, to be very frank, some of the churches were interested in the poverty program because 'what's in it for us.' 'Can we get a day care center, can my wife become director of the day care center,' or this, that, or the other thing. And I have some strong feelings about that. I think some of these people are more interested in their own personal power than the problems of the poor. I think this is very unfortunate. Some ministers have been very active, and have done an excellent job, but I think the majority of them, the ones that I've worked with, they have a church here in the neighborhood, and they live in Bethesda. Absentee pastors, or what have you. I think it doesn't speak well for the situation here.

Query: Are the ministers in the community involved in any significant role?

Well, I assume that we are talking off the record. The ministers and *you must never quote me on this*—they are a most ineffectual group. We have been trying to work out programs with them, but it's a lot of circle talk. They are terribly ineffective.

Query: What do you consider the major blocks?

Lack of ability to deal with practical problems in a practical way. Mostly exhortation and chest beating, and wanting to do something, but they don't know how. So we've been working with them, hoping that . . . offering them opportunities. Lately they came to us and said, 'Can't we do something about job upgrading?' Well, we said great. And we said, why don't you figure out a program of upgrading and we'll fund it and maybe tie it . . . but do the things that we are not now doing—there's a lot to be done. So we asked them to take the initiative here and do some planning and they came in with a page and a half proposal that was as thin and shallow as anything I've ever seen, so we worked with them and tried to beef it up, and we just kept on talking and talking in circles.

A number of national religious organizations have, however, taken a firm stand on the principles behind an effective community action program. The National Council of Churches has an Anti-Poverty Task Force. The United Church Women are embarked on a three-year program on "People, Poverty, Plenty." In January, 1966, leaders of the Synagogue Council of America, the National Catholic Welfare Conference, and the National Council of Churches founded the Inter-Religious Committee Against Poverty. The National Council's resolution on "Involvement of the Poor" adopted in January noted that

> WHEREAS, it is evident that difficulties are developing in this as in other human undertakings and that trends are emerging which may circumvent or subvert the involvement of the poor in community action programs before the OEO has had sufficient experience to evaluate the effectiveness of this approach; . . .

It stated that such involvement embodies two fundamental principles

> which commend themselves to the Christian conscience, viz., (a) a recognition that every human possesses inherent worth and dignity regardless of social or economic circumstances; and (b) recognition that every person in a democratic society is entitled to participate effectively in the decisions which shape the policies and programs affecting his life; . . .

In certain cities religious groups have given major backing to vigorous programs designed to alter the conditions of poverty. In Syracuse, for example, a grant from the Episcopal Diocese was offered to keep the CATC program alive for a space of time after the government withdrew support in the wake of a militant community action program. In Cleveland, the Protestant Ministry to Poverty sponsored a counter-program to protest what it considered the ineffectiveness of that city's community action program. PMP was supported by four denominations, the

American Baptists, the United Church of Christ, the Methodist Church, and the United Presbyterian Church. Protestant and Catholic Church leaders have been active in supporting Saul Alinsky's programs in the Woodlawn Organization in Chicago and other cities.

On the whole, Protestant groups seem to have been the most conspicuous in such programs, in particular the Episcopal and Presbyterian—interestingly enough and probably not irrelevantly, those churches least active in the Negro ghettos and in the communities of the poor, where Methodists, Baptists, and storefront sects are the most prevalent. In several cities studied the Roman Catholic Church has tended to shy away from militant social action programs and to identify with the more conservative elements in the community and the maintenance of the *status quo*.

One might raise a number of questions about these patterns, but perhaps the two central ones are these:

a. Has the church, generally, faced the implications of its responsibilities as property owner and partner, albeit a newer partner, in the Establishment, and of its identification as an institution with the community of affluence? and

b. If the church did fully face its realistic institutional role, would it find that it had real power to influence change in society?

One suspects that in Northern cities the answer would be "no" to both questions.

5. Programs to Protect the Interests of the Poor

In none of the cities where the OEO and PCJD have sponsored community action programs is there an independent group that can offer sustained and systematic critical evaluation and appraisal of the programs. There are attempts at governmental control of financial procedures, as with HARYOU, and of program, as with MFY, but control is *part* of program and does not offer independent assessment as to the effectiveness of the project in changing the lives of people. Most of the programs are proceeding on the still-to-be-confirmed assumption that their means will lead to the desired ends. There is no precedent in experience that would justify this faith.

The response of the poor to conditions of poverty has often been random, frustrated individual destructiveness, directed against self or others—as in drug addiction or crime—or in group destructiveness—as in the summer riots of 1964, 1965, 1966, and 1967. Since a number of the community action programs came *after* the first of these riots, and indeed in direct response to them, the effect of these programs in containing or sublimating violence cannot yet be weighed. Where such programs themselves have been subverted or diluted, the response of the poor and their surrogates may be a rising frustration and militance or a return to apathy. Or it may take the form of attempts by surrogates of the poor to organize a counter-program or a protective group to serve as watchdogs and centers of defensive power in behalf of the poor. These defensive counter-attacks can be categorized as follows:

A. *Ad hoc* programs organized by civil rights representatives or groups, church leaders, and the poor themselves to attack concrete issues, as in the Boston area where the city-wide community action program was deemed unsympathetic and ineffective.

B. Support of counter-programs of sustained service and/or action as in Cleveland's Protestant Ministry to Poverty, and Chicago's Woodlawn Organization.

C. Attempts to draw empathic professionals and intellectuals into a coalition with the poor on a local basis to provide a wider base of power, as in the lay clergy program PLUNGE in Chicago, the proposal for Chicago made by Students for a Democratic Society, and the Citizens' Committee for an Adequate Cleveland Community Action Program.

D. Attempts to organize conventions and councils of the poor on an all-city basis as in New York and Syracuse or on a state-wide basis, as in California, or a national basis, as in the People's War Council Against Poverty organized to support the Syracuse fight to retain federal funding.

E. Attempts to organize empathic intellectuals and institutional leaders from the ranks of labor, the academic world, religious institutions, the business community, civil rights groups, etc. on a national basis to aid the poor in planning action programs to protect their efforts through lobbying and to seek the means to abolish poverty. The only example of this is the Citizens' Crusade Against Poverty.

In none of these programs are the poor themselves in control of the protection of their interests in the apparatus and organizations of the poor.

A. *Ad Hoc Groups Dealing with Specific Limited Issues*

In various communities where citizens' groups are dissatisfied with the progress of community action programs, *ad hoc* committees have been set up to respond to a particular problem. For example in the Negro ghettos of Boston: The Roxbury–North Dorchester Parents Committee for Better Schools (later the Roxbury–North Dorchester–South End Parents Association) was formed by parents against a plan by the Boston School Committee to put certain elementary schools in the Negro section of the city on double sessions. This group, assisted by the Boston Action Group and the Northern Student Movement, sponsored "Operation Exodus" to bus 300 children to other schools.

Established civil rights groups, other newly formed civil rights and social agency groups consolidated themselves into the Roxbury–North Dorchester *Ad Hoc* Committee for the purpose of insuring that the poor of Boston, and primarily the Negro poor, would be included in the planning of the anti-poverty program. It has been said that the *Ad Hoc* Committee was instrumental in forcing Boston's community action program ABCD to hold elections for area boards. This *Ad Hoc* Committee was given a grant by ABCD to organize the Roxbury–

North Dorchester community, but difficulties arose when the civil rights groups and the social agencies involved found it hard to work together. When there was a poor turnout for the elections for the area boards, the civil rights groups blamed the social agencies.

Such programs seem to show the following characteristics:

The leadership tends to come from the community itself with help from outside organizations, particularly civil rights groups, for whom the direct action protest to a particular end has often previously proven successful.

Protests have tended to be concrete and specific and hostile to the majority culture, and have sought redress of grievances. They have not tended to provide program or a sustained effort themselves.

Protests have concerned themselves primarily with a few goals—in particular, the rehabilitation of *housing* but resistance to urban renewal; integrated and quality *education;* cessation of restrictive *hiring* and provision for *job training* and *placement.*

While the concerns are basic (*e.g.,* housing, education, jobs), the emphasis of protest has been upon the improvement of opportunities and conditions and not upon the basic transformation of social institutions leading to the abolition of poverty itself.

B. *Counter-Programs to Protect the Poor*

(1) *The Woodlawn Organization of Chicago* began in 1961, under the leadership of lay people, ministers, priests and the Woodlawn Block Council, who were dissatisfied with the social agencies within the community and felt they themselves were not adequately relevant to the pathology of the community. The group approached Saul Alinsky, originator of the Back Yards programs in Chicago and skilled in trade union organization. (Incidentally, a number of the leaders of community action programs which emphasize involvement of the poor have had trade union background.) Alinsky's orientation here and in other cities is based on his assumption that the underprivileged have no power over their lives and that they know it. The motto

of TWO, therefore, became "people and power." The group turned for funds to foundations and to the larger churches, as for example the Presbyterian—Alinsky has had support from various church groups, Protestant and Catholic, in the communities where he has been active.

The group then began a door-to-door canvassing in search of indigenous leadership and then began to assess community problems. Each group among the 104 organizations and churches involved sent a representative to a council, whose steering committee carried out the council's policies. Each neighborhood had a block captain to whom people of the area could come to express their problems; he, in turn, carried the problem back to the Council for strategy. The role of the organizer has been to give direction to the group but the suggestions for the solution of the problem come from the group itself.

In one case, to illustrate, the group visited the school principals to ask for improvement in the educational system. When nothing happened, TWO picketed the principals' and superintendents' homes until action resulted. An experimental schools program was set up for the summer of 1965. The organization has emphasized the concrete needs of the people of its community, not only schools, but jobs and housing. In one protest, against Marshall Field's hiring practices, a letter went to the president of the company threatening to picket the store and to organize a program of harassment. After much discussion 500 jobs were opened to Negroes within the Woodlawn area. In the field of housing TWO went directly to Mayor Daley, who apparently recognizes the power of the numbers which the group represents (out of a population of 100,000 it is estimated that about half are one way or another involved in the group). Through the urban renewal program, Mayor Daley allowed TWO to select sites for the housing development and saw to it that the development was scaled in rent so that persons displaced could move in without a substantial increase in rent.

TWO's emphasis assumes that the only limitations of the organization are in terms of the people themselves, that if the people have no interest in changing their situation, little can be done. The people have to be helped by professional organizers, however, to recognize their own power.

TWO is not concerned primarily with intervention in the larger social structure but concentrates instead on particular problems faced by the residents of its particular community, which is, incidentally, predominately Negro.

Warren C. Haggstrom of Syracuse's CATC says:

> On the other hand, TWO failed in several ways. It has not yet become financially self-supporting (contrary to its early intention). *It also became necessary to concentrate so much of the time of organizers in coordination and action in relation to existing structures that substantial portions of the lowest income population remain entirely outside TWO. There is no organizational structure which they see as effective, belonging to them, through which they can act. Finally, the tremendous task of increasing the income and available housing in TWO neighborhoods has barely begun. As yet, TWO has not acquired the power necessary to enable it to transform the economy of its area.**

Alinsky himself emphasizes the need to treat the causes of poverty not the symptoms alone:

> In criminology, for instance, all the experts agreed that the major causes of crime were poor housing, discrimination, economic insecurity, unemployment, and disease. So what did we do? We went in for supervised recreation, camping programs, something mysterious called 'character building.' We tackled everything but the actual issues, because the issues were controversial. Sometimes I'd say, 'come on, let's stop this crap, we know what the causes of crime are.' Then they'd say, 'Don't be radical.' ("A Professional Radical," *Harpers Magazine,* June, July, 1965)

There seems to be little evidence to date, however, that The Woodlawn Organization has succeeded in achieving major social change, nor is the rationale of self-help that lies behind the Alinsky programs genuinely radical in its assumptions.

* "Action Organizations of Minority Group Communities," essay dated November 16, 1965.

Norton E. Long, professor of politics at Brandeis University, is critical of the Alinsky philosophy:

The Alinsky formula assumes some kind of bootstrap magic by which individual neighborhoods can solve their problems through an almost Mao-like belief in the magic of efficacy of unaided human will. It seems doubtful in the extreme whether local communities can make up for an inadequate national growth rate and, in many, if not most cases, the local economy is a reflection of factors beyond its individual control. The Alinsky model may thus lead to profound conservatism in practice in which radical slogans and rent strikes serve as a substitute for coordinated programmatic national action. Neighborhood organization without adequate theory may produce no more than piecemeal noble gestures. On the other hand, these organizations could become limited to exert powerful pressure on behalf of their constituents. Frank Riessman's criticisms of Alinsky, which he passes off contemptuously, remain in point.*

It is ironic that the Alinsky community action programs, regarded as daring and radical by many, actually expect and demand the most from the poor, in effect placing the further burden of their own salvation upon them. This is not to say that organization of the poor is useless but rather to ask whether the poor should be held responsible for their own condition, or be asked to assume the major responsibility for reversing that condition.

(2) *The Protestant Ministry to Poverty* was organized in opposition to the Establishment-dominated Cleveland Action for Youth. PMP is directly related to the poor, and unlike CAY, is action-oriented as well as opportunities-oriented. It does not conceive of itself as a mere extension of the social welfare system.

More than eighty percent of its Board are poor and live in the area. The poor are directly involved in PMP's policy and plan-

* Norton E. Long, "The Politics of Social Welfare," paper prepared for the Columbia University School of Social Work Arden House Conference, November 18–21, 1965.

ning, nor has the organization of the poor seemed to present particular difficulties to PMP's leadership. Working with them are the young people of Students for a Democratic Society, who seem to be effective in working directly with Cleveland's poor.

The Protestant Ministry to Poverty has three goals: (a) To engage the Church of Christ and its churches in efforts to eliminate poverty; (b) to bring a Christian witness to Cleveland's war on poverty; (c) to assist the poor and poverty area people and organizations in work for the elimination of poverty.

PMP has worked with the Citizens' Committee for an Adequate Cleveland Community Action Program in critique and action aimed at improving the program of Cleveland's Council for Economic Opportunities. It has been a prod and goad to the official community action program and its director, Rev. Paul Younger, criticized the city's program with candor and bitterness at a hearing before Rep. Adam Clayton Powell's investigating group.

PMP's own program includes joint activities with a variety of community groups; development of a regional structure to work for increased state funds for public assistance programs; organization of a Neighborhood Youth Corps and Head Start proposals for the Council of Churches; rallying of Wade Park Churches to carry out the anti-poverty program; and counseling of church groups and individuals who wish to get involved in anti-poverty action.

Although PMP by no means provides an adequate substitute for an effective city-wide program, it does testify to the presence of concerned members of the majority culture, and it does provide an outlet for the frustrations of some of Cleveland's poor.

Certain characteristics of these counter-programs may be noted:

They occur in communities frustrated by apparent ineffectiveness of community action programs as related to the component of social change.

They tend to have support of certain intellectuals and religious leaders, who themselves are on the periphery of power, and to emphasize the necessity of sustained leadership from outside the community of poverty. But all insist that the involvement of the poor themselves is essential.

They emphasize the need of the people to help themselves by direct confrontation with the centers of power to achieve social cohesion, power, and individual and community rehabilitation. Despite the charges of radicalism inevitably lodged against them because of their often abrasive and melodramatic techniques of protest against the *status quo,* their programs are essentially conservative in their goals.

Their organizational model is one of highly structured participatory democracy, similar to the trade union movement, intended to be essentially autonomous but always conducted with the guidance of paid professionals.

Though they are power-oriented in articulation, they are primarily opportunity-oriented in program and tend to concentrate on concrete issues to ameliorate the conditions of poverty in a particular community; they do not tend to concern themselves with the transformation of the basic causes of poverty. They have had certain limited success in achieving their concrete goals.

Their financial support comes from foundations, churches, and in some instances from federal funds, usually threatened when action programs become involved in overt conflict.

Their most valuable contribution is that they have served to prevent the total ignoring of the needs of the poor in their communities. They have been a friend in court for the powerless.

Such programs are worthwhile in their own terms, but their impact is limited and the drama of occasional success may prove a deceptive illusion of greater effectiveness.

Fein and Miller point out that

As presently constituted, neighborhood-based groups are frequently grappling with problems that require national action. This is not

> true of, say, police brutality or a traffic light for a busy corner. But problems of jobs and decent housing can only partially be dealt with at local levels. There is a conflict between immediately accessible and local sources of power and the less visible but immediate national decision-makers. While neighborhood-based social action can be powerful in affecting local power groups and effective in reducing feelings of powerlessness, it is limited, as presently envisioned, in affecting large-scale national decisions. The very attractiveness of the programs for neighborhood residents lies in the immediacy and concreteness of the issues. This is also a major limitation. *Crucial problems are not always immediate and concrete. Even on the city level, a neighborhood view may be inadequate.* (Emphasis added)

The parallels between the trade union movement and current attempts to organize the poor are worth examining. Both rose out of similar conditions—powerlessness, social disorganization; both attempt to remedy lives of misery and exploitation. Both are organized primarily from sources outside the community. Both labor and the poor could threaten discomfort for the oppressor—for labor, through sit-downs, violence, but most important, withdrawal of labor via strikes; for the poor, through demonstrations, boycotts, riots. Both can be threatened in their turn by the opposition, for labor by lockouts and violence; for the poor by withdrawal of political and economic support, and by violence. Both considered their lot miserable enough so that they had little to lose by organized action. Both risked infiltration or take-over (labor by left-wing parties, and company unions; the poor by political capture, as in Powell's control of HARYOU). Labor unions moved from organization at the local to the national level; the poor have only begun to consider this. Both are related to political power; labor at first was opposed by the major parties, then won support and was dependent on the Democratic Party, deciding not to adopt (with a few state exceptions) the European system of labor-based political parties. The poor were and are politically dependent, particularly on the Democratic administration nationally, and on whoever is in charge locally. Labor has gained real power and a certain political independence; the poor have not.

But the model has important limitations that may be highly significant in planning for the poor. The poor are a minority in an affluent society. With Negroes dominant among the urban poor, the racism of the majority society further restricts the power of the poor. The poor are not concentrated in a structured environment engaged in common activity. They have little productive or consumer value (except potentially) and, therefore, with high unemployment in an affluent society, cannot claim power by withholding their labor. But most important, while labor's goal is to improve its lot, the poor wish to *abolish* the condition of poverty—and, at least the Negro poor, the racism that accompanies it. The only model for the organized poor's taking matters into their own hands is not the labor union model but the model of socialism. The central question facing American society is whether poverty can and will be abolished by the affluent society itself.

C. *Local Coalitions Between Professionals and the Poor*

(1) *The Citizens' Committee for an Adequate Cleveland Community Action Program (CCACCAP)* has been sponsored by the Protestant Ministry to Poverty (see IV, pp. 180–181) and was formed to oppose the Council for Economic Opportunities (CEO) in Greater Cleveland. The director of PMP serves on the Citizens' Committee as its Task Officer. CCACCAP is open for membership to anyone interested in the problems of the poor in Cleveland.

CCACCAP's Constitution (adopted November 17, 1965) states that the purposes of the committee are: (1) To organize the poor of Cleveland to achieve their own economic and political goals based upon their own interests and principles; (2) to cooperate with the poor at all levels in the Cleveland Economic Opportunities Program and to assist them by all ways and means to achieve an adequate anti-poverty program in Cleveland; (3) to secure funds for these purposes as a non-profit organization and to account for such funds in a public manner.

A letter from the CCACCAP to the Sub-Committee on Poverty Area Representation of the Council of Economic Opportunities says further:

"The following are principles that we believe are basic to any effective method for selecting representatives.

a. that all poverty area representatives meet the federal definition of poverty.

b. that all public and political officials such as councilmen, ward leaders, etc., be excluded from serving as representatives.

c. that nominees for representatives be people who are dedicated to alleviating poverty and concerned with the welfare of all people in the area without regard to race, creed, nationality, education, or political affiliation.

d. that every resident of the area have a right to vote on their representative.

e. that enough time be given between nomination and election for the area to become familiar with the nominees and their qualifications.

f. that local area councils should be elected by all residents, with power to review, veto, initiate and carry out anti-poverty programs in their areas."

The letter goes on further that they are "concerned

a. about the size of the five designated areas to be represented. Each person represents too large a population.

b. that the areas are too complex, having too many different people and problems for one person to represent adequately.

c. that any method of electing representatives depending primarily on using existing neighborhood organizations, notably the system of area conventions used in New York City, will not successfully involve the poor. Most street clubs, Area Councils, PTA's, etc., are composed of people who are not in poverty" (11/25/65).

The Citizens' Committee continued to protest through letters and demonstrations the structure of the Council for Economic Opportunities. In October, 1965, a little over a year after the Council was set up, a Citizens' Committee press release announced that "the Council is under pressure from the Office of Economic Opportunity to demonstrate how it plans to involve poverty area representatives meaningfully on their board and in their structure. Any further grants of federal money under Title II of the Economic Opportunity Act are being withheld from Cleveland until they come up with a concrete plan for 'maximum feasible involvement of the poor.' "

CCACCAP also developed and submitted to OEO its own proposal for program development involving the development of independent grass roots organizations in the poverty areas to plan anti-poverty programs and action. According to Younger's testimony before the Powell committee on November, 1965, the CCACCAP proposal,

> focusing mainly on community organizations for service, conflicted with the Greater Cleveland Neighborhood Centers Association (GCNCA) outreach services program. After several efforts to get representatives of the Citizens' Committee together with director Ralph Findley in Washington to attempt to resolve the conflict (all unsuccessful due to Mr. Findley's breaking the appointments), the OEO finally said they would have to fund GCNCA first and then see what they could do for the Citizens' Committee.

OEO said that CCACCAP should go to CEO for funds first (cf. OEO's response in the conflict between CATC and CFO in Syracuse), and in the event that they failed here, "the Citizens' Committee's project sponsor, the Protestant Ministry to Poverty, and the CEO would have to file separate briefs as to why or why not OEO should fund the project for review by them, after which a decision would be made."

Just as in Syracuse, OEO had proved here to be more sensitive to the demands of political exigencies than to the demands of the powerless poor and their articulate but outnumbered surrogates.

(2) *Students for a Democratic Society Proposal for Chicago*

A proposal for a coalition between intellectuals and the poor was described in a memorandum to the Stern Family Fund from Rennie Davis of the SDS. It speculated on the possibility of a union between the unemployed of JOIN and Chicago professionals. Excerpts from their proposal show a high degree of empathy:

A critical link between mainstream society and a militant community group could be found in the growing number of professionals in the social sciences. Intellectuals in their work often join together ideas and serve as 'translators' between ideas. If given the opportunity, some of these professionals will become involved in the problems of America's poor.

Generally, intellectuals tend to accept the condition of things as they are as a necessary limitation on their work. However, many times in Europe and on a smaller scale in the United States, intellectuals in numbers have linked up with social movements as they have become strong enough to offer the promise of a joint advance for the community and for the intellectuals affiliated with them.

The program rests on the assumption that an organization of urban poor must be built independent of established institutions, but that such an organization needs and can develop working relations of various kinds with established private and governmental agencies through effective utilization of the skills of intellectuals in those agencies.

This program would seek to develop relations between an interracial group of *unemployed* called JOIN and *professionals in welfare* agencies, local trade unions, Chicago universities, churches and private and public anti-poverty agencies. While it is important that the unemployed remain independent of the agencies they want to affect, they will be *politically irrelevant*—and *thus ineffectual*—unless they can win the support of other groups in the city—unless, in short, a coalition of groups come to have a stake in the program. It is thus to the advantage of JOIN to win support and assistance from some established groups.

It is also to the advantage of some established groups to see this insurgent group become politically relevant rather than operate outside the political arena where frustration and anger can easily reach a destructive pitch.

This project would develop a Full Employment Research Group in Chicago which could draw qualified people into such an effort. Participants would include trade union researchers, faculty and graduate students from local universities and colleges, (primarily the University of Chicago), research-oriented people from various groups in the fields of housing, education, health care and social services, research-oriented people in religious institutions. . . .

The involvement of students in part-time community organizing work is a relatively new phenomenon and one of great potential for shaping the role of the social science intellectual as sketched above.

These few attempts at organization of local coalitions of empathic professionals and the poor are characterized by the following:

They occur in areas frustrated by apparent ineffectiveness of community action programs as related to the component of basic social change.

They are organized by intellectuals *for* the poor but seem to escape the characteristics of welfare paternalism, due to their own empathy and their emphasis on reversing the condition of powerlessness of the poor.

Their leadership, from the student movement (SDS) and from religious institutions, tends to represent groups on the periphery of power.

They insist on autonomy for themselves as a group, but they seek funding from the federal government or national foundations and they do not move toward total self-determination for the poor; rather, the poor are to be guided *by* the professionals.

D. *Councils and Conventions of the Poor*

(1) *The People's War Council Against Poverty in Syracuse and the People's Convention for the Total Participation of the Poor*

The People's War Council in Syracuse is a coalition of neighborhood organizations representing the poor, organized to protest the federal government's withdrawal of funds from CATC-SCDA. The Council charged that "OEO is abandoning the idea that the poor should be helped to build organizations totally of, by, and for the poor . . . without giving it half a chance."* A delegation of the Council went to Shriver's office in Washington in December and tried in vain to see President Johnson. A few delegates went on to San Antonio in pursuit of the President and were arrested, then taken to meet aides of the President.

The Council called the People's Convention for January 15–16, 1966, the first national convention of the poor as such. To that convention came about 600 representatives of approximately 183 grass roots groups from twenty states. Mrs. Grace Cade, chairman of the People's War Council Against Poverty of New York City, told delegates, as recorded by one of this study's observers:

Hi, I'm late as usual. I'll make this short, but it's very important that the New York City People's War Council Against Poverty speak to this convention today. We resolved on December 12th at the Hotel Roosevelt, in the tradition of the People's War Council Against Poverty in Syracuse to set up a similar organization. A city-wide organization. The People's War Council in New York is a group of about 25 to 30 organizations from all the boroughs of New York, from Queens, Brooklyn, Bronx, Manhattan and we don't have Richmond. They don't seem to have any poverty over there.

We have resolved to support Syracuse, because we feel that all of the poverty programs all over the country are either in the process

* Jules Witcover and Erwin Knoll, "Politics and the Poor: Shriver's Second Thoughts," *The Reporter,* December 30, 1965.

of being attacked or can expect this kind of attack from either their local City Hall or eventually some city government agency. We feel that the poverty program has exposed the government in a way. . . . we understand today that the poverty money is really just buying votes. We are not going to be bought anymore. We're saying, all right, you want to get a poverty program for us. We want to operate it. We want the dominant voice, as a matter of fact, we want 100% total participation. No maximum feasible participation. 100%; we're the poor, we know what we need, it's our struggle, we want to operate and want our own programs. We want to make use of that money in the way we know how, better than any agencies, any official, any professional. Poor people can learn how to operate, they can be skilled and trained to operate their own program. These are some of the many issues. If we work together in some kind of communication system across the country, nation-wide, the thing that happened to Syracuse can be stopped.

This is the potential power that people said always existed, but poor people never used; so let's use it. Let's set up a communication system from California to New York, from Michigan to Georgia, Mississippi . . . the point is we can support each other and fight together because that kind of unity, nation-wide unity, among poor people has been unheard of. So I'm just hoping that out of today can come that kind of national support and that's what New York City's War Council people are here for. To learn how to independently without city or government money be a pressure group in your city, and in your state, and therefore, in your government. Learn how to fund-raise; poor people fund-raising. Learn how to get the skills and the training.

Now you've got the message. That's what we're here for. (Emphasis added)

The convention operated after the manner of the group dynamics-participatory democracy of the middle-class. This, from the tape of the convention, quoting the parliamentarian:

First of all, I hope that everybody here has their credentials. The first sheet in your packet is a credential sheet which explains how we've divided up this convention. Who can vote. If you haven't registered yet, please go downstairs as soon as we break up and register so that you are an official part of this convention. The second sheet is the convention rules. These rules cover tomorrow morning's session. From 10 to 1. They cover how we're going to handle the resolutions we expect to come out of today's afternoon session. I ask you to review those before tomorrow morning so that you know what to expect so that everybody knows how we're going to operate. The third sheet on a much more practical level is an information sheet which deals with housing and anybody here that hasn't signed a housing sheet at the housing desk downstairs should do so. If you're from out of town and you've got friends in the city and they put you up, please sign the housing sheet so we know where you're at. If you're from Syracuse and you want a ride home tonight, also stop down at the housing desk.

On the agenda sheet that was handed out as you came through the door is a list of 10 areas of interest. There will be a committee, a working session committee, for each one of these 10 areas, plus one other that was mentioned by people when they arrived here and looked over our list. The eleventh is participation. Maximum participation. And I guess as Mrs. Cade said, you can't get any more feasible than 100%.

A number of resolutions were passed at the convention. Excerpts show their tenor:

ACTION

Whereas the anti-poverty program as presently constituted does not attack the basic causes of poverty nor meet the needs of poor people,

Be it resolved that a national attack be made on OEO for a transferal of power from the politicians to the people by means of direct funding to neighborhood organizations.

We further resolve that a national demonstration be held by local groups to support the aforementioned.

Whereas independence of action and continuity of organization are largely dependent on a reliable and constant source of sympathetic income and

Whereas people who have a substantial and financial stake in their own future will work the best and most lasting change

Be it resolved that all organizations working for social change develop their own independent sources of income.

Be it further resolved that we demand the Community Chests and United Funds across the nation provide operating funds for mass local community organizations controlled by the people to the same extent that they provide operating funds for existing welfare agencies controlled by the paternalists.

Whereas large numbers of our community people are members of local AFL-CIO unions and

Whereas the national AFL-CIO unions are providing massive financial resources for the Citizens Crusade Against Poverty

Be it resolved that CCAP provide the necessary funds for recruiting and training local community organizers to insure participation of the poor in the War on Poverty policy making.

We recognize that the realities of life seem to dictate that OEO will not fund any community organization project on a mass base that fits the needs of the people, and therefore,

Be it resolved that we call on the major denominations of our nation as one of the last hopes the poor have for obtaining funds to develop such organizations.

We urge the denominations to make these funds available for community organizations across the country.

Be it further resolved that each organization represented here confront their local churches with the specific needs of their community organization.

The delegates proposed to undertake a great number of projects, including running of political candidates sympathetic to the poor, setting up an Economic Information Service in Swarthmore, Pennsylvania, setting up a training course, poor people's corporations and the like. They intended to establish themselves as a continuing organization.

One of the most significant characteristics of the Syracuse convention, as at later conventions of the poor, was the pervasive atmosphere of anger, but it seemed to be an anger not born of despair but of harsh vitality, fierce in its suggestion of suppressed violence:

The theme of our convention is total participation of the poor. A lot of people don't know what this means. But the power structures in just about every one of the cities knows what this means. It seems like we're not only fighting poverty, we're fighting the power structure too. And it was proven here in Syracuse, just how hard the power structure would go. They tried to kill the convention, but I see a lot of friendly faces out in the audience.

One of the things we came here for is to build better communications all over the nation in the poverty program. If we can get together and understand each other's problems, we can solve these problems. Not city hall, not the power structures, but the people. This is the whole idea of the war against poverty. I've talked to a lot of people all over the country, and they're starting to be a little suspicious of Washington, how they renege on their promises.

Syracuse is a good example. We had a very good working program here. But it was working too good. The power structure here in Syracuse tried to kill it right from the beginning. And finally, they set us back. I wouldn't say they succeeded, because they didn't and they never will, because we're not going to let it stop here. We're going to keep on fighting. Even if we have to fight with guns. We going to keep on fighting. Even if we have to fight with guns. We're them.

I don't know how sincere President Johnson was when he started this war, but when he handed it over to the people, we're going to show him how sincere we are.

(2) *Poor People's Convention of the Citizens' Crusade Against Poverty*

The Citizens' Crusade Against Poverty which was the only national "watchdog" project of review of programs for the poor, organized a tumultuous two-day "poor people's convention" in Washington on April 13–14, 1966. In attendance were delegates from Watts, Harlem, Appalachia, and the Mississippi Delta—in all about 1,000 persons from local organizations in poor neighborhoods and rural areas.

Delegates booed and jostled anti-poverty director Sargent Shriver when he spoke before the convention, and the distressed OEO director refused to stay for questions, declaring according to the *New York Times* (April 14, 1966): "I will not participate in a riot." When angry poor condemned the anti-poverty program as ineffective, some of the sponsors left the meeting. Said Jack T. Conway, AFL–CIO associate of Walter Reuther, whose UAW funds have supported Crusade, "They have turned on the people who wanted to help them."

For days thereafter liberal columnists attempted to explain the rude behavior of the poor. Michael Harrington pointed out that the war against poverty had introduced a subversive element of hope in the poor but said the delegates were "wrong" to harass Shriver and urged them to join with labor, the churches and liberals in a formidable coalition.

Roy Wilkins of the NAACP said, according to reports in the New York *Herald Tribune* and the New York *Post* that the spectacle was one of "self-degrading bad taste and bad language." "Many of these people are wholly unprepared beyond the recital of clichés to function in the existing political and economic environment," he said. "Unable or unwilling to grapple with the sharpened problems presented, they see intrigue and betrayal in every proposal. They react with the only technique they know: pure protest dressed in ranting invective."

The national committee of the CCAP sent Shriver a letter of apology expressing their regret and embarrassment.

It is ironic that the veterans of the labor movement, tumultuous and disorderly in its time, now find it so hard to understand the anger of her later movement for justice. The Citizens' Crusade said, in its original statement of policy, that it was imperative to break through the "apathy of the poor" and that "a national awakening of conscience" might help the poor "to find their voice and the will to help themselves." The poor have begun to speak, but the voice is not gentle. Who would have expected it to be?

The verbal confrontation between Shriver and the poor reflected among other things the fact that some of the more articulate representatives of the poor do not accept the usual rules and regulations which govern communication among middle-class and governmental officials. The language of the poor and their representatives is likely to be more direct, blunt, and accusatory. The etiquette of indirection, circumlocution, or equivocation does not seem to operate for the poor in their communication with officials. It would seem, therefore, that the poor are either passive or so overtly militant in such encounters as to make communication with middle-class representatives awkward, strained, or impossible. Shriver and other officials such as Eugene Carson Blake reacted to this style of the poor by denouncing them, rather than attempting to understand the difficulties in style and patterns of communication.

When bitterness and anger emerged at conventions of the poor, as they invariably did, after attacks on OEO (Syracuse, West Oakland, California, Citizens' Crusade convention), some observers tended to report patterns of manipulative organization by professionals or other disciplined individuals. One might speculate on whether, in fact, a core of agitators is stirring up such response or whether the observers infer that such response must necessarily be triggered by agitators. The discovery of conspiracy is often an effective means of discounting the evidence of rebellion. Further, extremists sometimes encourage this view, wishing to take "credit" for rebellions they never caused. On the other hand, the poor, and particularly the Negro poor, have been exploited for centuries by groups who view them as vulnerable. It would be especially tragic if such exploitation should now occur in the guise of protecting the interests of the poor. Surrogates for the poor have a special responsibility to be aware of such danger and to guard against it.

Conventions of the poor are a relatively new phenomenon growing out of community organization for social action and the increasing frustration of such groups to achieve their desired ends. They show the following characteristics:

All of the conventions—the city convention in Paterson sponsored by the local CAP itself, the State convention in California, the People's Convention for the Total Participation of the Poor, the Poor People's Convention—all seem to have been organized from the top down rather than from the bottom up. The Paterson convention was part of the executive director's strategy to arouse public interest and commitment to the city's program. The California meeting seems to have been guided, though relatively unobtrusively, by a small group of professional organizers. The People's Convention held in Syracuse was organized by the leaders of CATC to save the program from defeat. The Poor People's Convention was organized by the middle- and upper-class representatives of the Citizens' Crusade Against Poverty.

Omitting the unique "convention" in Paterson, atypical in its origin, the others were instruments of fierce protest, and express intense anger, suspicion, and bitterness toward the Establishment.

They were organized along the lines of a typical middle-class organizational convention in terms of procedures, and were carefully structured.

They addressed themselves to the root causes of poverty and hence sought to reach the central figures of public power locally and nationally, and tended to cover a vast territory of proposals rather than to concentrate on a few concrete community goals.

So far, they have had no noticeable effect in achieving their goals.

Local conferences designed to give the poor a sense of unity like that held in Paterson generally have been called only by the more effective community action programs. The others do not risk such a confrontation. The regional and national protest assemblies serve a very different purpose—as a channel of communication and as therapy for the frustrated and angry. Again, these attempts at preventing stagnation of programs bring similar problems: they are all initiated and organized by the non-poor. Conferences held at a distance also present certain logistic problems—the inability of the poor to pay transportation or conference living expenses, their unfamiliarity with parliamentary procedures. The question of the reality of the involvement of organization has not been solved. There is yet no evidence of the poor and of their effective participation in the apparatus that such middle-class methods will be adaptable to the needs and competence of the poor.

Such conventions may prove merely escape valves to release the energies of the poor through words, providing new futility when they achieve no consequences. Or perhaps conventions will become effective forms of power, influencing the appropriate local and federal agencies. The poor's lack of ability to make contact with power sources dictates, however, their need for surrogates to counter a sense of futility. As of now, it is clear that a formula for united action exists, but there is little evidence that the conferences held to date have addressed themselves to the central issues of the realities of power. There is danger rather of their confusion of the means with the desired ends. Conventions are only worthwhile in the long run, as contrasted with the short-run value of therapy, if they lead to basic social change in the conditions which the organized groups have met to condemn.

E. *National Organizations of Citizens to Protect the Poor*

The first national organization to protect the rights of the poor is the Citizens' Crusade Against Poverty.

> The Citizens' Crusade was announced on November 6, 1965, though set up some months before. It was designed to be 'the vehicle through which citizens throughout the country could voice their desire to help eliminate poverty from our midst and can participate actively and directly in this great and worthy effort. [CCAP] is committed to achieve a national awakening of conscience for we know that once Americans everywhere become aroused and indignant against the immorality of a needless poverty in the midst of plenty, they will act quickly and effectively to end this shame upon America. In the course of this effort, the poor will find their own voice and the will to help themselves. (Statement of Policy and Program, 11/13/65)

Walter Reuther, CCAP chairman, and the United Auto Workers made an initial contribution to CCAP of $1 million. The organization is nonpartisan and includes more than 125 organizations and leaders of religious, civil rights, labor, academic, business, farm, and student groups.

Its executive director, Richard W. Boone, formerly served on Shriver's staff, and before that worked with adolescent street gangs in Chicago, for the YMCA, and for the Ford Foundation. He was a member of the White House special projects staff and a consultant to the President's Committee on Juvenile Delinquency.

CCAP's program was described in an illuminating article in the *New York Times:*

The plan, if it works, carries profound significance for City Halls throughout the country. Big city Mayors, now resisting demands of the poor for a voice in shaping community antipoverty programs, may be confronted by a new force that will try to influence the patterns of municipal government generally.

The Citizens' Crusade Against Poverty and the Government's campaign are parallel efforts, broadly speaking, but it is the Crusade's further purpose to see that the Government drive does not falter and that Mayors do not exercise monopoly power over community action programs financed by the Federal Government.

Forty-five per cent of the $1.5 billion antipoverty fund this year is marked for citywide and neighborhood projects called community action programs.

The organization proposes to give vitality to a provision in the Economic Opportunity Act that defines a community action progam as one 'which is developed, conducted, and administered with the maximum feasible participation of residents of the areas and members of the groups served.'

The most militant champions of the antipoverty campaign view that phrase as the heart that distinguishes the campaign from traditional forms of social work and public assistance. They contend that making the poor mere recipients of aid perpetuates the poverty problem.

At least one member of the CCAP's commission on community activity and organization, Dr. Richard Cloward of Columbia University, believes that 'economic deprivation is fundamentally a political problem, and power will be required to solve it.' He so told the Senate Select Subcommittee on Poverty when it was considering renewal of the program this year.

A related view that is influential in the organization holds that poverty often is not solely the absence of money but the presence of hopelessness.

The Citizens' Crusade Against Poverty will also establish a nationwide information network of local organizations fighting poverty.

The training program is described as the first of such magnitude operated outside the Government. The Industrial Areas Foundation, directed by Saul Alinsky of Chicago, has trained community workers for years. The organization is consulting Mr. Alinsky as well as those who differ on his approach to community deprivation.

Mr. Boone said the CCAP would combine both protest and program, and would use either or both as circumstances indicate. It is important, he said, that local citizens be prepared to offer positive programs where a political establishment is willing to move but does not know how.

The organization will be prepared to help local groups that have achieved authority over an antipoverty project but lack the experience to execute it without publicity blemishes.

Several major training centers will be established. Some trainees will go out as 'interns' to work on programs that are already in operation. Others, carefully selected for leadership potential, will be brought in as 'fellows' and paid a salary during training and for 18 months afterward.

The trainees will be drawn from poor neighborhoods where they have shown leadership, from the civil rights movement, and from returning Peace Corps volunteers. Others are expected to be sent by national organizations on a contract basis.

The training program has been approved by CCAP's commission on community activity and organization whose chairman is Dr. Eugene Carson Blake, Stated Clerk of the United Presbyterian Church in the USA.

Dr. Blake, in a statement, declared: 'Empty exhortations to our ideals no longer suffice. Human dignity and self-esteem are denied all of us, not just the poor, when our affluence ignores the continued misery of poverty and its waste of human potential.'

Dr. Blake's group also directed the staff of the organization in designing a program to enable the poor to establish community centers in rural poverty areas of the South. These centers are intended to serve as rallying points for the poor to participate more effectively in antipoverty projects such as Head Start (preschool classes) and adult basic education.

James G. Patton, president of the National Farmers Union, heads the CCAP commission on national programs and policies, which has announced plans for white papers in three major areas to plan the total elimination of poverty. (November 7, 1965)

The Commission on Public Information and Education planned to produce two pamphlets: the first to deal with the successes and failures of the poor in action; the second with the role of non-professionals in anti-poverty programs. This Commission prepared to establish one task force to work on the problem of quality education in the slum and another to evaluate anti-poverty programs—those sponsored by OEO and all others. It planned to translate to community groups relevant academic material and government documents, established intra-group communication between groups and between grass roots people and professionals; and publicize an anti-poverty week, according to notes taken at a Commission Meeting (12/8/65).

The CCAP information network would be:

a system through which the CCAP would establish and maintain contact with about three to five thousand organizations of the poor or representatives of the poor at the neighborhood or sub-city level.

. . . The purpose of such a system would be to establish a two-way communication so that CCAP could inform local groups about available federal resources and help these groups establish contact with each other. Many of these organizations would likely be local community organizations totally unrelated either to the federal government program or national organizations.

Boone said that the training program plan "evolved from recognition within CCAP that there were limited numbers of people in poverty communities who had the leadership ability and the capability to exploit the mandate of Congress calling for maximum feasible participation of the poor in the federal anti-poverty program. It was the feeling of the staff and the officers that CCAP should take the lead in training about one thousand community workers over the next three-year period."

The leaders of the CCAP include many who represent organizations not previously identified with strong support for social change—colleges, churches, social welfare groups, labor unions, hospitals, scientific organizations and others actually supportive of the *status quo* in a number of community action programs. It also included some who represent civil rights militancy, such as Dr. Aaron Henry, though such members are in the minority. On the whole, it is a highly respectable organization from a variety of liberal elites—political intellectual, religious, business and labor, etc. Almost all have been regularly identified with liberal reform in a wide variety of areas. Some members, whose listing would seem superficially to indicate a lack of understanding of the problems of poverty, are actually more knowledgeable and socially involved than would immediately be apparent. For example, Dr. Benjamin Spock is more than a famous author on pediatrics; he has been a leader in such groups as SANE. Dr. Ralph Lapp of Quadri-Science, Inc., is more than a nuclear physicist; he was a leader in scientific groups supporting Kennedy and Johnson and is a controversial social critic.

Whether CCAP will prove to be action-oriented is still to be determined. At present their proposals seem to emphasize:

1. opportunities for the poor
2. communication-liaison between the poor and the Establishment
3. training of the poor for leadership
4. self-help, mobilization of energy of the poor
5. protest and programs to solve the problems of poverty
6. evaluation of research and of programs
7. lobbying in behalf of the poor.

CCAP does not emphasize direct transformation of social institutions. Nor is there any indication that such an emphasis is not intended. On the positive side, if Crusade's efforts were successful it may be because of the knowledge and experience and the toughmindedness and clarity of its executive director. The logical implication of the statements of consensus would suggest that fundamental action would follow but, as we have seen, clarity of proposals does not necessarily lead to clarity of action.

Through the Citizens' Crusade, as through the other programs to protect the poor, persons of prestige and some power have assumed a certain level of responsibility for seeing that the poor are not short-changed by the federal government and by local anti-poverty programs. The fact that Citizens' Crusade has to be financed by such institutions as labor unions, civil rights groups, and churches raises questions about the possibilities of total independence. Certainly labor unions have not been particularly concerned with opening up opportunities or mobilizing power for a change in the status of the minority poor. The churches and civil rights groups have consistently verbalized concern for the poor but so far have not found the formula for playing any effective role in existing programs, and themselves have not, for many and unclear reasons, been able to mount a national or direct local program for action in behalf of the poor. Such groups claim that their programs, methods, and goals and victories do in fact benefit the poor in the long run. This claim must be judged in the light of the hard facts that in spite of such victories, the predicament of the minority poor has become steadily even more desperate. Claims of indirect benefit are therefore not substantiated.

It remains to be seen how effective Citizens' Crusade can be; in the final analysis its effect might be a function of the extent to which, as a national lobby, it can mobilize the power and influence the power of the federal government, so it can act more consistently in terms of the interests of the poor, in terms of its own purposes:

The fight against poverty must not become merely a well-intentioned social welfare program in which the 'haves' do favors for the 'have-nots.' The poor must be enabled to share in the sense of dignity and belonging that only their personal and active participation in this struggle can provide. Apathy must give way to awakened interest. Frustration must surrender to realizable hope. Disorganized confusion must be fashioned into organized, united effort. Thus, the poor will contribute a new and dynamic dimension to the struggle to wipe out poverty. (Citizens' Crusade Against Poverty, Statement of Policy and Programs, New York City, October 13, 1964)

V
Criteria of Effectiveness of Community Action Programs

1. Ranking of Cities Studied

A serious war against poverty, like any other war, eventually has to be judged in terms of its consequences. Wars are not waged for their own sakes, but for identifiable and specific goals. Nor can the outcome of a war be determined by the excitements of isolated skirmishes, the drama of a particular battle, or by temporary advances or retreats. It is the ultimate victory that counts. Success in war depends upon intangibles and tangibles—the intangible resources of ideological strength, commitment, and morale; the imperative tangibles of human and material resources, superior organization and supplies, and the ability to mobilize the necessary manpower, resources, intelligence, and power.

The War Against Poverty, if it is to be taken seriously, must be understood in the same terms and must meet the same hard challenges. This war, too, must have identifiable, obtainable and specific goals; it must depend upon the sustaining intangibles of belief, commitment, ideology, and morale; and above all, it must be able to mobilize and organize the tangible resources and power—human, material, and financial—necessary to defeat the "enemies" who block the attainment of the desired goals. It is essential that there be some criteria by which to measure the strength of the resources and the degree of effectiveness of the anti-poverty programs.

It is not now possible, however, to determine with any high degree of confidence the absolute degree of effectiveness of any given anti-poverty program in a given city. The development of some "objective" basis for evaluating these programs is difficult because of these programs' short life—in operation only a few years. All these programs reflect in varying degrees the difficulties expected in attempts to organize new programs and to develop new approaches to the solution of long-standing social problems. Even estimates of comparative effectiveness must take into account the fact that conditions or circumstances differ from city to city, that some cities' programs began later than others, and therefore could profit from the mistakes of the older programs or could use them as models; and that the history of the city, the political climate and structure, the power of social agencies, the degree of social disorganization or the pathology of the poor, and the percentage of non-white poor vary observably from city to city.

Yet, if programs in process are not to proceed blindly, stumbling in a trial and error fashion toward one blind alley after another often in frustration and futility, they must be evaluated in terms of reasonable and appropriate criteria. The human importance of the community action programs; the promise of hope and positive action held out to the poor; the high cost of their implementation; the urgency of the need; and the tragic human, social, and political consequences of failure demand constant critical assessment of relevance and seriousness.

It may be of value then to attempt to assess the anti-poverty programs in the twelve cities visited and studied by the staff members of this project. Even such limited results may suggest clues for a more definitive future assessment based upon further evidence.

A relative ranking of the twelve cities studied was attained in the following manner: Each of the two staff members who visited these cities and interviewed the directors or top staff and others associated with the project was asked to rank these twelve cities in order of the effectiveness of their anti-poverty programs. They were instructed to use their own criteria of effectiveness: their impressions of the individuals directing these programs, and their general familiarity with the literature, problems, style, and successes of the project. Three other individuals also familiar to some degree with these projects were asked to rank them in terms of effectiveness based upon their own criteria of effectiveness. One of these three was the project director, who had direct knowledge of and contact with eight of the twelve cities, and knowledge of the other four through the reports of the staff observers and of a field investigator, and newspaper accounts. The second individual ranked the cities exclusively in terms of reading the staff reports, other literature and reports and newspaper accounts of these cities, necessary for the planning and writing of this report. The third was a member of the OEO investigation staff whose responsibilities and assignments required him to observe directly the projects in some of these cities; he had access to reports and information about projects in those cities which he did not directly observe.

Each of these five individuals were given the same instructions, namely, to rank the cities in order of effectiveness of their anti-poverty programs. The criteria used by each individual as the basis for his ranking were not shared with the others until after the completion of the various rankings. When an individual city such as Syracuse or New York had more than one anti-poverty project, the individual was instructed to rank his estimate of the cumulative impact of the most effective program as far as possible in terms of eventual change in the conditions of the poor in that city as a whole. Two individuals found this difficult to do and tended at first to rank individual program's effectiveness rather than the impact on the cities.

The decision to focus on cities rather than programs was based upon the assumption that significant and observable changes in the actual conditions of the poor would be a function of the most effective program in a given city. For example, if City A had two ineffective programs and one effective program the chances of improvement in the conditions of its poor would be greater than in City B, which had only one program which was ineffective. Similarly, no distinction was to be made as to the specific area of potential effectiveness—for example, education, or municipal services—since observable change in one could feed into another.

The ranking of the effectiveness of anti-poverty programs in the twelve cities can be seen in Tables 3 and 3A.

Although rankings were made independently and upon the basis of different criteria and different types of contacts with the projects and the cities, a surprisingly high degree of consistency resulted. For example, four out of the five individuals ranked New Haven as having the most "effective" anti-poverty program. The one person who did not rank it number one was one of the staff members who visited these twelve cities. She ranked New Haven number eight in her list, using the political administration's guidance of the program and the non-involvement of the poor at high policy level as her reason for doing so, but she also felt the program itself was in other respects highly effective. At the other extreme, Boston was ranked number twelve by three judges and number eleven by one and number nine by the OEO employee. Only one of the five judges* considered any of the three most "ineffective" programs—Chicago, Cleveland or Boston—effective. Similarly, no one considered any of the four relatively effective programs the reverse. While the five "mixed" cities tended to show somewhat more variability in the rankings of the judges, they tended to be ranked in the middle range by all the judges, again with the exception of the OEO official.

After each individual had completed his ranking of the twelve cities and prior to his knowledge of the cumulative rankings, each was asked to state the criteria or the reasons for ranking each city at a particular point. The listings of these reasons then suggested some of the critieria or common conditions for

* This was the OEO official who deviated from the other four judges more than any of them deviated from each other. It appeared that the OEO observer tended to determine the effectiveness or ineffectiveness of the anti-poverty programs in a given city in terms of the extent of controversy or conflict aroused by the program and which required the concern or activity of the investigatory staff of the National Office of Economic Opportunity. Cleveland and Chicago were ranked second and third respectively by this official. Controversy and conflict within the CAP have been kept to a minimum in Cleveland through the domination of the anti-poverty programs by the social welfare agencies and councils and the public school system; in Chicago the anti-poverty programs are dominated and controlled by the political apparatus of the mayor's office.

Table 3: Ranking of Community Action Programs in 12 Cities in Terms of Effectiveness

City	*Cumulative Rank*
Relatively Effective Programs	
1. New Haven	12
2. Syracuse	18
3. Newark	20
4. Paterson	22
5. Minneapolis	23
Presently Unclear Programs, combining ingredients of effectiveness and ineffectiveness	
6. New York	32
7. Washington, D.C.	40
8. San Francisco	40
9. Los Angeles	40
Relatively Ineffective Programs	
10. Chicago	41
11. Cleveland	46
12. Boston	57

Table 3A: Ranking by Individuals

Cities	*Judges*					*Cumulative Rank*
	A	B	C	D	E	
New Haven	1	1	8	1	1	12
Syracuse	5	2	1	4	5	17
Newark	3	3	3	2	9	20
Paterson	4	4	4	2	7	22
Minneapolis	2	5	2	10	4	23
New York	6	8	7	5	6	32
Washington	7	7	9	9	8	40
San Francisco	8	10	5	6	11	40
Los Angeles	9	6	6	7	12	40
Chicago	11	9	10	8	3	41
Cleveland	10	12	11	11	2	46
Boston	12	11	12	12	10	57

programs regarded as effective and some of the common characteristics for the mixed and less effective programs. It will be seen from the presentation and discussion below that some of the conditions found in "effective" programs are also found in "ineffective" ones. It remains, nonetheless, a relevant and important challenge in social analysis to determine the specific factors or pattern or combination of factors which would help in differentiating between anti-poverty programs that work and those that don't.

2. Characteristics of Relatively Effective Programs: Positives Dominant

It was generally agreed by the five judges that the five relatively effective Community Action Programs in New Haven, Syracuse (CATC), Newark, Paterson, and Minneapolis had in common the following characteristics:

—a clear statement of *purposes,* definitions and goals of community action;

—actual *programs* which seemed relevant to and compatible with the stated community action purposes and goals;

—effective, strong, and articulate staff *leadership,* generally backed by a sophisticated *board* with some base of realistic power;

—some form of *involvement or representation of the poor* on the policy making or the staff level;

—an early *confrontation* with the local political apparatus and progress toward the working out of an acceptable *accommodation* by which the community action program is permitted to operate either with minimum political interference and with integrity or with the political apparatus as an ally actively protecting the integrity and effectiveness of the anti-poverty program;

—some early evidence of actual *positive changes* in the conditions of the poor or evidence that through the activities of the program the poor have learned or developed methods and techniques by which to help themselves in the future.

The Community Action Programs in these five cities differ in the degree to which each demonstrates the importance of one or more—or the patterning—of the above criteria of program effectiveness. While each city with a relatively effective program had clarity of purposes and goals, compatibility and relevance of programs, and effective staff leadership and board support, the cities differed markedly in the constellation or combination of the other factors grouped around these crucial criteria of effectiveness. For example:

A. *New Haven*

The determinants of the effectiveness of the New Haven community action programs, generally believed to be the most effective of all the programs studied, were (1) program clarity and compatibility; (2) effective staff leadership; (3) the development and sustaining of a dependable alliance between the director of the program and the mayor; (4) the integral relationship between the anti-poverty program and the community's larger, and serious, political and economic commitment for large-scale urban redevelopment; and (5) some actual beneficial, if limited, changes in living conditions of the poor, perceived by the poor, *e.g.*, in education and housing. The effectiveness of the New Haven Community Action Program demonstrates the importance of the use of local political power to protect the integrity of the anti-poverty program and the related fact that an effective community action program need not be a political threat to the local political structure. The New Haven situation suggests further that evidence of actual positive changes in the living conditions of the poor is a necessary condition for a positive, dynamic relationship between political authorities and anti-poverty program leadership.

B. *Syracuse*

In some respects the designation of the program in Syracuse as effective seems a contradictory one. Unlike the situation in

New Haven, relationship of the CATC program in Syracuse with the local political apparatus was marked by mutual suspiciousness, antagonism, and overt hostility. The major, local welfare council and social agency officials saw the activities of CATC as politically threatening and disruptive. After prolonged conflict with the "official," politically dominated Crusade for Opportunity program, the CATC program was required by the OEO director, Sargent Shriver, to seek the funds for its additional fifteen months of research and training in community action from its avowed adversary, the Crusade for Opportunity. This denial of direct OEO funding came as a culmination of a year of controversy and open conflict over the fact that the University of Syracuse-based CATC program actually did send organizers into the neighborhood of the poor, held meetings of the poor, aided them in voter registration drives and helped them confront the political authorities and relevant governmental agencies on such practical problems as housing, welfare, and police protection.

While the fate of this program remains in question because it came in conflict with the interests and power of the local political apparatus and its independence was not supported by the OEO, incidentally demonstrating the non-partisan political sensitivity of OEO—it was a Republican mayor whose resistance had been aroused—it is nonetheless ranked as an effective community action program, increasing the chances of improvement in the status of the poor in Syracuse. In addition to the (1) clarity of its goals and purposes, (2) the relevance and compatibility of its programs, (3) the strength, clarity, persistence of its leadership, (4) its sensitivity to problems of supervision and evaluation, the Syracuse CATC program demonstrated the importance of (5) community action programs' attempts to organize and train and work with the poor in a realistic, non-sentimental way toward the end of confrontation and conflict, which it recognized as inevitable stages in any serious program designed to change the conditions of the poor; and (6) an unwillingness to dilute its program at the point of crisis or to retreat in the face of the consequences of such conflict. It sought allies in anticipation of conflict among academic and some church groups; when conflict came it intensified its organizational work with the poor. Confrontation resulted in what appeared to be at least a temporary defeat and the loss of independent funding, but the work that has already been done by CATC in attempting to organize and mobilize the poor may generate its own momentum for future independent action on the part of the poor and the allies of the poor.

C. *Newark and Paterson, New Jersey*

The Newark and Paterson Community Action Programs were similar in important aspects of their over-all pattern but differed significantly in the nature of their relationship to the local political structure. In Newark and in Paterson there were clear statements of the purposes, objectives and goals of community action programs—modelled, not surprisingly, after the HARYOU document since both directors had been part of the HARYOU planning staff. The proposed and actual programs appeared to be relevant and compatible with the stated rationale, objectives and goals; the staff leadership was clear, insightful, sophisticated, and experienced, and seemed to have had the confidence and backing of a representative and concerned board of directors. The poor had been involved or represented in serious and relevant areas of community action.

An additional strength of the Paterson program was a skillful method of organization by education of the poor through the conference and convention technique. The sensitivity to style allows greater contact with the poor than would otherwise be possible, particularly since these techniques are seen as means to ends and not as ends in themselves.

Only in the area of confrontation and conflict with the existing local political structure did these two programs differ. In the case of Newark, the controversy over whether the community action programs would be controlled by the mayor and his political apparatus or by an independent anti-poverty board arose early in the existence of this program. Again, one must assume that the Newark political authorities' insistence on control of this program reflected their awareness of the political threat inherent in an effective community action program. The fact that the Newark anti-poverty program had been able to resist political encroachment and take-over during its first year of operation may have been a testament of the skill of its leadership and the concern, sophistication, and power of its board of directors. A counteracting factor to cynical political take-over may be the fact that Negroes, who are generally identified with the poor, constitute a little more than half of Newark's population. Given the fact that Newark has no charismatic political leader after the fashion of Adam Powell who could exploit the grievances of the Negro population for his own political advantage, the high percentage of Negroes in Newark would seem to prevent more flagrant attempts at political domination of the community action components of its anti-poverty program.

In Paterson, the initial controversy between the mayor and the political apparatus and the anti-poverty program was not directly related to the issue of control of the anti-poverty program, but was concerned with the more mundane and immediate question of the relative salaries of the mayor and of the director of the Paterson anti-poverty program. This issue seemed to have been resolved to the mutual advantage of all concerned. The board of directors of the Paterson program continued to back its director, and the initial confrontation on the matter of salary did not spill over into other aspects of the relationship between the anti-poverty program and the Paterson political structure. The situation as of 1966 seemed to be one of respectful independence or distance. The mayor had publicly stated his support of the program and had not expressed directly any sense of threat about the community action components of these programs. On the other hand, it is clear that there has not been in Paterson the close working relationship and the identity of goals between the anti-poverty program and the local political structure which characterizes New Haven. After the 1967 riot, the community action project staff was under fire on charges of having contributed to the unrest.

D. *Minneapolis*

Minneapolis is ranked among the more effective community action programs not primarily because of the presence of affirmative reasons, but largely because of the absence of pronounced or retarding negatives. On the surface, Minneapolis had all the positives required for an effective program, yet there appears to be no evidence of ferment of dynamic involvement of the poor or of confrontation and conflict related to such involvement. The picture in Minneapolis—the trends, direction, or even evidence of movement—was not clear. All the available evidence supported the conclusion that there was a good, workmanlike program functioning according to the existing guidelines with a minimum of administrative difficulties, an optimal degree of political support, protection and domination, and little evidence of any eventual observable change in the conditions of the poor. The fact that there is such a small percentage of Negroes in Minneapolis may account for the lack of ferment, if not the stagnation of the Minneapolis program. These conditions seem consistent with the general atmosphere of liberalism and reform, and efficient government which is believed to characterize Minneapolis.

3. Characteristics of Presently Unclear Programs: Balance of Positive and Negative Forces

The community action programs in New York City, Washington, D.C., and San Francisco, and Los Angeles, California, are classified in the category of uncertain effectiveness.

A. *New York City*

In New York City, the MFY and HARYOU programs each in its own way gave promise of serving as models of an effective, new, community action approach to the solution of the problems of the poor. Both were precise in their definition of the nature and goals of social action. In the case of MFY, proposals were implemented by programs. In addition to its three years of planning, organizational tooling-up and program pretesting, MFY had nearly two years of actual operation of community action programs financially supported by the President's Committee on Juvenile Delinquency. The MFY staff was in fact organizing the people on the Lower East Side of New York to identify their problems in such areas as housing, jobs, welfare, and education and to determine methods for solving these problems and confronting the appropriate governmental agencies with grievances and demands for remedy.

Prior to the publication of the HARYOU document, *Youth in the Ghetto*—in which the political implications of the community action approach to the problems of the poor were more explicitly spelled out—the community action activities of MFY did not result in stark controversy and conflict with the press and city political officials. It is significant that the serious attacks on MFY, its philosophy, its methods and its top staff, came after the Harlem riots of June, 1964. Though MFY operated on the Lower East Side, MFY was charged by some members of the press with instigating the Harlem riot and publishing inflammatory material concerning the policeman who had killed the Negro youth. MFY was charged with harboring leftists and subversives on its staff and with poor administration. It was understood, however, that the local field superintendent of schools and the police department were irritated and disturbed by the fact that MFY staff was organizing the people in their community for direct confrontation and action.

The newspaper attacks on MFY, by no means unanimous,* were not countered by any meaningful support on the part of local political officials. In fact, Paul Screvane, then president of the City Council, conducted an "investigation" and released a report which failed to clarify the problems and in effect contributed to the distortions of the attacking press. The board of directors of MFY at times seemed sure and firm but at crucial times vacillated in its support of its top staff. The result of the MFY confrontation, conflict, and controversy was that two of its three top staff members resigned. The agency was "reorganized" under the direction of a distinguished social service administrator; during the first year of his tenure it tended to deemphasize its more abrasive or disruptive community action programs. MFY still works with groups of the poor and provides some of them with legal aid and representation in seeking redress from the Department of Welfare and the New York City Housing Authority, but its programs are now more service- than action-oriented. The results of the conflict add up to a victory for the anti-community action forces or at best a temporary defeat and regrouping of the forces for a more sophisticated and probably more effective war of the poor in the future. Like the Syracuse CATC conflict, it may be that the momentum of the

* The New York *Herald Tribune,* the *New York Times,* and the *World Telegram and Sun* sought to maintain objective balanced reporting and sometimes sought to counteract the more strident attacks of some of the other newspapers by supporting editorials.

past conflict-producing serious community action programs will evolve or erupt later into significant activity on the part of the poor and their allies.

The HARYOU controversy is not to be understoood in the same terms as the MFY conflict. In the case of MFY the conflict arose out of direct work with the poor and the threat inherent in their organization and their confrontation of the governmental agencies with their grievances. HARYOU's controversy arose out of a struggle for control of the program prior to any actual work with the poor of Harlem. Adam Clayton Powell was the first major political figure to understand the political implications and dynamite inherent in the community action components of the HARYOU planning document. Seeing this, he insisted that if it were going to operate in his district, it would have to be under his control. It is quite probable that his insight into the potential of the program and the public controversy which surrounded his intervention alerted other political officials in New York and in other cities to the built-in threat in community action programs, and set the stage for the controversies over MFY, CATC in Syracuse, and programs elsewhere.

The fact is that HARYOU's difficulties preceded any direct or serious attempts to organize the poor of Harlem for community action. The Powell forces were victorious in this initial stage of controversy and the program was damaged and its momentum stopped before any overt encounter with the institutions of the city and governmental leadership could take place. A former assistant to Powell was designated as executive director, and Powell supporters or accessories moved to dominate the board of directors of the new organization, a merger of the previously independent HARYOU and the Powell operation ACT into HARYOU-ACT. The Powell victory was made possible by the fact that the HARYOU board of directors was not insightful enough to understand or strong enough to resist the power, persuasiveness, and blandishments of the Powell forces; by the fact that the Federal government, the PCJD and the newly emerging OEO, dared not counter the desires of the then powerful chairman of the House Education and Labor Committee through which all anti-poverty legislation and appropriation must initially pass; and the fact that there was no disposition or sufficient concern or commitment on the part of the political officials in City Hall to cause them to cross swords with Adam Powell before a crucial mayoralty election.

Aside from the administrative and fiscal difficulties of HARYOU-ACT which reflected the inexperience, if not incompetence, of the top staff and a lack of clarity and general inefficiency in the staff responsible for various aspects of the over-all program, it remains a fact that HARYOU-ACT postponed throughout its first year and a half of existence the implementation of the core of its community action programs. Even at the present, the community action programs—organization of neighborhood councils and groups—is among the least effective of HARYOU-ACT programs and is less effective than even the present MFY community action programs. The controversy for control of the HARYOU program and the resolution of that controversy with victory for the Powell forces effectively blocked any systematic and serious work with or organization of the poor in Harlem. The poor were fought *about* but not for, another instance of the pathos of the poor. The poor were hostages, instruments to other peoples' profit and power. The Harlem poor did not have even the dubious satisfaction of the emotional catharsis obtained in certain other programs from conflict with governmental agencies. They did not even have the chance to be defeated in conflict as MFY did. HARYOU-ACT's programs during the first two years seemed confined to those social services of the maximum public relations value and those which purported to contain the disruptive and riot potential of the restless and frustrated youth and adults of the ghetto. Indeed, the leaders of HARYOU-ACT, the director and board members, based their claims to program effectiveness on the grounds that there was no riot in Harlem during the summer of 1965.

The Bedford-Stuyvesant and the anti-poverty programs

among the Puerto Ricans in New York City encountered similar difficulties in organization and in struggle for control. These programs also have failed to involve the poor in any direct-action confrontation and conflict-producing activity and have spent their available energy in intramural power struggles. Here, too, the needs of the poor were ignored while the struggle for control of them raged and waned.

The various forms and dimension of controversies which plague the anti-poverty programs in New York City suggest the possibility that there are problems related to the possible degree of effectiveness of these programs peculiar to New York City. Among the problems which might limit the effectiveness of even the most efficient community action program is the sheer size of the city itself and the related dimension and ponderousness of its agencies and bureaucracies. Then, too, New York City probably has a larger number of poor people in a given municipal unit than any other American city. The problems of New York's poor are complicated by population density, ethnic diversity among the poor, and the fact that the poor are distributed in large pockets throughout the five boroughs rather than concentrated in a given manageable location. Given these and related problems, it is not now possible to predict with any degree of confidence whether community action components of anti-poverty programs currently in operation can be effective solutions to the problems of the poor in New York City.

B. *Washington, D.C.*

The classification of the Washington, D.C. program in this middle category of indecisive community action programs reflects the fact that, while the Washington program is clear in its objectives, goals, and purposes, has seemingly compatible programs and articulate leadership, and has involved the poor at least on the staff level, nonetheless a clear picture of the effectiveness or potential effectiveness of this program did not emerge. The planning stage of the Washington program, under the direct sponsorship of the PCJD, was marked by its share of controversy and a prolonged study between the social welfare agencies and the new and independent staff for control of the project. The director and his top associates resigned when they were defeated. This initial controversy and its resolution, however, does not fully account for the lack of clarity of the program. Rather, the ambiguity of the Washington Community Action Program must be understood primarily in terms of the political ambiguity of the city. Washington is unique in that it does not have a local goovernmental structure directly responsible to the people; so far, the voters do not elect their mayor. The city's commissioners are appointed by the President of the United States subject to the approval of the Congress. In fact, the real source of political power is the District Committee of the House of Representatives, a group distant from the residents of Washington and not required to be directly responsive to their needs. Washington had no city hall to picket or demonstrate against.

In addition, Washington has the distinction of being the only major American city which is now predominantly Negro. As the middle-class white government workers and executives retreated to the surrounding suburbs of Virginia and Maryland, the inner-city of Washington was left to lower, working-class, and middle-class Negroes. The fact that the Negro population of Washington contained a large percentage of middle-class, middle- and upper-income government workers, school teachers, college professors, and other professionals, does not seem to affect positively the status of the Negro poor. The situation in Washington, like Los Angeles, to some extent Cleveland, and other cities, highlights the fact that there is a clear and probably increasing alienation between the Negro middle class and the marginal and lower-class Negro, an alienation marked by mutual suspiciousness, by insensitivity, and by a communication gap difficult to bridge short of some racial atrocity perpetrated upon a Negro by the white police or other governmental official. The quiet and undramatic problems of the poor do not ordinarily arouse empathic concern and sustained activity among the Negro middle class. This might be even more true in those communities with a large percentage of Negroes who have "made it" in spite of race—a demonstration of the fact that those Negroes who have not "made it" must in some way be personally inadequate or unworthy, tending to support the validity of negative racial stereotypes and thereby jeopardizing the status of all Negroes. Furthermore, given the fact that many of the policy-making and operational positions in Washington are held, at least nominally by Negroes—City Commissioner and Director of Housing Authority and Chairman of the Board of Education, and now the appointed Mayor—a serious and effective community action program in Washington would have to involve the organization of the Negro poor primarily by Negro middle-class professionals, with the help of some indigenous workers, for the purpose of confrontation of and conflict with Negro middle-class government officials. Such considerations may account for the present lack of clarity concerning the actual direction and potential effectiveness of the community action programs in Washington, D.C.

C. *San Francisco*

San Francisco originally experienced no major controversy within the anti-poverty program itself. There was apparent clarity and consistency on the part of the directors in terms of their view of what is required for an effective community action program. Furthermore, not only were the poor involved, but San Francisco represents one of the few cases in which the poor appeared to be successful in winning from the Mayor and other political officials control and domination of the program. It is now apparent, however, that the effectiveness of the program in terms of actual change in the conditions of the poor is unlikely. As a matter of fact, the Mayor of San Francisco seemed to be biding his time and awaiting the failure of this program before stepping in and taking it over. He was later proved to be correct in anticipating confusion and failure in a program dominated by the poor. The catharsis and the pride associated with control by the poor served as a temporary substitute for effective social change, offering the psychological benefits of "we are in control" without the power and access to actual decision-making forces in the social and political structure. The various groups in the city active in civil rights and in the anti-poverty program which had been effective in joint efforts in various campaigns against specific aspects of discrimination seemed unable to avoid destructive competition among themselves when the possibility of actual official power was at stake. Involvement of the poor itself may serve as a skillful device for containment, obscuring the failure to achieve social change. The riots of the fall of 1966 in San Francisco were a warning sign. Further, the failure of the representatives of the poor to be effective in a leadership role both discourages the poor and encourages in the non-poor and in civic leadership the conviction that potential strength does not exist in the poor themselves. It is, however, primarily a demonstration of the fact that those who have no effective power cannot exercise a power they do not have even when they are placed in positions that have the surface manifestations of power.

D. *Los Angeles*

The Los Angeles program is dominated and confused by a complexity of political problems intensified by the Watts riots of 1965. At the time of the Watts eruption, Sargent Shriver and other officials in Washington maintained that an anti-poverty program had failed to develop in Los Angeles largely because of political indecisiveness and confusion. Some observers suggested that the Watts outbreak could be explained partly by the fact that no anti-poverty program was operating there at that time. Whether this explanation is valid or not, it is true that the anti-poverty program in operation in Los Angeles was characterized by political confusion and indifference, amorphousness, irrelevance of structure and program, and lack of administrative clarity.

The peculiar characteristics of the minority poor in the Los

Angeles area are also significant. For example, while the Negro ghetto in Los Angeles is not overtly marked by the signs of deterioration, it does have all the other characteristics of northern urban ghettos, such as low income, underemployment and high unemployment, high welfare rates and so forth. In addition, the problems of Negroes in the Watts area are complicated by clear alienation between the Negro middle-class and professionals and the masses of working-class marginal Negroes, an alienation resulting in failure of the Negro middle class to assume responsible leadership of the Negro masses. Civil rights groups such as the NAACP and the Urban League do not appear to have any direct contact with or loyalty from the Negro majority. For these reasons, therefore, the Los Angeles anti-poverty community action program must be classified as unclear in terms of potential effectiveness. While is is possible for it to be galvanized into an effective program, it is also possible for it to remain essentially stagnant and ineffective. There seemed little evidence that the community is able to or will mobilize the resources necessary for serious organization of the poor and for realistic social change.

4. Characteristics of Relatively Ineffective Programs: Negatives Dominant

The designation of Cleveland, Chicago and Boston as examples of the three relatively ineffective programs of the twelve cities studied in depth for this study is based both upon characteristics which the three had in common and upon characteristics peculiar to each city. The outstanding common characteristic is the lack of an imaginative, dynamic, and creative leadership. In each case, the leadership seems totally dominated either by political control or by traditional social agency control or, in the case of Cleveland, both.

A. *Cleveland*

In Cleveland, the anti-poverty program was initially set up under the control of the social welfare agencies, the Board of Education, and a relatively weak political organization. The initial control and the planning of the program under the President's Committee on Juvenile Delinquency resulted in the domination of that stage of the program by the schools, social welfare and political interests. This domination has continued without a meaningful and dynamic program seeking to involve the poor directly or change their predicament significantly. The Protestant Ministry to the Poor and CORE made attempts to control the general stagnation and ineffectiveness of the official OEO operation. If any significant change in the predicament of the poor occurs in Cleveland, it is not likely to come as a consequent official OEO operation, nor is it likely to result from the activities of the Urban League or the NAACP in Cleveland, since these organizations have become a part of the control structure and Board of Directors of the official anti-poverty program. Furthermore, while the Negro middle class and professionals in Cleveland played an effective role in the protest against segregated public schools, their general alienation from the masses of the Negro poor has been reflected in the fact that they are not now playing a meaningful and effective role in the anti-poverty programs. The prognosis for Cleveland was poor. Whether the coalition of Negroes and a minority of whites that united to elect a Negro, Carl Stokes, Mayor of Cleveland would prove to have a long-range impact is still to be determined.

B. *Chicago*

In Chicago, there were no serious signs that the official OEO program is basically concerned with or operating programs which are primarily concerned with changing the actual conditions of the poor in that city. The Chicago programs have been almost exclusively social service-oriented, unimaginatively but somewhat effectively operated. The *realities* of the racial and political climate in Chicago, the fact that almost all aspects of life have been dominated by the Daly and Dawson machines, seem to suggest that any serious change in the conditions of the poor in Chicago is remote. In spite of demonstrations, picketings, boycotts, and other forms of protest organized and sustained by Raby's groups, there had been no observable ameliorations of the problem of segregation and inferior education in the public schools. A new superintendent has proposed various plans but there has not been time to test his effectiveness. However, the forces responsible for the maintenance of the status quo in education in Chicago remain entrenched; these same forces will probably work toward maintaining the status quo in the conditions of the poor. Two forces which might operate positively in Chicago are the Alinsky Woodland Organization program and Martin Luther King's operation in the Chicago slums. The Woodland Organization is discussed elsewhere in this report. It is too early to determine the long-range effects of the program begun by Martin Luther King. So far it does not seem to have any significant effect on the operations of the official anti-poverty program in Chicago.

C. *Boston*

Boston was unquestionably the least effective of the twelve anti-poverty programs studied in depth for this report. The problems and difficulties of the other OEO programs, found in different degrees and patterns elsewhere, were concentrated and intensified in the Boston program and suggest strongly that the chances of observable and meaningful changes in the conditions of the poor of Boston were practically nil. The Boston anti-poverty program was totally dominated by City Hall. Attempts on the part of some civil rights groups and some neighborhood groups to move in and participate in the decision-making boards of the Boston program have so far been unsuccessful. There have been no direct confrontations and conflicts between the anti-poverty programs and the political structure in behalf of the poor. The role of the clearly reactionary Boston School Committee in contributing to the ineffectiveness of the Boston anti-poverty program is not clear. What is clear, however, is that there had been in the anti-poverty program persistent evidence of maladministration; lack of clarity of goals; lack of relevance of programs to the need for change in conditions of the poor; inadequate quality control of programs; lack of meaningful organization, involvement or participation of the poor; and, above all, a general apathy, indifference, if not cynicism, on the part of the early leadership of this program. Boston has had the dubious distinction of being the only city whose funds were frozen by the OEO. Whether the new administration of City Hall will transform this depressing picture is not yet clear.

5. A Relative Achievement

As we have seen, the record of the community action programs in the cities studied is, even at best, a qualified success. Even the most effective show only tentative signs of observable social change. At their worst, they are a charade, an elaborate exploitation of the poor. But the criteria of effectiveness and ineffectiveness point the way toward assessment of such programs that may make such exploitation more apparent in the future and, hopefully, therefore, less likely.

VI
A Relevant War Against Poverty: Summary and Conclusions

1. Objectives of the Study

The objectives of this study of community action programs, conducted under the auspices of the Stern Family Fund, were:

A. To develop a preliminary inventory of community action programs.

B. To determine how each of these programs defines what is meant by a community action program.

C. To attempt to establish some objective criteria by which these programs could be evaluated.

A. *Inventory*

The community action programs of twelve cities—New York, Boston, New Haven, Syracuse, Washington, D.C., Newark, Paterson, Minneapolis, Chicago, Cleveland, Los Angeles, and San Francisco—were visited and studied in depth. In addition, information concerning community action programs was received by direct correspondence from or the analysis of 51 project proposals from other cities and regions. (Since the initiation of this study, the OEO has funded more than 200 anti-poverty programs with CAP components throughout the nation.)

B. *Definition and Goals of Programs*

"Community Action" has been defined in a variety of different ways by the different anti-poverty projects. These variations in definitions and differences in emphases probably reflect primarily the ambiguity of the statutory definition found in Title II A, Section 202(a) of the Economic Opportunity Act, which made it possible for "services, assistance, and other activities of sufficient scope and size to give promise of progress toward elimination of poverty." Section 202(b) of the Economic Opportunity Act recognized the generality of the statutory definition and permitted even greater latitude by the provision: "The director is authorized to prescribe such additional criterion for community programs as he shall deem appropriate." Because this act did not define community action programs explicitly and specifically, it was possible for anti-poverty projects to define community action, verbally and programmatically, in terms of a large number of traditional social services and community organization emphases and programs. The stated goals of community action programs tend to vary from the traditional emphasis on (1) a provision of *social services* for the poor; to (2) the opening up of *opportunities* for the poor; (3) through provision of organizations for *participation by the poor in securing necessary services and opportunities;* to (4) leadership by the poor in *independent action to secure the power* to deal with the basic causes of poverty.

The documents examined and the individuals interviewed have tended to define community action more in terms of the recent and fashionable *action* and *power* goals than in terms of traditional social services. This emphasis seemed to be due to the apparent demand embodied in the Economic Opportunity Act, and encouraged by OEO administration for a new approach to the solution of the problems of the poor. But this study on *A Relevant War Against Poverty* has discovered that it is easier to verbalize a novel approach to the problems of the poor than to develop and implement new programs compatible with those new theories and purposes. In the actual operation of community action programs, the traditional social services approach, not the action approach, dominated.

Among the often vaguely stated but clear implications of the stated goals of community action programs as interpreted from the evidence observed in this study were these:

The programs were intended:

As mediators between the poor and the more privileged members of the community.

As forces for social cohesion and harmony, to prevent social eruptions, community instability, and chaos.

As molders of individual behavior, so that the poor would become more "socially responsible" and more imitative of the middle class in manner, speech, values, and over-all behavior.

As agents for or instruments to facilitate self-help on the part of the poor to enable the poor, with help, to develop their own organizations for the mobilization and use of the power necessary to affect change in their condition.

The actual programs operated under the heading of community action programs were for the most part traditional social service, opportunity, or educational programs, and did not directly provide the poor with the opportunity or the skill to obtain and exercise the power required to bring about observable changes in their living conditions.

Of the 51 anti-poverty projects sampled, most (116) of the community action programs in operation were educational programs, including Head Start programs; 103 were traditional social services programs; 52 were job training and placement services programs, and 34 traditional community organization programs. Fifty-five programs could be classified as reflecting the more recent approach and emphasis in terms of a social change-and-action orientation toward community action; 23 of these were so classified because they stated that they used "indigenous" people on their staffs. Only 5 of these 55 had community action programs which involved actual organization of the poor for *action* directed in their own behalf or toward social change.

There seemed to be little relationship between the clarity, specificity, and action emphasis of the verbal definitions and goals of community action and the actual programs operated under the designation of community action programs. That is, some programs and directors were action-oriented verbally but tended to run social services programs, nevertheless, while other programs were unwilling to define community action programs verbally but could operate an action-oriented, social change type of program.

Practically no program—and certainly not the administration of the OEO—has defined the goals of the CAP component of the anti-poverty war, either verbally or programmatically, in terms of the elimination of poverty itself, or in terms of the words of President Johnson who, in his speech calling for a national war on poverty, named as the goal: "Our objective: total victory."

In actual operation there seems to be little difference, except verbal, and therefore little basis for any realistic expectation of different results, between the new anti-poverty community action programs and the traditional social services approaches to the problems of the poor. The programs in general seemed limited to the provision of services designed to ameliorate the conditions of poverty, or limited to the opening up of opportunities—some sporadic job training and employment information and the like—without attempting to cope with the central problems of the poor, for whom an "opportunity" defined is inadequate guarantee of the ability to get and to hold a self-respecting job after a lifetime of insufficient or irrelevant education, and physical and psychological deprivation. So, too, Head Start while useful in itself, does not begin to transform the deprived ghetto schools and often results in the stimulation of hopes that are then frustrated in the schools themselves. Neither the services nor the opportunities approach attempt to grapple with the elimination of the root causes of poverty.

C. *Criteria of Effectiveness*

In spite of the fact that this study was conducted at a time when most of the anti-poverty programs reviewed in depth were in operation less than two years and the fact that these programs varied in size, complexity of community in which they sought to operate, and in other factors seemingly related to success of program, an attempt was made to rank the twelve programs in order of effectiveness. Two members of the staff involved in collecting the basic data, two members with responsibility for organizing the data and writing the final report, and a member of the OEO national staff who had independent information on these programs, were asked to rank the twelve cities in terms of their own criteria of effectiveness. The cumulative rank of these five individuals was used as the basis for determining the effectiveness rank.

The ranking showed that the anti-poverty program in New Haven was considered to be the most effective program; others judged relatively effective, in order of degree of effectiveness, were Syracuse, Newark, Paterson, and Minneapolis. Programs generally considered to have determining ingredients both of effectiveness and ineffectiveness were, again in order of rank, New York City, Washington, D.C., San Francisco, and Los Angeles. The anti-poverty programs in Chicago, Cleveland, and Boston were considered to be relatively ineffective—and in that order.

A summation of the criteria used by each judge in determining the basis for ranking suggests the following prerequisites for a potentially effective anti-poverty program:

(1) a clear statement of purpose;

(2) actual programs consistent with that purpose;

(3) strong, effective and articulate leadership—staff and board—of courage, integrity, empathy, and intelligence, a board with some basis of realistic power, tight fiscal controls, and a system for determining quality, relevance, and accountability of programs;

(4) some form of involvement or representation of the poor on the staff at policy-making level;

(5) the development of dependable allies and an early confrontation with the local political and other leadership and the working out of the program either with minimum political interference and with integrity or with the political apparatus as an

ally actively protecting the integrity and effectiveness of the community action anti-poverty program;

(6) some early observable evidence of actual positive changes in the conditions of the poor.

Programs presently unclear in terms of effectiveness or judged to be relatively ineffective could be characterized as follows:

(1) lack of clarity of stated purpose;

(2) ambiguity of program in spite of clarity of verbal goals;

(3) weak, incompetent, or politically dominated board and staff;

(4) diversion of energies to preoccupation with the form rather than the substance of programs, as, for example, preoccupation with the problem of indigenous representation on boards, or the mobilizing of vast energy toward too modest goals, deluding with the appearance of activity or tendency to increase the cynicism or apathy of the poor;

(5) inadequate communication between those in the community of poverty and more privileged members of the staff and board, ineffective alliances with persons and groups with power;

(6) defeat through controversy over an internal struggle for power or retreat from community action programs in the face of direct confrontation and conflict with vested interests;

(7) failure to achieve genuine social change.

2. Implications of Evaluation

Some of the central questions that emerged in the study, as a result of an attempt to estimate relative effectiveness or ineffectiveness of community action programs, were these:

A. *What is the role of conflict and controversy in stimulating or impeding effectiveness of the community action programs?* This question is particularly important because conflict is feared by the local and federal establishments as disruptive, and cherished by many intellectual and reform-minded groups as necessary to positive change.

B. *Have the energies and resources available to community action programs been diverted or diluted?* If so, how? This question is significant as a guide to future strategy leading to greater program effectiveness.

C. *What is the extent of involvement of the poor, and has that involvement led to observable change in the conditions of the poor?* The answer to this question is vital because of the verbal focus of OEO and of many reform groups upon "maximum feasible participation" of the poor as a key to the success of the community action component of the anti-poverty program.

D. *What is the evidence of actual change in the conditions of the poor as a result of community action programs?* No community action program can be considered a success in the absence of an affirmative answer to that question.

A. *Conflict and Controversy*

The question of whether conflict and controversy are inhibiting threats to community action or invigorating stimuli to social change can be answered only by a complex response on the basis of the evidence.

When conflict has occurred in the community action programs, it has owed its impact to the presence of (1) an assumed threat to political power or other vested interests such as social agencies; (2) an organized power that resisted this threat; and (3) countervailing power that responded to the challenge. The absence of any one of these three has meant no conflict. New Haven and Cleveland prevented the emergence of threat and hence of conflict; Minneapolis has not resisted the program of its community action agency; Boston, Chicago, and Washington, D.C., produced no countervailing power within the anti-poverty program that was capable of resisting domination. But Syracuse and New York had a countervailing power in CATC and MFY, as well as assumed threat and organized resistance from the city government and some of the press.

It is necessary, however, to make a distinction between *con-*

flict, reflecting relevance of program, and *controversy,* reflecting competing vested interests seeking to control the internal apparatus of the program.

Controversy is strictly a power struggle for control of the community action program. Manifestations of this struggle were apparent initially in Newark and seemingly resolved there; in HARYOU in New York, where it tore the organization apart; in Syracuse, where it led to a schism between the public "umbrella" agency and the independent CATC, undermining the latter; in Los Angeles and Washington, D.C., where the social welfare organizations strove for control, and in San Francisco, where the representatives of the poor successfully maneuvered for dominance.

A tremendous amount of energy, not relevant specifically to the poor themselves, has been spent in this kind of controversy. In the area of power, controversy not only is not relevant to the predicament of the poor but the poor serve as pawns in a struggle in which their interests are not the primary concern. The leaders talk in the name of the poor, and extensive funds are appropriated and spent in their name without direct concern for, or serious attempts at, involvement of the poor. The argument about the indigenous and the involvement of the poor leads to competition among the non-poor for control of the poor and for the financial and potential organizational power attached to the poor. It is ironic how important the poor seem to be as an object of attention when money and power are related to their control. The presence of controversy in a community action program, therefore, does not mean that the poor will be served. Neither, however, it must be pointed out, does the absence of controversy.

While controversy is irrelevant to effectiveness, conflict, at least theoretically, is more relevant. It indicates that operation of program has reached a level of organizing of the poor through which the poor and their representatives confront the appropriate agency of government in terms of specific problems, such as education, housing or municipal services.

But, though conflict is defined here as a confrontation indicating relevance of program, its absence does not indicate the existence of ineffectiveness. New Haven exhibited minimum controversy, minimum conflict, but, relative to other programs, maximum improvement in the status of the poor. The absence of overt conflict can be noted both in some of the most effective and the most ineffective programs. It is not the case that ferment and demonstration are necessary concomitants of growth, as many suppose.

On the other hand, apparent serenity in the community action programs is in itself no evidence of civic health. The government officials who watch the summer season anxiously for riot symptoms have confused stagnation with peace, and the police who took false comfort in the decline of the violent gang failed to see that narcotics addiction, as a form of self-destruction, was as dangerous and perhaps even more long-ranging in its effects for the community as a whole than the more flamboyant expression of overt violence. But stagnation and destructive violence can coexist. In every one of the twelve cities studied, a major or a minor riot occurred in one of the summers from 1964 to 1967. Whether or not the community action program was effective seemed irrelevant to immediate civic peace.

Where conflict has been prevented in the community action programs studied here, it has been prevented by the identification of the community power structure with the action program and its consequent containment of the program. This is the case in both New Haven and Cleveland. In New Haven this strategy has led to effectiveness of at least some identifiable kind; in the case of Cleveland it has led to relative ineffectiveness. The difference in consequences in those two cities is due to (a) *the nature of the political power structure itself,* (b) *the imagination or constriction of its goals,* (c) *a sense of security or insecurity,* permitting or forbidding a certain degree of ferment without sense of threat, (d) *a commitment to social change or to the status quo,* (e) *an attitude of openness versus a resistance to ideas and experimentation in method.* In New Haven the power structure is primarily liberal-political; there was some evidence of resistance to community action on the part of professionals in the educational, civil service, and social agency establishments, but these groups were not central to the city's decisions. In Cleveland the power structure was a kind of interlocking directorate of press-social agency-school leadership with a weak political influence secondary; the action programs were neutralized and took on the conservative character of the power structure of the community itself.

One could not generalize, however, that political power is always more empathic to the poor and more daring in its programs than the school-social agency establishment, for in Syracuse political power intervened to disrupt an effective action program that had had university backing. Conflict in Syracuse was engendered by the political structure because it perceived the program as a threat, whereas in New Haven and Cleveland the community leadership was cohesive enough to contain any threat. In Boston, political power was used to dominate the program without conflict and despite elaborate initial CAP planning, little has been done to change the lives of the poor. In Chicago, political power has on the whole controlled the programs and dissipated their effectiveness. A liberal national political administration also intervened in Chicago as in Syracuse with initially curtailed program effectiveness the result. As we have seen, political resistance to community action programs is nonpartisan, particularly on the local level.

Conflict, therefore, does not necessarily mean that the poor will succeed in bringing about the desired changes. Even a direct confrontation of power can be aborted and evaded and the energies of the poor dissipated through the resilience, shrewdness, skillful parrying, intransigence, and the marshalling of superior power on the part of local political and governmental apparatus, or through federal action backing local resisting groups.

It is clear from available data that when conflicts have occurred, the consequences have not been beneficial to the poor.

The resolution of such conflicts seems invariably to be in the direction of the dilution of effective social action and a regression toward less abrasive community organization, particularly toward a substitution of social services for community action. The entire data gathered for this study reveal not a single instance in which conflict or controversy have resulted in intensification of community action or social change. On the contrary, conflict and controversy so far have meant either the stagnation or curtailment of programs as in Syracuse or the deemphasizing of programs or at least temporary return to social service, as in MFY in New York. The organized poor are not in themselves apparently able to sustain any momentum to continue the struggle once the apparatus has been diverted or diluted. Their allies in the churches and other groups tend to be exhausted or diverted or seem to be unable to sustain the necessary financial and psychological impetus. This is particularly true when the federal government either removes funds or insists that effective programs be funded through publicly controlled apparatus. This is a sign of total defeat.

In no case, then, has conflict or controversy led to effectiveness of program. But, in every case, effectiveness has been a contributing cause of conflict and potential effectiveness a contributing cause of controversy—even in HARYOU, where the effectiveness that led to controversy was potential and not actual, residing in the clarity and boldness of the plan and in the extent of funding available to support it. Although conflict has so far resulted in defeat for action, it is nevertheless evidence of ferment and potential strength and therefore to be considered a sign of community vitality and possible future change. All of the programs that were defeated or dissipated after open battle with the power structure seemed to offer more hope for genuine change than did the programs which were successfully implemented. HARYOU, MFY in New York, and CATC in Syracuse were all more daring and more promising than the programs of New Haven, Minneapolis, Newark, and Paterson: it seems clear that this fact was the major factor in the defeat of the one and the tentative success of the others. There is some evidence, moreover, that the vision of the defeated programs, and the circumstances of their defeat, have inspired and instructed the leaders of later programs.

B. *Diversion of Energies*

Energy was successfully diverted away from implementation of goals of community action programs in these twelve cities in a number of different ways. In Boston, elaborate planning and political maneuvering absorbed most of the available energy; in HARYOU, struggles for power sapped the strength of the participants; in MFY, charges of infiltration and the need to counteract them diverted resources from the main job and weakened public support; in San Francisco, the struggle for involvement of the poor in policy and leadership became the major effort with program itself secondary; in Chicago, independent protest groups directed much of their efforts to elaborate battles with worthwhile but minor goals—such as the cleaning up of a block. In Newark and Paterson, the achievement of coexistence between political power and program leadership may have given an exaggerated sense of accomplishment; in Cleveland, attempts at control of the program and defense of the *status quo* diverted much energy and resources into projects of limited potential. In Syracuse, energies were wasted in a political battle and a jurisdictional dispute with OEO.

Even the money available often served as a diversion, not only as a potential source of patronage and even of petty corruption but also as a temptation that lulled some with salaries beyond the mean of other jobs of social welfare or civic administration, taking into account the inexperience or degree of competence of many of those hired. Money so spent seemed almost an expression of community guilt or a substitute for action itself. It served also to increase the sense of alienation between the Negro poor and those Negroes who succeeded in obtaining CAP jobs and who thereby moved nearer middle-class status.

This is not to suggest that these dissipated energies were diverted through planned strategy. It is to suggest, however, that energies expended in one activity are not available for another, and that those seriously committed to social change have not succeeded in husbanding what power they do control in behalf of larger ends.

C. *Involvement of the Poor*

The community action component of the anti-poverty program assumed that the goals of the war against poverty could be attained only through the involvement of the victims of poverty themselves. The study has noted different varieties of assumptions about the nature of involvement desired, the degree of involvement possible, and the training of individuals to prepare them for effective involvement.

In all cases where a city's program has been judged relatively effective, the involvement of the poor has been an important factor but not necessarily at the level of policy-making. The poor were involved as staff in all effective programs and as participants in voter registration drives, rent strikes and the like, but the degree of their participation was guided and to a large extent controlled by leaders not themselves poor and, with only one exception, HARYOU, by leaders who did not represent the community itself. In no case of an effective program were elected poor influential in major decisions, though several programs envisioned gradual involvement of neighborhood boards at policy-making levels. The insistence on a certain proportion of poor in board or policy positions which became OEO's verbal criterion and the battle cry of many protest groups (*e.g.*, "participatory democracy"), seems to be irrelevant in practice as an index of observable change in the lives of the poor.* In

* *Note:* The CDGM Head Start Program in Mississippi, not studied for this report, may be an exception to this finding, due probably to the fact that the poor were not merely represented on boards, but were seriously involved with the board and the total program. In fact CDGM may also be an exception to the general finding that effective protest and conflict

fact, where it *was* the emphasis, programs seemed *less* effective. In HARYOU, for example, youth were represented on the board yet they proved particularly susceptible to blandishments and the outright "buying" of support by flattery or financial advantage, a weakness to be understood in terms of the predicament of the poor itself. A vote on a board is not a guarantee of independence. The poor are still poor and financially, as well as psychologically, vulnerable.

The abrasive militance often characteristic of representatives of the poor on boards is itself easily absorbed and handled by condescending indulgence. The poor are permitted to blow off steam; a proportion of agenda time is, as it were, allocated to the group therapy. But it seldom affects the outcome of policy. So, too, the passivity characteristic of other representatives of the poor weakens their effectiveness on boards. The total context of deprivation tends to lead to passivity among many who, when chosen to represent the poor, are pleased to be accepted by middle-class leadership and function with docility. Others compensate by extreme and incoherent demands or retreat into negativism. Further, the presence of a socially stratified group, a number of whom represent real power is likely to influence the opinions of those who have no power. When the president of the First National Bank or a college president, a spokesman for city hall, or a pastor with high status from a financially powerful church speaks on a community action board, he is listened to as a representative of real power and taken seriously.

The poor are self-conscious in their assigned role of "indigenous," aware that they have been involved not because of genuine acceptance of their individual worth, but as symbols of the poor, chosen for show. The poor are seen by the non-poor, on the other hand, either as exotic creatures, quaint, different in kind rather than degree from others, and controllable; or as alarming and uncontrollable. The underlying condescension and

invariably lead to the neutralization of community action programs and a retreat into non-threatening social service programs. The CDGM conflict developed after the collection of data, analysis, and writing of this report.

alienation reflects the power realities typical of any stratified authority.

The indigenous representatives are generally not taken seriously unless they demonstrate tremendous charisma or clarity of vision or articulateness, consistency, or integrity or are seen as a disruptive threat—and such persons generally have been able to use such skills to remove themselves from the status of the poor long ago. Individuals with those characteristics that would be consistent with eliciting a serious response from others have found it possible, even mandatory, to rise out of that status called indigenous into the middle class. The poor themselves often feel betrayed by or resentful of such "desertion" and reject such persons as their representatives. The artificial involvement of the poor as window dressing for programs not of their making is instinctively understood by the masses of the poor themselves and is doubtless responsible in large measure for the failure of the poor to take seriously the "elections" of representatives of the poor that have been held by a number of local governments at considerable expense and with indifferent if not disastrous results.

Where involvement of the poor has been genuine, although limited, as in Syracuse, or in the abortive conventions of the poor, the authorities have tended to fear and curtail or circumvent it, leading the poor to conclude with much justification that official plans for involvement must represent a fraud.

There is, indeed, a sense in which the "involvement" of the poor seems an attempt to draw the poor in as accessories to policy but to reject them when they challenge the central goals and the methods of traditional welfare. The relationship of governmental and private agencies to the poor has never been structured as a relationship of peers, but of clients, or patients, or delinquents.

The statutory requirement that community action programs be "developed, conducted and administered with the maximum feasible participation of residents of the areas and members of the group served" is, based on the evidence in these twelve cities, no assurance of effectiveness of these programs. The involvement of the indigenous or the clients in the operation of these programs, while theoretically and democratically sound, is more illusory than real. For one thing, the definition of the indigenous is as ambiguous as the definition of community action programs, if not more so. Techniques for the identification and selection of the indigenous who will be asked or permitted to participate in these programs are unclear. Equally unclear is the level on which the indigenous will be permitted to or required to participate in fulfillment of the statutory requirement—on the level of the board, staff, volunteer or recipient of services. The problems related to effective functioning of the poor in anti-poverty programs are many, complex, and subtle. Until these problems are faced squarely, and objective and realistic solutions to them are found, the "involvement of the poor" will remain either a sentimental gesture or another cynical exploitation of the poor which the more sophisticated indigenous will exploit as another "hustle," thereby reducing these programs to a charade and limiting their effectiveness.

D. *Actual Change in the Conditions of the Poor*

The key sign of effectiveness in an anti-poverty program is observable evidence of social change, not only the modifying of poverty itself but of the psychological context of poverty.

The obsession with the requirement of the involvement of the poor has obscured the primary goals: to alter the conditions of the poor and to abolish poverty. The anti-poverty program has tended to confuse the means with the end. It is, in effect, asking the victims of long-standing social injustice to change injustice on their own, in effect asking the sick person to get himself well. When the poor *are* involved and social change still fails, society tends to say, if you can't do it, no one else will. Although a resounding defeat for a community action program can come through irrelevance of purpose and program, through controversy and chaos, through conflict and confrontation, the most insidious defeat comes with the best intentions through the placing of the burden of transformation of society on the victims, who by virtue of the very nature of their problem, are unequipped to engage more sophisticated adversaries.

Taking into account the limitations of this study—the ambiguity of the statutory definition of community action programs and the variety of definitions which resulted, the fact that these programs were studied at a time when many of them were either in their first year or two of operation or were just beginning to operate, and the need for and difficulty in finding adequate staff to service the programs in the various cities—the data collected lead to the considered judgment that federally financed community action programs have so far not resulted in any observable changes in the predicament of the poor. The rationale and stated purposes of these programs are almost invariably action- and social-change-oriented. The actual implementation of these programs, however, almost invariably falls back on traditional social services which have been found in the past to be generally ineffective in terms of social change and, indeed, are likely to reinforce the dependency and powerlessness of the poor.

When one seeks to speculate about the reasons for this general ineffectiveness, a number of factors emerge. Foremost among them is the fact that the community action programs attempt to bring about regulated changes in the conditions of the poor by organizations financed by federal and local governmental agencies controlled by elected or appointed political officials. The factor of political control is inevitable; it is not likely even in the most effective of these programs that political and governmental officials will permit any type of program or any degree of intensity of community action program which would directly or indirectly threaten the maintenance of their own political power.

The federal government's instrument of power in influencing community action programs has been money. Appropriation has made possible the establishment of program, the indirect control of program, and the curtailing of program. In no case studied has the federal government supported a program against city or state resistance. In no case, apparently, has a program been disciplined or curtailed because of failure to change the condition of the poor. In no case studied has such effectiveness been a criterion for federal support.

Since it has become increasingly clear that a truly serious war on poverty would have to include and result in significant and observable positive changes in the predicament of the poor, the crucial question is whether such changes can occur without major modifications in the political structure and organization within which the problems of the poor develop and are perpetuated. Is it then possible for the poor to be organized effectively, for them to mobilize their power to bring about desired changes in their condition without at the same time threatening the power and the privilege of the privileged community and the political officials who represent the community of privileged? So far, the data of this study and general observations would seem to provide negative answers to these questions.

More relevant to program effectiveness than involvement of the poor as representatives on policy-making boards seems to be the degree of independence of the community action program itself. In Syracuse, Newark, and Paterson the successful programs were sponsored by independent corporations: CATC in Syracuse with support of the university and federal funding but with independent leadership; Newark's United Community Corporation originally designed as an independent agency with consulting area boards; Paterson's Task Force for Community Action operating independently. But in Syracuse the program was derailed because of its independence; in Newark and Paterson city officials were on the board and involved in policy, and the effective leaders of both groups have resigned. The extent and continuance of the program's independence is not yet clear. The New Haven program was not independent structurally but its independence of spirit was supported by a city administration which found its program useful to its own ends and therefore protected the integrity of the program. It is not yet clear whether the resignation of the director will have a negative impact on this relatively successful program.

The goal of obtaining meaningful, sustained, and positive changes in the conditions of the poor would seem to require the identification, development, and use of techinques through which the latent power of the poor is mobilized and organized for sustained action on their own behalf without interference from government. This recognition of the relationship between the organization and use of power of disadvantaged people and the attainment of social change poses a number of problems. Among them is the determination of the nature, depth, and extent of potential power of the disadvantaged:

Is the maximum power inherent or available to the poor sufficient to attain the desired social change in the face of the resistance and power which can be mobilized by more advantaged people?

What are the limits of social change which the advantaged, affluent, and powerful will permit for the disadvantaged?

So far, the data suggest that the threshold of tolerability for significant changes in the predicament of the poor is rather low for politicians and may be somewhat higher but not particularly high for middle-class professionals and even those staff members who are charged with the responsibility for directing community action and other programs on behalf of the poor. Generally, the staff members responsible for these programs are directly responsible to political officials or those in control of traditional social service agencies. And almost invariably these staff members tend to identify with the middle class in style, speech, dress, education, and the types of methods considered acceptable or unacceptable for achievement of social change. This identification with middle-class patterns tends to result either in the maintenance of the status quo or in the restriction of community action programs to techniques and methods acceptable to the middle class, thereby limiting the rate or the amount of change permitted to the poor.

An inescapable present fact is that the poor are powerless.

Their powerlessness is reflected not only in their present disadvantaged predicament, but also in the fact that the poor at present are not able to plan, regulate, or determine their own community action programs. The poor must, therefore, inevitably depend upon surrogates as an avenue to power. The surrogates upon which the poor at present depend are middle-class individuals in staff leadership roles in programs for the poor, but the poor have not been educated to confront such individuals in any systematic or rational way even when there is flagrant evidence that the interest of the poor has been subordinated to the maintenance of the status quo. The poor can be exploited flagrantly or subtly even by those programs that are designed for their benefit and even by programs designed to protect them from the abuses of governmental programs.

Politicians, social workers, social scientists, community actionists, and some indigenous workers have all benefitted to one degree or another from anti-poverty programs. The poor seem to have benefitted less.

The general ineffectiveness of CAP anti-poverty programs studied—the general absence of any observable improvement in the conditions of the poor and any evidence of social change—has led to various attempts to protect the interest of the poor: they have sought to counter:

(1) indecisiveness and inconsistencies of the federal OEO administration;

(2) local political control which seeks to limit the extent of political organization and power of the poor;

(3) maladministration of the local anti-poverty programs;

(4) the power of social agencies and allied civic groups seeking to maintain these programs in traditional social services orientation and control.

In some cities *ad hoc* groups of the poor, or a coalition of civil rights groups, have been set up to monitor the administration of poverty programs. Civil rights groups have, however, generally not proved particularly effective monitors of anti-poverty programs either because of indifference, inadequacy of staff, or because their local leaders have been co-opted onto the governing boards of these programs.

Saul Alinsky has organized the poor as a counterforce to the anti-poverty programs in a few cities. There is, however, no evidence that the Alinsky approach, in spite of the extensive publicity and success in a few skirmishes with power groups, has contributed to any observable changes of real significance in the basic conditions of the poor in those communities in which he has worked.

In some communities independent coalition between organized churches and the poor has attempted to counteract the ineffectiveness of the community action programs. These coalitions have been characterized by marked dedication and commitment of the professionals and/or students, by active involvement of some selected poor, and by the psychological gratification of relevant effort, but so far there has been little evidence that they have been able to influence positively the dicisions and actions of the anti-poverty programs' boards or staffs or to change basic conditions of poverty in their cities.

Conferences or Councils of the Poor have also been organized in an attempt to provide a forum for the poor. These conferences are generally initiated by professionals who seek to involve the poor—the more articulate poor—in an essentially middle-class approach to dealing with problems; namely, discussions, resolutions, and organizations for follow-up. So far these conferences have not demonstrated the ability to do anything other than to provide some of the more vocal poor with an opportunity to release some of their hostility and frustrations. There is little evidence of effective follow-up.

The Citizens' Crusade Against Poverty, a national organization which seeks to protect the poor and provide the machinery for follow-up, intends to use both protest and program in order to see that the government's anti-poverty program is run in the interest of the poor. Its top sponsors included Walter Reuther and Martin Luther King. It is not yet clear how effective the

Citizens' Crusade approach can be without involvement in a direct political battle, or without contamination from the influences it was organized to combat.

Since the preparation of the main body of this report, a union of public welfare recipients has been organized, under the leadership of George Wiley, former associate director of CORE, and Richard Cloward; its purpose is to see that welfare recipients are not short-changed by local welfare administrators and that their rights as citizens are not abridged or ignored.

Without regard to such individual or collective effectiveness in protecting the interest of the poor, the existence and proliferation of these independent programs testify to the fact that the present anti-poverty programs are generally perceived to be ineffective. This judgment seems to be justified by the available evidence assembled for this report.

3. *A Coalition of Professionals and the Poor*

The poor themselves have so far not been able to plan, sustain, and bring to a positive conclusion effective programs for social change. To expect that they can—as so many community action programs do—may be viewed as a subtle rationalization for the maintenance of the *status quo* in the face of inevitable failure. The alternative may be for concerned, committed, and independent professionals to develop machinery and organizations which would mobilize the power of intelligence and concern on behalf of the poor. These surrogates would be required to work in a systematic, sustained, and diligent manner as if they were working on behalf of themselves, as indeed they are if one accepts the view that the problems which affect the poor affect the stability of the entire society and the future of all persons—in fact, the general public welfare. To the extent possible, in view of the erosion and distortion of energy inherent in poverty, realistic programs would be developed to train and provide the poor with the necessary skills for realistic confrontation of public officials, and for rational, systematic social and political action until the professional is no longer necessary or until his role is determined by decision of the people.

In a program that utilizes such professionals, special skills will be needed:

(a) the ability to operate without a condescension which contributes to powerlessness and dependency;

(b) the ability to maximize whatever power does reside within the poor; and

(c) the ability to define as accurately as possible what power is really there.

The ultimate skill of the leader is demonstrated by the extent to which he is no longer required. There is latent power in the poor—not merely the power of life, but a level of energy that is really harnessable—and the leader must mobilize these energies and sustain them until change is effected. If there is sufficient energy among the poor, such mobilization would require not just organization of the poor, but observable external changes coincident with the harnessing of energy. The experience of the past has indicated that the community of poverty is debilitating and that those who can mobilize the energy to escape do so. This natural process will continue. Therefore it follows that realistic organization of the community of poverty cannot be done with static continuation of that community. There must be concomitant evidence of changes in the conditions of poverty and ultimately an end to poverty itself. The failure to produce such evidence is that rock on which anti-poverty programs fail.

The alternative to such a realistic systematic program of empathic and non-exploitative use of intelligence and power would seem to be a continuation of the frustrations of the poor and the perpetuation of the capricious threats of urban eruptions, riots, and rebellions.

It is reasonable to speculate that the frustrations of disadvantaged peoples are increased when verbal promises are not followed within a reasonable time by observable positive changes. These programs have made promises they have so far not been able to fulfill. The available evidence strongly suggests that they are not likely to be able to fulfill these promises. The failure of the community action phase of the anti-poverty programs as presently constituted has contributed significantly to the fuel of urban conflagration, increased the power of demagogues, and added to the restlessness, the alienation, and the sense of hopelessness of the deprived. Such ingredients make for profound social instability. Serious and considered analysis of the data of this study lead to the inescapable conclusion that only the development of an empathic, identified, independent coalition of trained, intelligent, committed professionals and the poor can increase the chances of a successful war against poverty and reduce the chances of social chaos. Yet even such a coalition must function in light of the probability that deprivation in many areas, such as education and employment, may not be responsive to programs of amelioration and community action. The problems of poverty cannot be resolved as if they were isolated from the wider economic, social and political patterns of the nation.

Afterword:
A Theory of Power

One of the noticeable lacks in all of the proposals for community action studied and all of the statements of goals and methods is any rationale based on a systematic philosophical and psychological theory of the effective uses of social power. The failure of social scientists to develop such a theory upon which strategy can be based doubtless contributes significantly to the ineffectiveness of the present programs. If one does not understand what power is and how it is achieved, sustained, and utilized, it is easy to stumble up blind alleys into sentimentality or cynicism.

If power is defined as that energy necessary to create, to sustain, or to prevent observable social change, it becomes immediately clear that the poor are powerless and that community action programs have not succeeded where the poor have failed.

A number of tentative premises might be derived from such a theory of power: (1) that power is amoral, capable of rational or irrational, constructive or destructive uses; (2) that power implies the possibilities of choice and decision and the ability to implement such decisions; (3) that power may be manifested in psuedo-forms that are illusory and cannot prevail in the face of conflict, or latent forms that may respond to challenge or active forms mobilized for defense of choice; (4) that power operates by laws of economy, exerting no more energy than necessary to deal with challenge unless the power-holder itself is not stable or sane; (5) that power operates by laws of response, selecting the form and intensity to meet the nature of crisis; (6) that power can be non-functional, withheld by non-decision or hoarding, or atrophied by disuse, or inert due to inhibition of conflicting interests; (7) that power cannot be voluntarily transferred or shared and that the attempt to do so may reflect the sharing of appearence rather than substance of power; (8) that clusters of power tend to operate in dynamic gestalt in any integrated and efficient social system, usually reacting to threats by mobilization and defense or offense, but sometimes reacting by the incorporation of change and by an increase in the integrity and stability of the system.

All such premises are implied in the evidence revealed in this study of community action programs. They need to be tested further, and other premises need to be postulated, as for example on the nature of conflict, of victory and defeat, of acquiescence and accommodation, on the nature of progress itself. Without such rational understanding of the phenomena of power and of social change, much trial and error and waste motion can consume the energies of society and reinforce the tragedy of the deprived, whose lives are the object of society's random experimentation.

Appendix

Outline of a Community Action Program

What Is Community Action?

The Community Action Programs will provide technical and financial assistance for urban and rural communities to fight poverty. Individual communities will decide how to do the job with private and public resources that will be augmented by this new Federal assistance.

The problems of poverty are a network of social ills like illiteracy, unemployment, poor health and dilapidated housing. To alleviate them will require a network of anti-poverty attacks that are varied while they are coordinated. This combination—fashioned by local talent and leadership—is the major aim of the Community Action Programs.

Specifically, remedial reading, literacy courses, job training, employment counseling, homemaker services, job development and training, vocational rehabilitation, health services are only some of the individual programs that can be supported and coordinated with a detailed local anti-poverty program.

In the past, many of these separate programs have been scattered and uncoordinated. A remedial reading program, for example, has limited effect if there is no literacy program to permit the parent to guide and help his child. Both programs have limited effect if the parents have no marketable skills and live in squalor. A program that addresses all of these difficulties in a systematic fashion will truly help that child and his family to remove the shackles of poverty. And this is the intent of Community Action.

The Federal Government will help local communities to develop and support these anti-poverty programs. However, Federal assistance will depend on the community's determination to:

1. Mobilize its own public and private resources for this attack.
2. Develop programs of sufficient scope and size that give promise of eliminating a cause or causes of poverty.
3. Involve the poor themselves in developing and operating the anti-poverty programs.
4. Administer and coordinate the Community Action Programs through public or private non-profit agencies or a combination of these.

In smaller communities and in those with more limited resources, local leaders can begin a Community Action Program in stages. For example, a community might start with a pre-school program coupled with a health service clinic for these youngsters. These would be followed by other specific programs all linked to each other in a coordinated campaign.

All local programs should use the talents of persons living in and affected by the poverty-stricken neighborhoods in planning and operating programs. As workers in projects, they could be used as aides to professionals, as recreational and day care assistants, and as helpers in homemaker and health services. Some other examples are community research aides, library aides, tutoring assistants, probation aides, and family service workers.

Further, Community Action Programs should see that existing local, State and Federal programs are linked to each other in a concentrated drive against poverty. Assistance now available to States and local communities under the Manpower Development and Training Act, the 1962 Public Welfare Amendments, vocation education, and the various programs under the Housing and Home Finance Agency all should be joined with any total community anti-poverty effort.

Community Action Programs, in short, will fuse the old, scattered programs while providing the technical and financial assistance to initiate the new attack against the varied problems that have ensnared the poor.

What Kind of Programs Might Be Developed?

Community Action Programs will vary as the needs of the people vary in different parts of the nation. They must be part of a total effort to help people escape poverty, not to make it more bearable. Here are some illustrations that might be part of a Community Action Program:

1. Service and activities to develop new employment opportunities;
2. Providing special and remedial education, with particular emphasis on reading, writing, and mathematics;*
3. Providing comprehensive academic counseling and guidance services and school social work services;
4. Providing after-school study centers, after-school tutoring, and summer, weekend and after-school academic classes;
5. Establishing programs for the benefit of pre-school children;
6. Reducing adult illiteracy;
7. Developing and carrying out special education or other programs for migrant or transient families;
8. Improving the living conditions of the elderly;
9. Arranging for or providing health examinations and health education for school children;
10. Rehabilitation and retraining of physically or mentally handicapped persons;
11. Providing health, rehabilitation, employment, educational and related services to young men not qualified for military services;
12. Providing community child-care centers and youth activity centers;
13. Improving housing and living facilities and home management skills;
14. Providing services to enable families from rural areas to meet problems of urban living;
15. Providing recreation and physical fitness services and facilities.

Excerpts from memo,
President's Task Force on
War Against Poverty,
Office of Economic Opportunity,
Community Action Programs,
Washington, D.C., August 21, 1964

* General aid to elementary or secondary education in any school or school system is prohibited by the legislation, and thus funds could not be provided for general reduction in class size, school construction, general teachers' salaries (as opposed to those special remedial reading instructors), religious instruction, or established curriculum.

Index

ABCD (Action for Boston Community Development)
  See 'Boston'
ACT (Associated Community Teams), 220
Action for Boston Community Development (ABCD)
  See 'Boston'
Ad Hoc Students Committee
  See 'San Francisco'
Addams, Jane, 78
AFL-CIO, 193, 195
Alinsky, Saul, 127, 175, 253
  and CCAP (Syracuse), 200
  criticism of, 145–146, 147, 148, 181
  and New Haven CATC, 153
  and The Woodlawn Organization (Chicago), 178 ff., 228
American Negro Association
  See 'Newark'
Appalachia, 194
Asbury Park (N.J.)
  community action programs, 62
Athens (Ga.)
  community action programs, 62

Back Yards programs
  See 'Chicago'
Baltimore (Md.)
  community action programs, 62
Baptists, American, 174
Barbourville (Ky.)
  community action programs, 62
Baxley (Ga.)
  community action programs, 62
Black Nationalists, 115
Blake, Eugene Carson, 201
Boone, Richard W., 199, 200, 202
Boston (Mass.)
  Action for Boston Community Development (ABCD), 94, 177
    and Roxbury–North Dorchester *Ad Hoc* Committee, 177–178
  board of education, 68
  community action programs, 12, 136, 160, 233, 239, 242, 244
    effectiveness, 210, 211, 226, 237
    goals, 27–28, 40–41, 50–51, 176, 228–229
  "Operation Exodus," 177
  Roxbury–North Dorchester *Ad Hoc* Committee, 177–178
  Roxbury–North Dorchester Parents Committee for Better Schools, 177
  Roxbury North Dorchester South End Parents Association, 177
  School Committee, 177
Bowser, Charles W., 113
Boy Scouts, 72
Brandon, Everett P., 122
Bridgeport (Conn.) community action programs, 62

Brooks, Deton, 32, 43
Brown, Rap, 169

Cade, Grace, 190, 192
Cardoza Project
  See 'Washington, D.C.—UPO'
CATC ([Syracuse University] Community Action Training Center)
  See 'Syracuse'
Cavanagh, Jerome (mayor, Detroit), 142
CAY (Cleveland Action for Youth)
  See 'Cleveland'
CCACCAP (Citizens' Committee for an Adequate Cleveland Community Action Program)
  See 'Cleveland'
CCAP (Citizens' Crusade Against Poverty)
  See 'Syracuse'
CCC
CCUO (Chicago Committee on Urban Opportunity)
  See 'Chicago'
CDGM (Child Development Group of Mississippi), 245*n.*–246*n.*
CEO (Council for Economic Opportunity)
  See 'Cleveland'
CFO (Crusade for Opportunity)
  See 'Syracuse'
Chattanooga (Tenn.)
  community action programs, 62
Chicago (Ill.)
  anti-poverty board appointments, 111
  Back Yards programs, 178
  board of education, 68
  Chicago Committee on Urban Opportunity (CCUO), 43
  Commission on Youth Welfare (CYW), 44, 49, 94, 95
    Neighborhood Extension Service, 169
Chicago (Ill.) (*Cont.*)
  community action programs, 12, 133, 136, 152, 167, 233, 239, 242, 244
    effectiveness, 210, 211, 226, 227–228, 237
  Joint Youth Development Committee, 49
  and Martin Luther King, 228
  PLUNGE (lay clergy program), 176
  SDS, 176, 188–189, 228
  Urban League, 171
  Urban Training Center, 48
  The Woodlawn Organization (TWO), 54, 85, 126, 153, 176, 228
    activities, 179
    and the churches, 174
    formation, 178
    rationale, 179–180
Chicago Committee on Urban Opportunity (CCUO)
  See 'Chicago'
Chicago, University of, 189
Church of Christ, 182
Cincinnati (O.)
  Community Action Commission, 92
  community action programs, 63
Citizen Participation Committee
  See 'New Haven—CPI'
Citizens' Committee for an Adequate Cleveland Community Action Program (CCACCAP)
  See 'Cleveland'
Citizens' Crusade Against Poverty (CCAP)
  See 'Syracuse'
Civilian Conservation Corps (CCC), 3
Cleveland, 166, 167, 223
  board of education, 68
  Citizens' Committee for an Adequate Cleveland Community Action Program (CCACCAP), 176, 182

Cleveland (*Cont.*)
Citizens' Committee for an Adequate Cleveland Community Action Program (CCACCAP) (*Cont.*)
and CEO, 185, 187
formation, 185
and GCNCA, 187
and PMP, 182, 185
purposes, 185–186
Cleveland Action for Youth (CAY), 40–41, 53, 94–95, 161
organization and leadership, 162 ff.
community action programs, 12, 21, 60, 133, 160, 233, 239, 241, 242, 244
effectiveness, 210, 211, 226, 227, 237
CORE, 169
Council for Economic Opportunity (CEO), 165, 182, 185, 187
Greater Cleveland Neighborhood Centers Association (GCNCA), 187
NAACP, 164, 168, 170
and OEO, 187–188
Protestant Ministry to Poverty (PMP), 168, 174–175, 176, 185, 187
and CCACCAP, 182, 185
formation, 181
goals, 182
organization, 181–182
Urban League, 164, 166, 168, 170
Cleveland Action for Youth (CAY)
See 'Cleveland'
Cloward, Richard, 200, 254
Cloward, Richard, and Lloyd Ohlin, *Delinquency and Opportunity: A Theory of Delinquent Gangs,* 29–30
Collins, John (mayor, Boston), 79
Columbia (Mo.)
community action programs, 63
Columbia University Mobilization for Youth Training Institute Workshop, 149*n.*
Commission on Youth Welfare (CYW)
See 'Chicago'
Committee to Preserve Racial Peace
See 'Newark'
"The Community Action Agency and Resident Participation"
See 'National Association for Community Development'
Community Action Commission
See 'Cincinnati'
Community Action Training Center (CATC)
See 'Syracuse'
Community Progress, Inc. (CPI)
See 'New Haven'
Conway, Jack T., 195
Coordination Council of Community Organizations
See 'Chicago'
CORE (Congress of Racial Equality), 112, 170
Also, see under specific cities
Corinth (Miss.)
community action programs, 62
Corpus Christi (Tex.)
community action programs, 63
Council for Economic Opportunity (CEO)
See 'Cleveland'
CPI (Community Progress, Inc.)
See 'New Haven'
Craven Operation Progress
See 'New Bern'
Crusade for Opportunity (CFO)
See 'Syracuse'
CYW (Commission on Youth Welfare)
See 'Chicago'

Dade County (Miami) (Fla.)
community action programs, 62
Daley, Richard (mayor, Chicago), 79, 155, 179, 228

Davis, Rennie, 188
Delinquency and Opportunity: A Theory of Delinquent Gangs (Richard Cloward and Lloyd Ohlin), 29–30
"The Demonstration as a Strategy of Change" (S. M. Miller and Morton Fein), 149, 183–184
Denver (Colo.)
community action programs, 63
Detroit (Mich.)
community action programs, 14, 63
Mayor's Committee, Total Action Against Poverty, 92
Urban League, 171
Detroit Metropolitan Fund
community action programs, 63
Durham (No. Car.)
community action programs, 62

Economic Information Service, 193
Economic Opportunities Development Corporation
See 'San Antonio'
Economic Opportunity Act of 1964, 21, 26, 69, 76, 122, 199
its passage, 11
Title I B, 99
Title I C, 99
Title II A, Section 202, 6–7, 22, 234
Title II B, 99–100
Economic and Youth Opportunities Agency (EYOA)
See 'Los Angeles'
Eloise (Mich.)
community action programs, 63
Emergency Relief, 3
EYOA (Economic and Youth Opportunities Agency)
See 'Los Angeles'

Fein, Morton, and S. M. Miller, "The Demonstration as a Strategy of Change," 149, 183–184
Findley, Ralph, 164, 187
Ford Foundation, 156, 169, 199
4H, 72
Frankel, Hy, 40

Gainesville (Ga.)
community action programs, 62
GATEWAY
See 'St. Louis'
GCNCA (Greater Cleveland Neighborhood Centers Association)
See 'Cleveland'
Gila River Indians (Ariz.)
community action programs, 63
Girl Scouts, 72
"Good Samaritan–Lady Bountiful Tradition" (of social welfare), 19–20, 27
Greater Cleveland Neighborhood Centers Association (GCNCA)
See 'Cleveland'

Haggstrom, Warren C., 85, 86, 180
Harlan (Ky.)
community action programs, 62
Harlem Youth Opportunities Unlimited (HARYOU)
See 'New York City'
Harrington, Michael, 195
Hartford (Conn.)
community action programs, 62
HARYOU (Harlem Youth Opportunities Unlimited)
See 'New York City'
HARYOU-ACT
See 'New York City'
Head Start, 60, 66, 182, 201, 235, 236, 245*n.*–246*n.*
Henry, Aaron, 202
House of Representatives, 223
Housing and Home Finance Agency, 262
Houston (Tex.)
community action programs, 37
Hunter, David, 9

Hunters Point Youth Opportunity Center
  See 'San Francisco'
Hyden (Ky.)
  community action programs, 62

Industrial Areas Foundation, 200
Inter-Religious Committee Against Poverty, 174

Johnson, Lyndon B., 190, 194, 202
  message on poverty to Congress (March 16, 1964), 2, 3, 6, 236
JOIN (Job Orientation in Neighborhoods), 188
Joint Youth Development Committee
  See 'Chicago'
Juneau (Alaska)
  community action programs, 63

Kennedy, John F., 202
  and juvenile delinquency, 3–4
Kennedy, Robert
  and PCJD, 4
Keyser (W. Va.)
  community action programs, 62
King, Martin Luther, 169, 228, 253
Knoll, Erwin, and Jules Witcover, "Politics and the Poor . . .," 155, 155*n.*, 190, 190*n.*

Lafayette (La.)
  community action programs, 62
LaGrange (Ga.)
  community action programs, 62
Lansing (Mich.)
  community action programs, 63
Lapp, Ralph, 202
Lee, Richard (mayor, New Haven), 135
Leech Lake Reservation (Minn.)
  community action programs, 63
Locher, Ralph (mayor, Cleveland), 165
Long, Norton E.
  on Saul Alinsky, 181
Los Angeles, 223
  anti-poverty board appointments, 111
  community action programs, 12, 120, 121, 167, 233, 240
    effectiveness, 211, 225, 237
    goals, 27–28, 33, 38, 42
  Economic and Youth Opportunities Agency (EYOA), 33, 92, 93, 119
  NAACP, 226
  United Civil Rights Committee (NAACP, CORE, SCLC, SNCC, Urban League, et al.), 168
  Urban League, 226
  Watts, 168, 194, 225
  Youth Opportunities Board (YOB), 93
Louisville (Ky.)
  community action programs, 62

Malcolm X, 6
Manpower Development and Training Act, 262
Marburger, Carl, 142
Marshall Field's, 179
McGuire, Edward, 155*n.*
Methodist Church, 174
MFY (Mobilization for Youth)
  See 'New York City'
Miller, S. M., and Morton Fein, "The Demonstration as a Strategy of Change," 149, 183–184
Milwaukee (Wisc.)
  community action programs, 63
Minneapolis (Minn.)
  community action programs, 12, 133, 170–171, 233, 239, 243
    effectiveness, 211, 217, 237
    goals, 29, 37, 51
  NAACP, 170–171
  Urban League, 171
  Youth Development Program (YDP), 30–31, 32, 171
Mobilization for Youth (MFY)
  See 'New York City'
Mogulof, Melvin B., 122

Moriarty, Robert T., 118
Muslims, 115

NAACP (National Association for the Advancement of Colored People)
See under specific city
National Association for the Advancement of Colored People (NAACP)
See under specific city
National Association for Community Development
position paper, "The Community Action Agency and Resident Participation," 75–77, 98, 108–109, 123, 156–158
National Association of Social Workers, 77
National Capital Area Health and Welfare Council, 105
National Catholic Welfare Conference, 174
National Council of Churches, 174, 182
National Farmers Union, 201
National Institute of Mental Health, 106
National Urban League, 110, 170
National Youth Administration, 3
Navaho Tribe (Ariz.)
community action programs, 63
Neighborhood Advancement Service
See 'Syracuse—CFO'
Neighborhood Extension Service
See 'Chicago—CYW'
New Bedford (Mass.)
community action programs, 62
New Bern (No. Car.)
community action programs, 62
Craven Operation Progress, 32
New Deal, 3, 20
New Haven (Conn.)
anti-poverty programs and the churches, 172 ff.
New Haven (Conn.) (*Cont.*)
community action program, 12, 124, 133, 158, 233, 239, 241–242, 243, 250
effectiveness, 210, 211, 212, 213, 237
goals, 27, 29, 33–34, 38, 44
Community Progress, Inc. (CPI), 92, 93, 94, 110
activities, 80–81
Citizen Participation Committee, 80–81, 138
CORE and NAACP, 138, 144, 169
expansion provisions, 98–101, 103, 137–138
and "participation," 137, 138, 145–148
its paternalism, 149–150
political orientation, 135–136, 139–145, 149, 151, 160, 161
rationale, 134–135, 136–137
New Rochelle (N.Y.)
community action programs, 62
New York City (N.Y.)
anti-poverty board appointments, 111
community action programs, 12, 15, 101, 176, 209, 233
effectiveness, 211, 218–222, 237
Harlem Youth Opportunities Unlimited (HARYOU), 4–6, 34–36, 80, 81, 166–167, 175, 184, 240, 243, 245, 246
document, *Youth in the Ghetto,* 5–6, 13, 35, 36, 38, 61, 68, 79, 215, 218
its recommendations, 5
reviewed by PCJD, 5–6
effectiveness, 8, 34, 35–36, 39
funded by PCJD, 4
Project Uplift, 171
rationale, 8, 34, 35–36, 39
and Urban League, 171
HARYOU-ACT, 220–221

New York City (N.Y.) (*Cont.*)
Mobilization for Youth (MFY), 4, 5, 34–35, 49, 68, 72, 79, 160, 161, 176, 218 ff., 239, 243, 244
activities, 80–81
effectiveness, 218 ff.
rationale, 8, 30, 34–35, 39, 46, 51
People's War Council Against Poverty, 190
Urban League, 171
New York *Herald Tribune,* 117–118, 195, 219
New York *Post,* 195
New York Times, 105, 119, 120, 122, 195, 199 ff., 219
New York *World Telegram and Sun,* 219
Newark (N.J.)
American Negro Association, 171
Committee to Preserve Racial Peace, 171
community action programs, 12, 36, 124, 133, 152, 161, 233, 240, 243, 244
CORE, 171
NAACP, 171
United Community Corporation (UCC), 250
effectiveness, 211, 215–216, 237
structure, 152, 171
Urban League, 171
NYA
See 'National Youth Administration'

Oakland (Calif.)
community action programs, 63
Office of Economic Opportunity (OEO), 9, 21, 23, 30, 31, 106, 112, 113, 120, 121–122, 125, 127, 144, 152, 153, 155, 156 ff., 174, 175, 190, 192, 196, 209, 210, 214, 220, 227, 233, 234, 236, 239, 244, 245, 252
and Boston, 228, 229
and Cleveland, 187–188
funds Syracuse Crusade for Opportunity, 83, 154–155
PCJD programs transferred to, 11
President's Task Force memo (1964), 261–263
Workbook, 75–77, 98, 106, 108, 123
Ohlim, Lloyd, and Richard Cloward, *Delinquency and Opportunity: A Theory of Delinquent Gangs,* 29–30
Omaha (Neb.)
community action programs, 63
Oneida-Scott County Community Action Program
See 'San Antonio'
"Operation Exodus"
See 'Boston'

PAAC (Philadelphia Anti-Poverty Action Committee)
See 'Philadelphia'
Palace Hotel (San Francisco), 168
Paterson (N.J.)
community action programs, 12, 36, 133, 161, 197, 233, 243, 244
Task Force for Community Action, 81, 250
effectiveness, 211, 215–217, 237
organization, 150–152
political orientation, 150, 160
Patton, James G., 201
PCJD: See 'President's Committee on Juvenile Delinquency'
Peace Corps, 200
Pennsylvania, University of, 111

People's Convention for the Total Participation of the Poor
See 'Syracuse'
People's War Council Against Poverty
See 'New York City,' 'Syracuse'
Philadelphia (Pa.)
anti-poverty election program, 111–118, 119, 120
Philadephia Anti-Poverty Action Committee (PAAC), 111 ff.
Urban League, 112, 171
Philadelphia Anti-Poverty Action Committee (PAAC)
See 'Philadelphia"
Pittsburgh (Pa.)
anti-poverty board appointments, 111
community action programs, 14, 62
PLUNGE
See 'Chicago'
"The Plunge," 48
PMP (Protestant Ministry to Poverty)
See 'Cleveland'
"Politics and the Poor: Shriver's Second Thoughts" (Jules Witcover and Erwin Knoll), 155, 155*n.*, 190, 190*n.*
Populist movement, 20
Powell, Adam Clayton, 79–80, 164, 182, 184, 216, 220–221
President's Committee on Juvenile Delinquency (PCJD), 3–4, 9, 10, 20, 21, 50, 82, 175, 199, 218, 220, 222
and HARYOU, 4–6
programs transferred to OEO, 11
Project Uplift
See 'New York City—HARYOU'
"Promoting Participation of the Poor: Philadelphia's Unique Anti-Poverty Program" (Arthur B. Shostak), 111 ff.
"Prophet Amos–New Deal Tradition" (of social welfare), 20
Protestant Ministry to Poverty (PMP)
See 'Cleveland'
Public Welfare Amendments (1962), 262
"Puritan–Horatio Alger Tradition" (of social welfare), 19, 20

Quadri-Science, Inc., 202

Raby, Albert, 169, 228
Reuther, Walter, 195, 199, 253
Riessman, Frank, 181
Ripley (Mo.)
community action programs, 63
Riverside (Calif.)
community action programs, 63
Rockefeller Foundation, 110
Roman Catholic Church, 175
Roosevelt, Franklin D., 3
Roxbury–North Dorchester *Ad Hoc* Committee
See 'Boston'
Roxbury–North Dorchester Parents Committee for Better Schools
See 'Boston'
Roxbury North Dorchester South End Parents Association
See 'Boston'
Rustin, Bayard, 144

Sacramento (Calif.)
community action programs, 63
St. Louis (Mo.)
community action programs, 14, 63
GATEWAY, 33
San Antonio (Tex.)
Economic Opportunities Development Corporation, 32
Oneida-Scott County Community Action Program, 92
San Francisco (Calif.)
Ad Hoc Students Committee, 168
community action programs, 12, 120–123, 160, 233, 240, 244

San Francisco (Calif.) (*Cont.*)
Community action programs (*Cont.*)
effectiveness, 211, 224–225, 237
goals, 33
CORE, 168
Hunters Point Youth Opportunity Center, 39–40, 41, 49, 51–52
United Negro Freedom Movement, 168
SANE (National Committee for a Sane Nuclear Policy), 202
Santa Clara County (Calif.)
community action programs, 63
Savannah (Ga.)
community action programs, 63
SAY (Syracuse Action for Youth)
See 'Syracuse'
SCDA (Syracuse Community Development Association)
See 'Syracuse'
SCLC
See 'Southern Christian Leadership Conference'
Screvane, Paul, 219
SDS
See 'Students for a Democratic Society'
Senate Select Subcommittee on Poverty, 200
Shelley, John F. (mayor, San Francisco), 122
Shostak, Arthur B., 111
Shottland, Charles I., 77
Shriver, Sargent, 146, 190, 195, 196, 214, 225
SNCC (Student Nonviolent Coordinating Committee), 168, 169, 171
Social Dynamics Research Institute, 9
Southern Christian Leadership Conference (SCLC), 168, 169
Spock, Benjamin, 202
Springfield (Mass.)
community action programs, 62
Stamford (Conn.)
community action programs, 62
Stanley, Frank, 171
Stern Family Fund, 9, 233
Stokes, Carl (mayor, Cleveland), 165, 226
Students for a Democratic Society (SDS), 170, 176, 182
and Chicago, 188–189, 228
Svirdoff, Mitchell, 135
Swarthmore (Penn.), 193
Synagogue Council of America, 174
Syracuse (N.Y.)
anti-poverty programs and the churches, 172 ff.
Citizens' Crusade Against Poverty (CCAP), 54, 177
formation, 198
organization and program, 199–204, 253–254
"poor people's convention," 194 ff.
community action programs, 12, 15, 119, 133, 151, 152, 160, 176, 196, 209, 211, 233, 242, 243, 244, 247
goals, 28
(Syracuse University) Community Action Training Center (CATC), 37, 52–53, 79, 81 84, 85, 86, 87, 88, 101–102, 219, 220, 239, 240, 243, 250
and CFO, 187
and civil rights groups, 169
development, funding, functions, 83–84, 156
effectiveness, 211, 212, 213–215, 237
and Episcopal Diocese, 174
and People's War Council, 190
political involvement, 153–154, 161
rationale, 153
and Saul Alinsky, 153
takes over research and training component of SAY

Syracuse (N.Y.) (*Cont.*)
(Syracuse University) Community Action Training Center (CATC) (*Cont.*)
Community Development, 83
voter registration drive, 152–153
CORE, 169
Crusade for Opportunity (CFO), 44, 79, 82, 83, 158, 161–162, 187, 214
Neighborhood Advancement Service, 44, 79
organization and functions, 88, 154–155
supplants SAY, 83
NAACP, 169
People's War Council Against Poverty
formation, 154, 177, 190
and People's Convention for the Total Participation of the Poor, 190 ff.
Syracuse Action for Youth (SAY), 49
Community Development program, 49–50, 83
becomes CFO, 83, and SCDA, 83
funded by PCJD, 82
proposals, 82–83
Syracuse Community Development Association (SCDA), 81–82, 190
formation, funding, functions, 83, 88, 154, 156
takes over action component of SAY Community Development, 83
Syracuse Action for Youth (SAY)
See 'Syracuse'
Syracuse Community Development Association (SCDA)
See 'Syracuse'
Syracuse University, 83, 84, 169
Tacoma (Wash.)
community action programs, 63
Task Force for Community Action
See 'Paterson'
Temple University, 117
trade union movement, 20, 184–185
Trenton (N.J.)
community action programs, 14, 118–119
United Progress, Inc., (UPI)
goals, 109–110
Tulare County Community Action Agency
See 'Visalia (Calif.)'
TWO (The Woodlawn Organization)
See 'Chicago'

UAW
See 'United Auto Workers'
UCC (United Community Corporation)
See 'Newark'
United Auto Workers (UAW), 195, 199
United Church of Christ, 174
United Church Women, 174
United Civil Rights Committee
See 'Los Angeles'
United Community Corporation (UCC)
See 'Newark'
United Negro Freedom Movement
See 'San Francisco'
United Planning Organization (UPO)
See 'Washington, D.C.'
United Presbyterian Church, 174, 178, 201
United Progress, Inc. (UPI)
See 'Trenton'
U.S. Conference of Mayors, 155
University Neighborhood Councils
See 'Washington, D.C.'
UPI (United Progress, Inc.)
See 'Trenton'

UPO (United Planning Organization)
See 'Washington, D.C.'
Urban League
See 'National Urban League' and under specific cities
Urban Training Center
See 'Chicago'

Visalia (Calif.)
community action programs, 42, 63
Tulare County Community Action Program, 92
Vista, 66

Wagner, Robert F. (mayor, New York), 79
Wald, Lillian, 78
Walsh, William (mayor, Syracuse), 79, 84, 153, 154, 155
War Against Poverty, 20, 207
President's Task Force memo, 261–263
Washington, D.C., 47, 89, 90, 95–98, 194
anti-poverty programs and the churches, 172 ff.
community action programs, 12, 15, 124, 233, 239, 240
effectiveness, 211, 222–224, 237
United Planning Organization (UPO), 31, 38, 39, 41–42, 46–47, 51, 52, 91, 95, 159–160
Cardoza Project, 47–48
University Neighborhood Councils, 45, 89
Urban League, 96
Watts
See 'Los Angeles'
Welch (W. Va.)
community action programs, 62
Wendell, Donald, 31–32
West Oakland (Calif.), 196
Whitesburgh (Ky.)
community action programs, 62
Wiley, George, 254
Wilkins, Roy, 195
Willis, Benjamin, 169
Wingate, Livingston, 171
Witcover, Jules, and Erwin Knoll, "Politics and the Poor . . .," 155, 155*n.*, 190, 190*n.*
Wolfe City (Ky.)
community action programs, 62
(The) Woodlawn Organization (TWO)
See 'Chicago'
Works Project Administration (WPA), 3
WPA
See 'Works Project Administration'

YDP (Youth Development Program)
See 'Minneapolis'
YMCA
See 'Young Men's Christian Association'
YOB (Youth Opportunities Board)
See 'Los Angeles'
Yorty, Samuel (mayor, Los Angeles), 119
Young Men's Christian Association (YMCA), 199
Younger, Paul A., 168, 182
Powell Committee brief, 164, 165
Youth Development Program (YDP)
See 'Minneapolis'
Youth in the Ghetto
See 'New York City—HARYOU'
Youth Opportunities Board (YOB)
See 'Los Angeles'

Zuni Tribe (N. Mex.)
community action programs, 63

69 70 71 72 73 8 7 6 5 4 3 2 1